EBEN HOLDEN

A TALE OF THE NORTH COUNTRY

By

Irving Bacheller

CONTENTS

PREFACE

Early in the last century the hardy wood-choppers began to come west, out of Vermont. They founded their homes in the Adirondack wildernesses and cleared their rough acres with the axe and the charcoal pit. After years of toil in a rigorous climate they left their sons little besides a stumpy farm and a coon-skin overcoat. Far from the centres of life their amusements, their humours, their religion, their folk lore, their views of things had in them the flavour of the timber lands, the simplicity of childhood. Every son was nurtured in the love of honour and of industry, and the hope of sometime being president. It is to be feared this latter thing and the love of right living, for its own sake, were more in their thoughts than the immortal crown that had been the inspiration of their fathers. Leaving the farm for the more promising life of the big city they were as men born anew, and their second infancy was like that of Hercules. They had the strength of manhood, the tireless energy of children and some hope of the highest things. The pageant of the big town—its novelty, its promise, its art, its activity—quickened their highest powers, put them to their best effort. And in all great enterprises they became the pathfinders, like their fathers in the primeval forest.

This book has grown out of such enforced leisure as one may find in a busy life. Chapters begun in the publicity of a Pullman car have been finished in the cheerless solitude of a hotel chamber. Some have had their beginning in a sleepless night and their end in a day of bronchitis. A certain pious farmer in the north country when, like Agricola, he was about to die, requested the doubtful glory of this epitaph: 'He was a poor sinner, but he done his best' Save for the fact that I am an excellent sinner, in a literary sense, the words may stand for all the apology I have to make.

The characters were mostly men and women I have known and who left with me a love of my kind that even a wide experience with knavery and misfortune has never dissipated. For my knowledge of Mr Greeley I am chiefly indebted to David P. Rhoades, his publisher, to Philip Fitzpatrick, his pressman, to the files of the Tribune and to many books.

IRVING BACHELLER New York City, 7 April 1900

BOOK ONE

Chapter I

Of all the people that ever went west that expedition was the most remarkable.

A small boy in a big basket on the back of a jolly old man, who carried a cane in one hand, a rifle in the other; a black dog serving as scout, skirmisher and rear guard—that was the size of it. They were the survivors of a ruined home in the north of Vermont, and were travelling far into the valley of the St Lawrence, but with no particular destination.

Midsummer had passed them in their journey; their clothes were covered with dust; their faces browning in the hot sun. It was a very small boy that sat inside the basket and clung to the rim, his tow head shaking as the old man walked. He saw wonderful things, day after day, looking down at the green fields or peering into the gloomy reaches of the wood; and he talked about them.

'Uncle Eb—is that where the swifts are?' he would ask often; and the old man would answer, 'No; they ain't real sassy this time o' year. They lay 'round in the deep dingles every day.'

Then the small voice would sing idly or prattle with an imaginary being that had a habit of peeking over the edge of the basket or would shout a greeting to some bird or butterfly and ask finally: 'Tired, Uncle Eb?'

Sometimes the old gentleman would say 'not very', and keep on, looking thoughtfully at the ground. Then, again, he would stop and mop his bald head with a big red handkerchief and say, a little tremor of irritation in his voice: 'Tired! who wouldn't be tired with a big elephant like you on his back all day? I'd be 'shamed o' myself t' set there an' let an old man carry me from Dan to Beersheba. Git out now an' shake yer legs.'

I was the small boy and I remember it was always a great relief to get out of the basket, and having run ahead, to lie in the grass among the wild flowers, and jump up at him as he came along.

Uncle Eb had been working for my father five years before I was born. He was not a strong man and had never been able to carry the wide swath of the other help in the fields, but we all loved him for his kindness and his knack of story-telling. He was a bachelor who came over the mountain from Pleasant Valley, a little bundle of clothes on his shoulder, and bringing a name that enriched the nomenclature of our neighbourhood. It was Eben Holden.

He had a cheerful temper and an imagination that was a very wilderness of oddities. Bears and panthers growled and were very terrible in that strange country. He had invented an animal more treacherous than any in the woods, and he called it a swift. 'Sumthin' like a panther', he described the look of it: a fearsome creature that lay in the edge of the woods at sundown and made a noise like a woman crying, to lure the unwary. It would light one's eye with fear to hear Uncle Eb lift his voice in the cry of the swift. Many a time in the twilight when the bay of a hound or some far cry came faintly through the wooded hills, I have seen him lift his hand and bid us hark. And when we had listened a moment, our eyes wide with wonder, he would turn and say in a low, half-whispered tone: "S a swift' I suppose we needed more the fear of God, but the young children of the pioneer needed also the fear of the woods or they would have strayed to their death in them.

A big bass viol, taller than himself, had long been the solace of his Sundays. After he had shaved—a ceremony so solemn that it seemed a rite of his religion—that sacred viol was uncovered. He carried it sometimes to the back piazza and sometimes to the barn, where the horses shook and trembled at the roaring thunder of the strings. When he began playing we children had to get well out of the way, and keep our distance. I remember now the look of him, then—his thin face, his soft black eyes, his long nose, the suit of broadcloth, the stock and standing collar and, above all, the solemnity in his manner when that big devil of a thing was leaning on his breast.

As to his playing I have never heard a more fearful sound in any time of peace or one less creditable to a Christian. Weekdays he was addicted to the milder sin of the flute and, after chores, if there were no one to talk with him, he would sit long and pour his soul into that magic bar of boxwood.

Uncle Eb had another great accomplishment. He was what they call in the north country 'a natural cooner'. After nightfall, when the corn was ripening, he spoke in a whisper and had his ear cocked for coons. But he loved all kinds of good fun.

So this man had a boy in his heart and a boy in his basket that evening we left the old house. My father and mother and older brother had been drowned in the lake, where they had gone for a day of pleasure. I had then a small understanding of my loss, hat I have learned since that the farm was not worth the mortgage and that everything had to be sold. Uncle Eb and I—a little lad, a very little lad of six—were all that was left of what had been in that home. Some were for sending me to the county house; but they decided, finally, to turn me over to a dissolute uncle, with some allowance for my keep. Therein Uncle Eb was to be reckoned with. He had set his heart on keeping me, but he was a farm-hand without any home or visible property and not, therefore, in the mind of the authorities, a proper guardian. He had me with him in the old house, and the very night he heard they were coming after me in the morning, we started on our journey. I remember he was a long time tying packages of bread and butter and tea and boiled eggs to the rim of the basket, so that they hung on the outside. Then he put a woollen shawl and an oilcloth blanket on the bottom, pulled the straps over his shoulders and buckled them, standing before the looking-glass, and, hang put on my cap and coat, stood me on the table, and stooped so that I could climb into the basket—a pack basket, that he had used in hunting, the top a little smaller than the bottom. Once in, I could stand comfortably or sit facing sideways, my back and knees wedged from port to starboard. With me in my place he blew out the lantern and groped his way to the road, his cane in one hand, his rifle in the other. Fred, our old dog—a black shepherd, with tawny points—came after us. Uncle Eb scolded him and tried to send him back, but I pleaded for the poor creature and that settled it, he was one of our party.

'Dunno how we'll feed him,' said Uncle Eb. 'Our own mouths are big enough t' take all we can carry, but I hain' no heart t' leave 'im all 'lone there.'

I was old for my age, they tell me, and had a serious look and a wise way of talking, for a boy so young; but I had no notion of what lay before or behind us.

'Now, boy, take a good look at the old house,' I remember he whispered to me at the gate that night "Tain't likely ye'll ever see it ag'in. Keep quiet now,' he added, letting down the bars at the foot of the lane. 'We're goin' west an' we mustn't let the grass grow under us. Got t'be purty spry I can tell ye.'

It was quite dark and he felt his way carefully down the cow-paths into the broad pasture. With every step I kept a sharp lookout for swifts, and the moon shone after a while, making my work easier.

I had to hold my head down, presently, when the tall brush began to whip the basket and I heard the big boots of Uncle Eb ripping the briars. Then we came into the blackness of the thick timber and I could hear him feeling his way over the dead leaves with his cane. I got down, shortly, and walked beside him, holding on to the rifle with one hand. We stumbled, often, and were long in the trail before we could see the moonlight through the tree columns. In the clearing I climbed to my seat again and by and by we came to the road where my companion sat down resting his load on a boulder.

'Pretty hot, Uncle Eb, pretty hot,' he said to himself, fanning his brow with that old felt hat he wore everywhere. 'We've come three mile er more without a stop an' I guess we'd better rest a jiffy.'

My legs ached too, and I was getting very sleepy. I remember the jolt of the basket as he rose, and hearing him say, 'Well, Uncle Eb, I guess we'd better be goin'.'

The elbow that held my head, lying on the rim of the basket, was already numb; but the prickling could no longer rouse me, and half-dead with weariness, I fell asleep. Uncle Eb has told me since, that I tumbled out of the basket once, and that he had a time of it getting me in again, but I remember nothing more of that day's history.

When I woke in the morning, I could hear the crackling of fire, and felt very warm and cosy wrapped in the big shawl. I got a cheery greeting from Uncle Eb, who was feeding the fire with a big heap of sticks that he had piled together. Old Fred was licking my hands with his rough tongue, and I suppose that is what waked me. Tea was steeping in the little pot that hung over the fire, and our breakfast of boiled eggs and bread and butter lay on a paper beside it. I remember well the scene of our little camp that morning. We had come to a strange country, and there was no road in sight. A wooded hill lay back of us, and, just before, ran a noisy little brook, winding between smooth banks, through a long pasture into a dense wood. Behind a wall on the opposite shore a great field of rustling corn filled a broad valley and stood higher than a man's head.

While I went to wash my face in the clear water Uncle Eb was husking some ears of corn that he took out of his pocket, and had them roasting over the fire in a moment. We ate heartily, giving Fred two big slices of bread and butter, packing up with enough remaining for another day. Breakfast over we doused the fire and Uncle Eb put on his basket He made after a squirrel, presently, with old Fred, and brought him down out of a tree by hurling stones at him and then the faithful follower of our camp got a bit of meat for his breakfast. We climbed the wall, as he ate, and buried ourselves in the deep corn. The fragrant, silky tassels brushed my face and the corn hissed at our intrusion, crossing its green sabers in our path. Far in the field my companion heaped a little of the soft earth for a pillow, spread the oil cloth between rows and, as we lay down, drew the big shawl over us. Uncle Eb was tired after the toil of that night and went asleep almost as soon as he was down. Before I dropped off Fred came and licked my face and stepped over me, his tail wagging for leave, and curled upon the shawl at my feet. I could see no sky in that gloomy green aisle of corn. This going to bed in the morning seemed a foolish business to me that day and I lay a long time looking up at the rustling canopy overhead. I remember listening to the waves that came whispering out of the further field, nearer and nearer, until they swept over us with a roaring swash of leaves, like that of water flooding among rocks, as I have heard it often. A twinge of homesickness came to me and the snoring of Uncle Eb gave me no comfort. I remember covering my head and crying softly as I thought of those who had gone away and whom I was to meet in a far country, called Heaven, whither we were going. I forgot my sorrow, finally, in sleep. When I awoke it had grown dusk under the corn. I felt for Uncle Eb and he was gone. Then I called to him.

'Hush, boy! lie low,' he whispered, bending over me, a sharp look in his eye.' 'Fraid they're after us.'

He sat kneeling beside me, holding Fred by the collar and listening. I could hear voices, the rustle of the corn and the tramp of feet near by. It was thundering in the distance—that heavy, shaking thunder that seems to take hold of the earth, and there were sounds in the corn like the drawing of sabers and the rush of many feet. The noisy thunder clouds came nearer and the voices that had made us tremble were no longer heard. Uncle Eb began to fasten the oil blanket to the stalks of corn for a shelter. The rain came roaring over us. The sound of it was like that of a host of cavalry coming at a gallop. We lay bracing the stalks, the blanket tied above us and were quite dry for a time. The rain rattled in the sounding sheaves and then came flooding down the steep gutters. Above us beam and rafter creaked, swaying, and showing glimpses of the dark sky. The rain passed—we could hear the last battalion leaving the field—and then the tumult ended as suddenly as it began. The corn trembled a few moments and hushed to a faint whisper. Then we could hear only the drip of raindrops leaking through the green roof. It was dark under the corn.

Chapter 2

We heard no more of the voices. Uncle Eb had brought an armful of wood, and some water in the teapot, while I was sleeping. As soon as the rain had passed he stood listening awhile and shortly opened his knife and made a little clearing in the corn by cutting a few hills.

'We've got to do it,' he said, 'er we can't take any comfort, an' the man tol' me I could have all the corn I wanted.'

'Did you see him, Uncle Eb?' I remember asking.

'Yes,' he answered, whittling in the dark. 'I saw him when I went out for the water an' it was he tol' me they were after us.'

He took a look at the sky after a while, and, remarking that he guessed they couldn't see his smoke now, began to kindle the fire. As it burned up he stuck two crotches and hung his teapot on a stick' that lay in them, so it took the heat of the flame, as I had seen him do in the morning. Our grotto, in the corn, was shortly as cheerful as any room in a palace, and our fire sent its light into the long aisles that opened opposite, and nobody could see the warm glow of it but ourselves.

'We'll hev our supper,' said Uncle Eb, as he opened a paper and spread out the eggs and bread and butter and crackers. 'We'll jest hev our supper an' by 'n by when everyone's abed we'll make tracks in the dirt, I can tell ye.'

Our supper over, Uncle Eb let me look at his tobacco-box—a shiny thing of German silver that always seemed to snap out a quick farewell to me before it dove into his pocket. He was very cheerful and communicative, and joked a good deal as we lay there waiting in the firelight. I got some further acquaintance with the swift, learning among other things that it had no appetite for the pure in heart.

'Why not?' I enquired.

'Well,' said Uncle Eb, 'it's like this: the meaner the boy, the sweeter the meat.'

He sang an old song as he sat by the fire, with a whistled interlude between lines, and the swing of it, even now, carries me back to that far day in the fields. I lay with my head in his lap while he was singing.

Years after, when I could have carried him on my back' he wrote down for me the words of the old song. Here they are, about as he sang them, although there are evidences of repair, in certain lines, to supply the loss of phrases that had dropped out of his memory:

I was goin' to Salem one bright summer day,

I met a young maiden a goin' my way;

O, my fallow, faddeling fallow, faddel away.

An' many a time I had seen her before,

But I never dare tell 'er the love thet I bore.

O, my fallow, etc.

'Oh, where are you goin' my purty fair maid?'

'O, sir, I am goin' t' Salem,' she said.

O, my fallow, etc.

'O, why are ye goin' so far in a day?

Fer warm is the weather and long is the way.'

O, my fallow, etc.

'O, sir I've forgorten, I hev, I declare,

But it's nothin' to eat an' its nothin' to wear.'

O, my fallow, etc.

'Oho! then I hev it, ye purty young miss!

I'll bet it is only three words an' a kiss.'

O, my fallow, etc.

'Young woman, young woman, O how will it dew

If I go see yer lover 'n bring 'em t' you?'

O, my fallow, etc.

''S a very long journey,' says she, 'I am told,

An' before ye got back, they would surely be cold.'

O, my fallow, etc.

'I hev 'em right with me, I vum an' I vow,

An' if you don't object I'll deliver 'em now.'

O, my fallow, etc.

She laid her fair head all on to my breast,

An' ye wouldn't know more if I tol' ye the rest

O, my fallow, etc.

I went asleep after awhile in spite of all, right in the middle of a story. The droning voice of Uncle Eb and the feel of his hand upon my forehead called me back, blinking, once or twice, but not for long. The fire was gone down to a few embers when Uncle Eb woke me and the grotto was lit only by a sprinkle of moonlight from above.

'Mos' twelve o'clock,' he whispered. 'Better be off.'

The basket was on his back and he was all ready. I followed him through the long aisle of corn, clinging to the tall of his coat. The golden lantern of the moon hung near the zenith and when we came out in the open we could see into the far fields. I climbed into my basket at the wall and as Uncle Eb carried me over the brook, stopping on a flat rock midway to take a drink, I could see the sky in the water, and it seemed as if a misstep would have tumbled me into the moon.

'Hear the crickets holler,' said Uncle Eb, as he followed the bank up into the open pasture.

'What makes 'em holler?' I asked.

'O, they're jes' filin' their saws an' thinkin'. Mebbe tellin' o' what's happened 'em. Been a hard day fer them little folks. Terrible flood in their country. Everyone on em hed t' git up a steeple quick 'she could er be drownded. They hev their troubles an' they talk 'bout 'em, too.'

'What do they file their saws for?' I enquired.

'Well, ye know,' said he, 'where they live the timber's thick an' they hev hard work clearin' t' mek a home.'

I was getting too sleepy for further talk. He made his way from field to field, stopping sometimes to look off at the distant mountains then at the sky or to whack the dry stalks of mullen with his cane. I remember he let down some bars after a long walk and stepped into a smooth roadway. He stood resting a little while, his basket on the top bar, and then the moon that I had been watching went down behind the broad rim of his hat and I fell into utter forgetfulness. My eyes opened on a lovely scene at daylight. Uncle Eb had laid me on a mossy knoll in a bit of timber and through an opening right in front of us I could see a broad level of shining water, and the great green mountain on the further shore seemed to be up to its belly in the sea.

'Hello there!' said Uncle Eb; 'here we are at Lake Champlain.'

I could hear the fire crackling and smell the odour of steeping tea.

'Ye flopped 'round like a fish in thet basket,' said Uncle Eb. "Guess ye must a been drearnin' O' bears. Jumped so ye scairt me. Didn't know but I had a wil' cat on my shoulders.'

Uncle Eb had taken a fish-line out of his pocket and was tying it to a rude pole that he had cut and trinmed with his jack-knife.

'I've found some crawfish here,' he said, 'an' I'm goin' t' try fer a bite on the p'int O' rocks there.'

'Goin' t' git some fish, Uncle Eb?' I enquired.

'Wouldn't say't I was, er wouldn't say't I wasn't,' he answered. 'Jes goin' t' try.'

Uncle Eb was always careful not to commit himself on a doubtful point. He had fixed his hook and sinker in a moment and then we went out on a rocky point nearby and threw off into the deep water. Suddenly Uncle Eb gave a jerk that brought a groan out of him and then let his hook go down again, his hands trembling, his face severe.

'By mighty! Uncle Eb,' he muttered to himself, 'I thought we hed him thet time.'

He jerked again presently, and then I could see a tug on the line that made me jump. A big fish came thrashing into the air in a minute. He tried to swing it ashore, but the pole bent and the fish got a fresh hold of the water and took the end of the pole under. Uncle Eb gave it a lift then that brought it ashore and a good bit of water with it. I remember how the fish slapped me with its wet tail and sprinkled my face shaking itself between my boots. It was a big bass and in a little while we had three of them. Uncle Eb dressed them and laid them over the fire on a gridiron of green birch, salting them as they cooked. I remember they went with a fine relish and the last of our eggs and bread and butter went with them.

Our breakfast over, Uncle Eb made me promise to stay with Fred and the basket while he went away to find a man who could row us across. In about an hour I heard a boat coming and the dog and I went out on the point of rocks where we saw Uncle Eb and another man, heading for us, half over the cove. The bow bumped the rocks beneath us in a minute. Then the stranger dropped his oars and stood staring at me and the dog.

'Say, mister,' said he presently, 'can't go no further. There's a reward offered fer you an' thet boy.'

Uncle Eb called him aside and was talking to him a long time.

I never knew what was said, but they came at last and took us into the boat and the stranger was very friendly.

When we had come near the landing on the 'York State' side, I remember he gave us our bearings.

'Keep t' the woods,' he said, 'till you're out o' harm's way. Don't go near the stage road fer a while. Ye'll find a store a little way up the mountain. Git yer provisions there an' about eighty rod farther ye'll strike the trail. It'll take ye over the mountain north an' t' Paradise Road. Then take the white church on yer right shoulder an' go straight west.'

I would not have remembered it so well but for the fact that Uncle Eb wrote it all down in his account book and that has helped me over many a slippery place in my memory of those events. At the store we got some crackers and cheese, tea and coffee, dried beef and herring, a bit of honey and a loaf of bread that was sliced and buttered before it was done up. We were off in the woods by nine o'clock, according to Uncle Eb's diary, and I remember the trail led us into thick brush where I had to get out and walk a long way. It was smooth under foot, however, and at noon we came to a slash in the timber, full of briars that were all aglow with big blackberries. We filled our hats with them and Uncle Eb found a spring, beside which we built a fire and had a memorable meal that made me glad of my hunger.

Then we spread the oilcloth and lay down for another sleep. We could see the glow of the setting sun through the tree-tops when we woke, and began our packing.

'We'll hev t' hurry,' said Uncle Eb, 'er we'll never git out o' the woods t'night 'S 'bout six mile er more t' Paradise Road, es I mek it. Come, yer slower 'n a toad in a tar barrel.'

We hurried off on the trail and I remember Fred looked very crestfallen with two big packages tied to his collar. He delayed a bit by trying to shake them off, but Uncle Eb gave him a sharp word or two and then he walked along very thoughtfully. Uncle Eb was a little out of patience that evening, and I thought he bore down too harshly in his rebuke of the old dog.

'You shif'less cuss,' he said to him, 'ye'd jes' dew nothin' but chase squirrels an' let me break my back t' carry yer dinner.'

It was glooming fast in the thick timber, and Uncle Eb almost ran with me while the way was plain. The last ringing note of the wood thrush had died away and in a little while it was so dark I could distinguish nothing but the looming mass of tree trunks.

He stopped suddenly and strained his eyes in the dark. Then he whistled a sharp, sliding note, and the sound of it gave me some hint of his trouble.

'Git down, Willie,' said he, 'an' tek my hand. I'm 'fraid we're lost here 'n the big woods.'

We groped about for a minute, trying to find the trail.

'No use,' he said presently, 'we'll hev t' stop right here. Oughter known berter 'n t' come through s' near sundown. Guess it was more 'n anybody could do.'

He built a fire and began to lay out a supper for us then, while Fred sat down by me to be relieved of his bundles. Our supper was rather dry, for we had no water, but it was only two hours since we left the spring, so we were not suffering yet. Uncle Eb took out of the fire a burning brand of pine and went away into the gloomy woods, holding it above his head, while Fred and I sat by the fire.

''S lucky we didn't go no further,' he said, as he came in after a few minutes. 'There's a big prec'pice over yender. Dunno how deep 't is. Guess we'd a found out purty soon.'

He cut some boughs of hemlock, growing near us, and spread them in a little hollow. That done, we covered them with the oilcloth, and sat down comfortably by the fire. Uncle Eb had a serious look and was not inclined to talk or story telling. Before turning in he asked me to kneel and say my prayer as I had done every evening at the feet of my mother. I remember, clearly, kneeling before my old companion and hearing the echo of my small voice there in the dark and lonely woods.

I remember too, and even more clearly, how he bent his head and covered his eyes in that brief moment. I had a great dread of darkness and imagined much evil of the forest, but somehow I had no fear if he were near me. When we had fixed the fire and lain down for the night on the fragrant hemlock and covered ourselves with the shawl, Uncle Eb lay on one side of me and old Fred on the other, so I felt secure indeed. The night had many voices there in the deep wood. Away in the distance I could hear a strange, wild cry, and I asked what it was and Uncle Eb whispered back, ''s a loon.' Down the side of the mountain a shrill bark rang in the timber and that was a fox, according to my patient oracle. Anon we heard the crash and thunder of a falling tree and a murmur that followed in the wake of the last echo.

'Big tree fallin'!' said Uncle Eb, as he lay gaping. 'It has t' break a way t' the ground an' it must hurt. Did ye notice how the woods tremble? If we was up above them we could see the hole thet tree hed made. Jes' like an open grave till the others hev filed it with their tops.'

My ears had gone deaf with drowsiness when a quick stir in the body of Uncle Eb brought me back to my senses. He was up on his elbow listening and the firelight had sunk to a glimmer. Fred lay shivering and growling beside me. I could hear no other sound.

'Be still,' said Uncle Eb, as he boxed the dog's ears. Then he rose and began to stir the fire and lay on more wood. As the flame leaped and threw its light into the tree-tops a shrill cry, like the scream of a frightened woman, only louder and more terrible to hear brought me to my feet, crying. I knew the source of it was near us and ran to Uncle Eb in a fearful panic.

'Hush, boy,' said he as it died away and went echoing in the far forest. 'I'll take care o' you. Don't be scairt. He's more 'fraid uv us than we are o' him. He's makin' off now.'

We heard then a great crackling of dead brush on the mountain above us. It grew fainter as we listened. In a little while the woods were silent.

'It's the ol' man o' the woods,' said Uncle Eb. 'E's out takin' a walk.'

'Will he hurt folks?' I enquired.

'Tow!' he answered, 'jest as harmless as a kitten.'

Chapter 3

Naturally there were a good many things I wanted to know about 'the ol' man o' the woods,' but Uncle Eb would take no part in any further conversation.

So I had to lie down beside him again and think out the problem as best I could. My mind was never more acutely conscious and it gathered many strange impressions, wandering in the kingdom of Fear, as I looked up at the tree-tops. Uncle Eb had built a furious fire and the warmth of it made me sleepy at last. Both he and old Fred had been snoring a long time when I ceased to hear them. Uncle Eb woke me at daylight, in the morning, and said we must be off to find the trail. He left me by the fire a little while and went looking on all sides and came back no wiser. We were both thirsty and started off on rough footing, without stopping to eat. We climbed and crawled for hours, it seemed to me, and everywhere the fallen tree trunks were heaped in our way. Uncle Eb sat down on one of them awhile to rest.

'Like the bones o' the dead,' said he, as he took a chew of tobacco and picked at the rotten skeleton of a fallen tree. We were both pretty well out of breath and of hope also, if I remember rightly, when we rested again under the low hanging boughs of a basswood for a bite of luncheon. Uncle Eb opened the little box of honey and spread some of it on our bread and butter. In a moment I noticed that half a dozen bees had lit in the open box.

'Lord Harry! here's honey bees,' said he, as he covered the box so as to keep them in, and tumbled everything else into the basket. 'Make haste now, Willie, and follow me with all yer might,' he added.

In a minute he let out one of the bees, and started running in the direction it flew. It went but a few feet and then rose into the tree-top.

'He's goin' t' git up into the open air,' said Uncle Eb. 'But I've got his bearins' an' I guess he knows the way all right.'

We took the direction indicated for a few minutes and then Uncle Eb let out another prisoner. The bee flew off a little way and then rose in a slanting course to the tree-tops. He showed us, however, that we were looking the right way.

'Them little fellers hev got a good compass,' said Uncle Eb, as we followed the line of the bees. 'It p'ints home ev'ry time, an' never makes a mistake.'

We went further this time before releasing another. He showed us that we had borne out of our course a little and as we turned to follow there were half a dozen bees flying around the box, as if begging for admission.

'Here they are back agin,' said Uncle Eb, 'an' they've told a lot o' their cronies 'bout the man an' the boy with honey.'

At length one of them flew over our heads and back in the direction we had come from.

'Ah, ha,' said Uncle Eb, 'it's a bee tree an' we've passed it, but I'm goin' t' keep lettin' 'em in an' out. Never heard uv a swarm o' bees goin' fur away an' so we mus' be near the clearin'.'

In a little while we let one go that took a road of its own. The others had gone back over our heads; this one bore off to the right in front of us, and we followed. I was riding in the basket and was first to see the light of the open through the tree-tops. But I didn't know what it meant until I heard the hearty 'hurrah' of Uncle Eb.

We had come to smooth footing in a grove of maples and the clean trunks of the trees stood up as straight as a granite column. Presently we came out upon wide fields of corn and clover, and as we looked back upon the grove it had a rounded front and I think of it now as the vestibule of the great forest.

'It's a reg'lar big tomb,' said Uncle Eb, looking back over his shoulder into the gloomy cavern of the woods.

We could see a log house in the clearing, and we made for it as fast as our legs would carry us. We had a mighty thirst and when we came to a little brook in the meadow we laid down and drank and drank until we were fairly grunting with fullness. Then we filled our teapot and went on. Men were reaping with their cradles in a field of grain and, as we neared the log house, a woman came out in the dooryard and, lifting a shell to her lips, blew a blast that rushed over the clearing and rang in the woods beyond it A loud halloo came back from the men.

A small dog rushed out at Fred, barking, and, I suppose, with some lack of respect, for the old dog laid hold of him in a violent temper and sent him away yelping. We must have presented an evil aspect, for our clothes were torn and we were both limping with fatigue. The woman had a kindly face and, after looking at us a moment, came and stooped before me and held my small face in her hands turning it so she could look into my eyes.

'You poor little critter,' said she, 'where you goin'?'

Uncle Eb told her something about my father and mother being dead and our going west Then she hugged and kissed me and made me very miserable, I remember, wetting my face with her tears, that were quite beyond my comprehension.

'Jethro,' said she, as the men came into the yard, 'I want ye t' look at this boy. Did ye ever see such a cunnin' little critter? Jes' look at them bright eyes!' and then she held me to her breast and nearly smothered me and began to hum a bit of an old song.

'Yer full o' mother love,' said her husband, as he sat down on the grass a moment 'Lost her only baby, an' the good Lord has sent no other. I swan, he has got putty eyes. Jes' as blue as a May flower. Ain't ye hungry? Come right in, both o' ye, an' set down t' the table with us.'

They made room for us and we sat down between the bare elbows of the hired men. I remember my eyes came only to the top of the table. So the good woman brought the family Bible and sitting on that firm foundation I ate my dinner of salt pork and potatoes and milk gravy, a diet as grateful as it was familiar to my taste.

'Orphan, eh?' said the man of the house, looking down at me.

'Orphan,' Uncle Eb answered, nodding his head.

'God-fearin' folks?'

'Best in the world,' said Uncle Eb.

Want t' bind 'im out?' the man asked.

'Couldn't spare 'im,' said Uncle Eb, decisively.

'Where ye goin'?'

Uncle Eb hesitated, groping for an answer, I suppose, that would do no violence to our mutual understanding.

'Goin' t' heaven,' I ventured to say presently—an answer that gave rise to conflicting emotions at the table.

'That's right,' said Uncle Eb, turning to me and patting my head. 'We're on the road t' heaven, I hope, an' ye'll see it someday, sartin sure, if ye keep in the straight road and be a good boy.'

After dinner the good woman took off my clothes and put me in bed while she mended them. I went asleep then and did not awake for a long time. When I got up at last she brought a big basin of water and washed me with such motherly tenderness in voice and manner that I have never forgotten it. Uncle Eb lay sleeping on the lounge and when she had finished dressing me, Fred and I went out to play in the garden. It was supper time in a little while and then, again, the woman winded the shell and the men came up from the field. We sat down to eat with them, as we had done at noon, and Uncle Eb consented to spend the night after some urging. He helped them with the milking, and as I stood beside him shot a jet of the warm white flood into my mouth, that tickled it so I ran away laughing. The milking done, I sat on Uncle Eb's knee in the door-yard with all the rest of that household, hearing many tales of the wilderness, and of robbery and murder on Paradise Road. I got the impression that it was a country of unexampled wickedness and ferocity in men and animals. One man told about the ghost of Burnt Bridge; how the bridge had burnt one afternoon and how a certain traveller in the dark of the night driving down the hill above it, fell to his death at the brink of the culvert.

'An' every night since then,' said the man, very positively, ye can hear him drivin' down thet hill—jes' as plain as ye can hear me talkin'—the rattle o' the wheels an' all. It stops sudden an' then ye can hear 'im hit the rocks way down there at the bottom O' the gulley an' groan an' groan. An' folks say it's a curse on the town for leavin' thet hole open.'

'What's a ghost, Uncle Eb?' I whispered.

'Somethin' like a swift,' he answered, 'but not so powerful. We heard a panther las' night,' he added, turning to our host. 'Hollered like sin when he see the fire.'

'Scairt!' said the man o' the house gaping. 'That's what ailed him. I've lived twenty year on Paradise Road an' it was all woods when I put up the cabin. Seen deer on the doorstep an' bears in the garden, an' panthers in the fields. But I tell ye there's no critter so terrible as a man. All the animals know 'im—how he roars, an' spits fire an' smoke an' lead so it goes through a body er bites off a leg, mebbe. Guess they'd made friends with me but them I didn't kill went away smarting with holes in 'em. An' I guess they told all their people 'bout me—the terrible critter that walked on its hind legs an' lied a white face an' drew up an' spit 'is teeth into their vitals 'cross a ten-acre lot. An' putty soon they concluded they didn't want t' hev no truck with me. They thought thin clearin' was the valley o' death an' they got very careful. But the deer they kep' peekin' in at me. Sumthin' funny 'bout a deer—they're so cu'rus. Seem's though they loved the look o' me an' the taste o' the tame grass. Mebbe God meant em t' serve in the yoke some way an' be the friend o' man. They're the outcasts o' the forest—the prey o' the other animals an' men like 'em only when they're dead. An' they're the purtiest critter alive an' the spryest an' the mos' graceful.'

'Men are the mos' terrible of all critters, an' the meanest,' said Uncle Eb. 'They're the only critters that kill fer fun.'

'Bedtime,' said our host, rising presently. 'Got t' be up early 'n the morning.'

We climbed a ladder to the top floor of the cabin with the hired men, of whom there were two. The good lady of the house had made a bed for us on the floor and I remember Fred came up the ladder too, and lay down beside us. Uncle Eb was up with the men in the morning and at breakfast time my hostess came and woke me with kisses and helped me to dress. When we were about going she brought a little wagon out of the cellar that had been a playing of her dead boy, and said I could have it. This wonderful wagon was just the thing for the journey we were making. When I held the little tongue in my hand I was half-way to heaven already. It had four stout wheels and a beautiful red box. Her brother had sent it all the way from New York and it had stood so long in the cellar it was now much in need of repair. Uncle Eb took it to the tool shop in the stable and put it in shipshape order and made a little pair of thills to go in place of the tongue. Then he made a big flat collar and a back-pad out of the leather in old boot-legs, and rigged a pair of tugs out of two pieces of rope. Old Fred was quite cast down when he stood in harness between the shafts.

He had waited patiently to have his collar fitted; he had grinned and panted and wagged his tail with no suspicion of the serious and humiliating career he was entering upon. Now he stood with a sober face and his aspect was full of meditation.

'You fightin' hound!' said Uncle Eb, 'I hope this'll improve yer character.'

Fred tried to sit down when Uncle Eb tied a leading rope to his collar. When he heard the wheels rattle and felt the pull of the wagon he looked back at it and growled a little and started to run. Uncle Eb shouted 'whoa', and held him back, and then the dog got down on his belly and trembled until we patted his head and gave him a kind word. He seemed to understand presently and came along with a steady stride. Our hostess met us at the gate and the look of her face when she bade us goodbye and tucked some cookies into my pocket, has always lingered in my memory and put in me a mighty respect for all women. The sound of her voice, the tears, the waving of her handkerchief, as we went away, are among the things that have made me what I am.

We stowed our packages in the wagon box and I walked a few miles and then got into the empty basket. Fred tipped his load over once or twice, but got a steady gait in the way of industry after a while and a more cheerful look. We had our dinner by the roadside on the bank of a brook, an hour or so after midday, and came to a little village about sundown. As we were nearing it there was some excitement among the dogs and one of them tackled Fred. He went into battle very promptly, the wagon jumping and rattling until it turned bottom up. Re-enforced by Uncle Eb's cane he soon saw the heels of his aggressor and stood growling savagely. He was like the goal in a puzzle maze all wound and tangled in his harness and it took some time to get his face before him and his feet free.

At a small grocery where groups of men, just out of the fields, were sitting, their arms bare to the elbows, we bought more bread and butter. In paying for it Uncle Eb took a package out of his trouser pocket to get his change. It was tied in a red handkerchief and I remember it looked to be about the size of his fist. He was putting it back when it fell from his hand, heavily, and I could hear the chink of coin as it struck. One of the men, who sat near, picked it up and gave it back to him. As I remember well, his kindness had an evil flavour, for he winked at his companions, who nudged each other as they smiled knowingly. Uncle Eb was a bit cross, when I climbed into the basket, and walked along in silence so rapidly it worried the dog to keep pace. The leading rope was tied to the stock of the rifle and Fred's walking gait was too slow for the comfort of his neck.

'You shifless cuss! I'll put a kink in your neck fer you if ye don't walk up,' said Uncle Eb, as he looked back at the dog, in a temper wholly unworthy of him.

We had crossed a deep valley and were climbing a long hill in the dusky twilight.

'Willie,' said Uncle Eb, 'your eyes are better'n mine—look back and see if anyone's comin'.'

'Can't see anyone,' I answered.

'Look 'way back in the road as fur as ye can see.

I did so, but I could see no one. He slackened his pace a little after that and before we had passed the hill it was getting dark. The road ran into woods and a river cut through them a little way from the clearing.

'Supper time, Uncle Eb,' I suggested, as we came to the bridge.

'Supper time, Uncle Eb,' he answered, turning down to the shore.

I got out of the basket then and followed him in the brush. Fred found it hard travelling here and shortly we took off his harness and left the wagon, transferring its load to the basket, while we pushed on to find a camping place. Back in the thick timber a long way from the road, we built a fire and had our supper. It was a dry nook in the pines—'tight as a house,' Uncle Eb said—and carpeted with the fragrant needles. When we lay on our backs in the firelight I remember the weary, droning voice of Uncle Eb had an impressive accompaniment of whispers. While he told stories I had a glowing cinder on the end of a stick and was weaving fiery skeins in the gloom.

He had been telling me of a panther he had met in the woods, one day, and how the creature ran away at the sight of him.

'Why's a panther 'fraid o' folks?' I enquired.

'Wall, ye see, they used t' be friendly, years 'n years ago—folks 'n panthers—but they want eggszac'ly cal'lated t' git along t'gether some way. An' ol' she panther gin 'em one uv her cubs, a great while ago, jes t' make frien's. The cub he grew big 'n used t' play 'n be very gentle. They wuz a boy he tuk to, an' both on 'em got very friendly. The boy 'n the panther went off one day 'n the woods—guess 'twas more 'n a hundred year ago—an' was lost. Walked all over 'n fin'ly got t' goin' round 'n round 'n a big circle 'til they was both on 'em tired out. Come night they lay down es hungry es tew bears. The boy he was kind o' 'fraid 'o the dark, so he got up clus t' the panther 'n lay 'tween his paws. The boy he thought the panther smelt funny an' the panther he didn't jes' like the smell o' the boy. An' the boy he hed the legache 'n kicked the panther 'n the belly, so 't he kin' o' gagged 'n spit an' they want neither on 'em reel comf'able. The sof paws o' the panther was jes' like pincushions. He'd great hooks in 'em sharper 'n the p'int uv a needle. An' when he was goin' t' sleep he'd run 'em out jes' like an ol' cat—kind o' playfull—'n purr 'n pull. All t' once the boy felt sumthin' like a lot o' needles prickin' his back. Made him jump 'n holler like Sam Hill. The panther he spit sassy 'n riz up 'n smelt o' the ground. Didn't neither on 'em know what was the matter. Bime bye they lay down ag'in. 'Twant only a little while 'fore the boy felt somethin' prickin' uv him. He hollered 'n kicked ag'in. The panther he growled 'n spit 'n dumb a tree 'n sot on a limb 'n peeked over at thet queer little critter. Couldn't neither on 'em understan' it. The boy c'u'd see the eyes o' the panther 'n the dark. Shone like tew live coals eggszac'ly. The panther 'd never sot 'n a tree when he was hungry, 'n see a boy below him. Sumthin' tol' him t' jump. Tail went swish in the leaves like thet. His whiskers quivered, his tongue come out. C'u'd think o' nuthin' but his big empty belly. The boy was scairt. He up with his gun quick es a flash. Aimed at his eyes 'n let 'er flicker. Blew a lot o' smoke 'n bird shot 'n paper waddin' right up in t' his face. The panther he lost his whiskers 'n one eye 'n got his hide fill' o' shot 'n fell off the tree like a ripe apple 'n run fer his life. Thought he'd never see nuthin' c'u'd growl 'n spits powerful es thet boy. Never c'u'd bear the sight uv a man after thet. Allwus made him gag 'n spit t' think o' the man critter. Went off tew his own folks 'n tol' o' the boy 'at spit fire 'n smoke 'n growled so't almos' tore his ears off An' now, whenever they hear a gun go off they allwus thank it's the man critter growlin'. An' they gag 'n spit 'n look es if it made 'em sick t' the stomach. An' the man folks they didn't hev no good 'pimon o' the panthers after thet. Haint never been frien's any more. Fact is a man, he can be any kind uv a beast, but a panther he can't be nuthin' but jest a panther.'

Then, too, as we lay there in the firelight, Uncle Eb told the remarkable story of the gingerbread hear. He told it slowly, as if his invention were severely taxed.

'Once they wuz a boy got lost. Was goin' cross lots t' play with 'nother boy 'n lied t' go through a strip o' woods. Went off the trail t' chase a butterfly 'n got lost. Hed his kite 'n' cross-gun 'n' he wandered all over 'til he was tired 'n hungry. Then he lay down t' cry on a bed o' moss. Putty quick they was a big black bear come along.

'"What's the matter?" said the bear.

'"Hungry," says the boy.

'"Tell ye what I'll dew," says the bear. "If ye'll scratch my back fer me I'll let ye cut a piece o' my tail off t' eat."

'Bear's tail, ye know, hes a lot o' meat on it—heam tell it was gran' good fare. So the boy he scratched the bear's back an' the bear he grinned an' made his paw go patitty-pat on the ground—it did feel so splendid. Then the boy tuk his jack-knife 'n begun t' cut off the bear's tail. The bear he flew mad 'n growled 'n growled so the boy he stopped 'n didn't dast cut no more.

'"Hurts awful," says the bear. "Couldn't never stan' it. Tell ye what I'll dew. Ye scratched my back an' now I'll scratch your'n."

'Gee whiz!' said I.

'Yessir, that's what the bear said,' Uncle Eb went on. 'The boy he up 'n run like a nailer. The bear he laughed hearty 'n scratched the ground like Sam Hill, 'n flung the dirt higher'n his head.

'"Look here," says he, as the boy stopped, "I jes' swallered a piece o mutton. Run yer hand int' my throat an I'll let ye hev it."

'The bear he opened his mouth an' showed his big teeth.'

'Whew!' I whistled.

'Thet's eggszac'ly what he done,' said Uncle Eb. 'He showed 'em plain. The boy was scairter'n a weasel. The bear he jumped up 'an down on his hind legs 'n laughed 'n' hollered 'n' shook himself.

'"Only jes' foolin," says he, when he see the boy was goin' t' run ag'in. "What ye 'fraid uv?"

'"Can't bear t' stay here," says the boy, "'less ye'll keep yer mouth shet."

'An the bear he shet his mouth 'n pinted to the big pocket 'n his fur coat 'n winked 'n motioned t' the boy.

'The bear he reely did hev a pocket on the side uv his big fur coat. The boy slid his hand in up t' the elbow. Wha' d'ye s'pose he found?'

'Durmo,' said I.

'Sumthin' t' eat,' he continued. 'Boy liked it best uv all things.'

I guessed everything I could think of, from cookies to beefsteak, and gave up.

'Gingerbread,' said he, soberly, at length.

'Thought ye said bears couldn't talk,' I objected.

'Wall, the boy 'd fell asleep an' he'd only dreamed o' the bear,' said Uncle Eb. 'Ye see, bears can talk when boys are dreamin' uv 'em. Come daylight, the boy got up 'n ketched a crow. Broke his wing with the cross-gun. Then he tied the kite swing on t' the crow's leg, an' the crow flopped along 'n the boy followed him 'n bime bye they come out a cornfield, where the crow'd been used t' comin' fer his dinner.'

'What 'come o' the boy?' said I.

'Went home,' said he, gaping, as he lay on his back and looked up at the tree-tops. 'An' he allwus said a bear was good comp'ny if he'd only keep his mouth shet—jes' like some folks I've hearn uv.'

'An' what 'come o' the crow?'

'Went t' the ol' crow doctor 'n got his wing fixed,' he said, drowsily. And in a moment I heard him snoring.

We had been asleep a long time when the barking of Fred woke us. I could just see Uncle Eb in the dim light of the fire, kneeling beside me, the rifle in his hand.

'I'll fill ye full o' lead if ye come any nearer,' he shouted.

Chapter 4

We listened awhile then but heard no sound in the thicket, although Fred was growling ominously, his hair on end. As for myself I never had a more fearful hour than that we suffered before the light of morning came.

I made no outcry, but clung to my old companion, trembling. He did not stir for a few minutes, and then we crept cautiously into the small hemlocks on one side of the opening.

'Keep still,' he whispered, 'don't move er speak.'

Presently we heard a move in the brush and then quick as a flash Uncle Eb lifted his rifle and fired in the direction of it Before the loud echo had gone off in the woods we heard something break through the brush at a run.

''S a man,' said Uncle Eb, as he listened. 'He ain't a losin' no time nuther.'

We sat listening as the sound grew fainter, and when it ceased entirely Uncle Eb said he must have got to the road. After a little the light of the morning began sifting down through the tree-tops and was greeted with innumerable songs.

'He done noble,' said Uncle Eb, patting the old dog as he rose to poke the fire. 'Putty good chap I call 'im! He can hev half o' my dinner any time he wants it.'

'Who do you suppose it was?' I enquired.

'Robbers, I guess,' he answered, 'an' they'll be layin' fer us when we go out, mebbe; but, if they are, Fred'll find 'em an' I've got Ol' Trusty here 'n' I guess thet'll take care uv us.'

His rifle was always flattered with that name of Ol' Trusty when it had done him a good turn.

Soon as the light had come clear he went out in the near woods with dog and rifle and beat around in the brush. He returned shortly and said he had seen where they came and went.

'I'd a killed em deader 'n a door nail,' said he, laying down the old rifle, 'if they'd a come any nearer.'

Then we brought water from the river and had our breakfast. Fred went on ahead of us, when we started for the road, scurrying through the brush on both sides of the trail, as if he knew what was expected of him. He flushed a number of partridges and Uncle Eb killed one of them on our way to the road. We resumed our journey without any further adventure. It was so smooth and level under foot that Uncle Eb let me get in the wagon after Fred was hitched to it The old dog went along soberly and without much effort, save when we came to hills or sandy places, when I always got out and ran on behind. Uncle Eb showed me how to brake the wheels with a long stick going downhill. I remember how it hit the dog's heels at the first down grade, and how he ran to keep out of the way of it We were going like mad in half a minute, Uncle Eb coming after us calling to the dog. Fred only looked over his shoulder, with a wild eye, at the rattling wagon and ran the harder. He leaped aside at the bottom and then we went all in a heap. Fortunately no harm was done.

'I declare!' said Uncle Eb as he came up to us, puffing like a spent horse, and picked me up unhurt and began to untangle the harness of old Fred, 'I guess he must a thought the devil was after him.'

The dog growled a little for a moment and bit at the harness, but coaxing reassured him and he went along all right again on the level. At a small settlement the children came out and ran along beside my wagon, laughing and asking me questions. Some of them tried to pet the dog, but old Fred kept to his labour at the heels of Uncle Eb and looked neither to right nor left. We stopped under a tree by the side of a narrow brook for our dinner, and one incident of that meal I think of always when I think of Uncle Eb. It shows the manner of man he was and with what understanding and sympathy he regarded every living thing. In rinsing his teapot he accidentally poured a bit of water on a big bumble-bee. The poor creature struggled to lift hill, and then another downpour caught him and still another until his wings fell drenched. Then his breast began heaving violently, his legs stiffened behind him and he sank, head downward, in the grass. Uncle Eb saw the death throes of the bee and knelt down and lifted the dead body by one of its wings.

'Jes' look at his velvet coat,' he said, 'an' his wings all wet n' stiff. They'll never carry him another journey. It's too bad a man has t' kill every step he takes.'

The bee's tail was moving faintly and Uncle Eb laid him out in the warm sunlight and fanned him awhile with his hat, trying to bring back the breath of life.

'Guilty!' he said, presently, coming back with a sober face. 'Thet's a dead bee. No tellin' how many was dependent on him er what plans he bed. Must a gi'n him a lot o' pleasure t' fly round in the sunlight, workin' every fair day. 'S all over now.'

He had a gloomy face for an hour after that and many a time, in the days that followed, I heard him speak of the murdered bee.

We lay resting awhile after dinner and watching a big city of ants. Uncle Eb told me how they tilled the soil of the mound every year and sowed their own kind of grain—a small white seed like rice—and reaped their harvest in the late summer, storing the crop in their dry cellars under ground. He told me also the story of the ant lion—a big beetle that lives in the jungles of the grain and the grass—of which I remember only an outline, more or less imperfect.

Here it is in my own rewording of his tale: On a bright day one of the little black folks went off on a long road in a great field of barley. He was going to another city of his own people to bring helpers for the harvest. He came shortly to a sandy place where the barley was thin and the hot sunlight lay near to the ground. In a little valley close by the road of the ants he saw a deep pit, in the sand, with steep sides sloping to a point in the middle and as big around as a biscuit. Now the ants are a curious people and go looking for things that are new and wonderful as they walk abroad, so they have much to tell worth hearing after a journey. The little traveller was young and had no fear, so he left the road and went down to the pit and peeped over the side of it.

'What in the world is the meaning of this queer place?' he asked himself as he ran around the rim. In a moment he had stepped over and the soft sand began to cave and slide beneath him. Quick as a flash the big lion-beetle rose up in the centre of the pit and began to reach for him. Then his legs flew in the caving sand and the young ant struck his blades in it to hold the little he could gain.

Upward he struggled, leaping and floundering in the dust. He had got near the rim and had stopped, clinging to get his breath, when the lion began flinging the sand at him with his long feelers. It rose in a cloud and fell on the back of the ant and pulled at him as it swept down. He could feel the mighty cleavers of the lion striking near his hind legs and pulling the sand from under them. He must go down in a moment and he knew what that meant. He had heard the old men of the tribe tell often—how they hold one helpless and slash him into a dozen pieces. He was letting go, in despair, when he felt a hand on his neck. Looking up he saw one of his own people reaching over the rim, and in a jiffy they had shut their fangs together. He moved little by little as the other tagged at him, and in a moment was out of the trap and could feel the honest earth under him. When they had got home and told their adventure, some were for going to slay the beetle.

'There is never a pit in the path o' duty,' said the wise old chief of the little black folks. 'See that you keep in the straight road.'

'If our brother had not left the straight road,' said one who stood near, 'he that was in danger would have gone down into the pit.'

'It matters much,' he answered, 'whether it was kindness or curiosity that led him out of the road. But he that follows a fool hath much need of wisdom, for if he save the fool do ye not see that he hath encouraged folly?'

Of course I had then no proper understanding of the chiefs counsel, nor do I pretend even to remember it from that first telling, but the tale was told frequently in the course of my long acquaintance with Uncle Eb.

The diary of my good old friend lies before me as I write, the leaves turned yellow and the entries dim. I remember how stern he grew of an evening when he took out this sacred little record of our wanderings and began to write in it with his stub of a pencil. He wrote slowly and read and reread each entry with great care as I held the torch for him. 'Be still, boy—be still,' he would say when some pressing interrogatory passed my lips, and then he would bend to his work while the point of his pencil bored further into my patience. Beginning here I shall quote a few entries from the diary as they cover, with sufficient detail, an uneventful period of our journey.

AUGUST 20 Killed a partridge today. Biled it in the teapot for dinner. Went good. 14 mild.

AUGUST 21 Seen a deer this morning. Fred fit ag'in. Come near spilin' the wagon. Hed to stop and fix the ex. 10 mild.

AUGUST 22 Clumb a tree this morning after wild grapes. Come near falling. Gin me a little crick in the back. Willie hes got a stun bruze. 12 mild.

AUGUST 23 Went in swinmun. Ketched a few fish before breakfus'. Got provisions an' two case knives an' one fork, also one tin pie-plate. Used same to fry fish for dinner. 14 mild.

AUGUST 24 Got some spirits for Willie to rub on my back. Boots wearing out. Terrible hot. Lay in the shade in the heat of the day. Gypsies come an' camped by us tonight. 10 mild.

I remember well the coming of those gypsies. We were fishing in sight of the road and our fire was crackling on the smooth cropped shore. The big wagons of the gypsies—there were four of them as red and beautiful as those of a circus caravan—halted about sundown while the men came over a moment to scan the field. Presently they went back and turned their wagons into the siding and began to unhitch. Then a lot of barefooted children, and women under gay shawls, overran the field gathering wood and making ready for night. Meanwhile swarthy drivers took the horses to water and tethered them with long ropes so they could crop the grass of the roadside.

One tall, bony man, with a face almost as black as that of an Indian, brought a big iron pot and set it up near the water. A big stew of beef bone, leeks and potatoes began to cook shortly, and I remember it had such a goodly smell I was minded to ask them for a taste of it. A little city of strange people had surrounded us of a sudden. Uncle Eb thought of going on, but the night was coming fast and there would be no moon and we were footsore and hungry. Women and children came over to our fire, after supper, and made more of me than I liked. I remember taking refuge between the knees of Uncle Eb, and Fred sat close in front of us growling fiercely when they came too near. They stood about, looking down at us and whispered together, and one young miss of the tribe came up and tried to kiss me in spite of Fred's warnings: She had flashing black eyes and hair as dark as the night, that fell in a curling mass upon her shoulders; but, somehow, I had a mighty fear of her and fought with desperation to keep my face from the touch of her red lips. Uncle Eb laughed and held Fred by the collar, and I began to cry out in terror, presently, when, to my great relief, she let go and ran away to her own people. They all went away to their wagons, save one young man, who was tall with light hair and a fair skin, and who looked like none of the other gypsies.

'Take care of yourself,' he whispered, as soon as the rest had gone. 'These are bad people. You'd better be off.'

The young man left us and Uncle Eb began to pack up at once. They were going to bed in their wagons when we came away. I stood in the basket and Fred drew the wagon that had in it only a few bundles. A mile or more further on we came to a lonely, deserted cabin close to the road. It had began to thunder in the distance and the wind was blowing damp.

'Guess nobody lives here,' said Uncle Eb as he turned in at the sagging gate and began to cross the little patch of weeds and hollyhocks behind it 'Door's half down, but I guess it'll de better'n no house. Goin' t' rain sartin.'

I was nodding a little about then, I remember; but I was wide awake when he took me out of the basket The old house stood on a high hill, and we could see the stars of heaven through the ruined door and one of the back windows. Uncle Eb lifted the leaning door a little and shoved it aside. We heard then a quick stir in the old house—a loud and ghostly rattle it seems now as I think of it—like that made by linen shaking on the line. Uncle Eb took a step backward as if it had startled him.

'Guess it's nuthin' to be 'fraid of;' he said, feeling in the pet of his coat He had struck a match in a moment. By its flickering light I could see only a bit of rubbish on the floor.

'Full o' white owls,' said he, stepping inside, where the rustling was now continuous. 'They'll do us no harm.'

I could see them now flying about under the low ceiling. Uncle Eb gathered an armful of grass and clover, in the near field, and spread it in a corner well away from the ruined door and windows. Covered with our blanket it made a fairly comfortable bed. Soon as we had lain down, the rain began to rattle on the shaky roof and flashes of lightning lit every corner of the old room.

I have had, ever, a curious love of storms, and, from the time when memory began its record in my brain, it has delighted me to hear at night the roar of thunder and see the swift play of the lightning. I lay between Uncle Eb and the old dog, who both went asleep shortly. Less wearied I presume than either of them, for I had done none of the carrying, and had slept along time that day in the shade of a tree, I was awake an hour or more after they were snoring. Every flash lit the old room like the full glare of the noonday sun. I remember it showed me an old cradle, piled full of rubbish, a rusty scythe hung in the rotting sash of a window, a few lengths of stove-pipe and a plough in one corner, and three staring white owls that sat on a beam above the doorway. The rain roared on the old roof shortly, and came dripping down through the bare boards above us. A big drop struck in my face and I moved a little. Then I saw what made me hold my breath a moment and cover my head with the shawl. A flash of lightning revealed a tall, ragged man looking in at the doorway. I lay close to Uncle Eb imagining much evil of that vision but made no outcry.

Snugged in between my two companions I felt reasonably secure and soon fell asleep. The sun, streaming in at the open door, roused me in the morning. At the beginning of each day of our journey I woke to find Uncle Eb cooking at the fire. He was lying beside me, this morning, his eyes open.

'Fraid I'm hard sick,' he said as I kissed him.

'What's the matter?' I enquired.

He struggled to a sitting posture, groaning so it went to my heart.

'Rheumatiz,' he answered presently.

He got to his feet, little by little, and every move he made gave him great pain. With one hand on his cane and the other on my shoulder he made his way slowly to the broken gate. Even now I can see clearly the fair prospect of that high place—a valley reaching to distant hills and a river winding through it, glimmering in the sunlight; a long wooded ledge breaking into naked, grassy slopes on one side of the valley and on the other a deep forest rolling to the far horizon; between them big patches of yellow grain and white buckwheat and green pasture land and greener meadows and the straight road, with white houses on either side of it, glorious in a double fringe of golden rod and purple aster and yellow John's-wort and the deep blue of the Jacob's ladder.

'Looks a good deal like the promised land,' said Uncle Eb. 'Hain't got much further t' go.'

He sat on the rotting threshold while I pulled some of the weeds in front of the doorstep and brought kindlings out of the house and built a fire. While we were eating I told Uncle Eb of the man that I had seen in the night.

'Guess you was dreamin',' he said, and, while I stood firm for the reality of that I had seen, it held our thought only for a brief moment. My companion was unable to walk that day so we lay by, in the shelter of the old house, eating as little of our scanty store as we could do with. I went to a spring near by for water and picked a good mess of blackberries that I hid away until supper time, so as to surprise Uncle Eb. A longer day than that we spent in the old house, after our coming, I have never known. I made the room a bit tidier and gathered more grass for bedding. Uncle Eb felt better as the day grew warm. I had a busy time of it that morning bathing his back in the spirits and rubbing until my small arms ached. I have heard him tell often how vigorously I worked that day and how I would say: 'I'll take care o' you, Uncle Eb—won't I, Uncle Eb?' as my little hands flew with redoubled energy on his bare skin. That finished we lay down sleeping until the sun was low, when I made ready the supper that took the last of everything we had to eat. Uncle Eb was more like himself that evening and, sitting up in the corner, as the darkness came, told me the story of Squirreltown and Frog Ferry, which came to be so great a standby in those days that, even now, I can recall much of the language in which he told it.

'Once,' he said, 'there was a boy thet hed two grey squirrels in a cage. They kep' thinkin' o' the time they used t' scamper in the tree-tops an' make nests an' eat all the nuts they wanted an' play I spy in the thick leaves. An they grew poor an' looked kind o' ragged an' sickly an' downhearted. When he brought 'em outdoors they used t' look up in the trees an' run in the wire wheel as if they thought they could get there sometime if they kep' goin'. As the boy grew older he see it was cruel to keep 'em shet in a cage, but he'd hed em a long time an' couldn't bear t' give 'em up.

'One day he was out in the woods a little back o' the clearin'. All t' once he heard a swift holler. 'Twas nearby an' echoed so he couldn't tell which way it come from. He run fer home but the critter ketched 'im before he got out o' the woods an' took 'im into a cave, an' give 'im t' the little swifts t' play with. The boy cried terrible. The swifts they laughed an' nudged each other.

'"O ain't he cute!" says one. "He's a beauty!" says another. "Cur'us how he can git along without any fur," says the mother swift, as she run er nose over 'is bare foot. He thought of 'is folks waitin' fer him an' he begged em t' let 'im go. Then they come an' smelt 'im over.

'"Yer sech a cunnin' critter," says the mother swift, "we couldn't spare ye."

'"Want to see my mother," says the boy sobbing.

'"Couldn't afford t' let ye go—yer so cute," says the swift. "Bring the poor critter a bone an' a bit o' snake meat."

'The boy couldn't eat. They fixed a bed fer him, but 'twant clean. The feel uv it made his back ache an' the smell uv it made him sick to his stomach.

'"When the swifts hed comp'ny they 'd bring 'em overt' look at him there 'n his dark corner." "S a boy," said the mother swift pokin' him with a long stick "Wouldn't ye like t' see 'im run?" Then she punched him until he got up an' run 'round the cave fer his life. Happened one day et a very benevolent swift come int' the cave.

'"'S a pity t' keep the boy here," said he; "he looks bad."

'"But he makes fun fer the children," said the swift.

'"Fun that makes misery is only fit fer a fool," said the visitor.

'They let him go thet day. Soon as he got hum he thought o' the squirrels an' was tickled t' find 'em alive. He tak 'em off to an island, in the middle of a big lake, thet very day, an' set the cage on the shore n' opened it He thought he would come back sometime an' see how they was ginin' along. The cage was made of light wire an' hed a tin bottom fastened to a big piece o' plank. At fust they was 'fraid t' leave it an' peeked out o' the door an' scratched their heads's if they thought it a resky business. After awhile one stepped out careful an' then the other followed. They tried t' climb a tree, but their nails was wore off an' they kep' fallin' back. Then they went off 'n the brush t' find some nuts. There was only pines an' poppies an' white birch an' a few berry bushes on the island. They went t' the water's edge on every side, but there was nuthin there a squirrel ud give a flirt uv his tail fer. 'Twas near dark when they come back t' the cage hungry as tew bears. They found a few crumbs o' bread in the cup an' divided 'em even. Then they went t' bed 'n their ol' nest.

'It hed been rainin' a week in the mount'ins. Thet night the lake rose a foot er more an' 'fore mornin' the cage begun t' rock a teenty bit as the water lifted the plank. They slep' all the better fer thet an' they dreamed they was up in a tree at the end uv a big bough. The cage begun t' sway sideways and then it let go o' the shore an' spun 'round once er twice an' sailed out 'n the deep water. There was a light breeze blowin' offshore an' purty soon it was pitchin' like a ship in the sea. But the two squirrels was very tired an' never woke up 'til sunrise. They got a terrible scare when they see the water 'round 'em an' felt the motion o' the ship. Both on 'em ran into the wire wheel an' that bore down the stern o' the ship so the under wires touched the water. They made it spin like a buzz saw an' got their clothes all wet. The ship went faster when they worked the wheel, an' bime bye they got tired an' come out on the main deck. The water washed over it a little so they clim up the roof thet was a kin' uv a hurricane deck. It made the ship sway an' rock fearful but they hung on 'midships, an' clung t' the handle that stuck up like a top mast. Their big tails was spread over their shoulders, an' the wind rose an' the ship went faster 'n faster. They could see the main shore where the big woods come down t' the water 'n' all the while it kep' a comin' nearer 'n' nearer. But they was so hungry didn't seem possible they could live to git there.

'Ye know squirrels are a savin' people. In the day o' plenty they think o' the day o' poverty an' lay by fer it. All at once one uv 'em thought uv a few kernels o' corn, he hed pushed through a little crack in the tin floor one day a long time ago. It happened there was quite a hole under the crack an' each uv 'em bad stored some kernels unbeknown t' the other. So they hed a good supper 'n' some left fer a bite 'n the mornin'. 'Fore daylight the ship made her pott 'n' lay to, 'side liv a log in a little cove. The bullfrogs jumped on her main deck an' begun t' holler soon as she hove to: "all ashore! all ashore! all ashore!" The two squirrels woke up but lay quiet 'til the sun rose. Then they come out on the log 'et looked like a long dock an' run ashore 'n' foun' some o' their own folks in the bush. An' when they bed tol' their story the ol' father o' the tribe got up 'n a tree an' hollered himself hoarse preachin' 'bout how 't paid t' be savin'.

'"An' we should learn t' save our wisdom es well es our nuts," said a sassy brother; "fer each needs his own wisdom fer his own affairs."

'An the little ship went back 'n' forth 'cross the cove as the win' blew. The squirrels hed many a fine ride in her an' the frogs were the ferrymen. An' all 'long thet shore 'twas known es Frog Ferry 'mong the squirrel folks.'

It was very dark when he finished the tale an' as we lay gaping a few minutes after my last query about those funny people of the lake margin I could hear nothing but the chirping of the crickets. I was feeling a bit sleepy when I heard the boards creak above our heads. Uncle Eli raised himself and lay braced upon his elbow listening. In a few moments we heard a sound as of someone coming softly down the ladder at the other end of the room. It was so dark I could see nothing.

'Who's there?' Uncle Eb demanded.

'Don't p'int thet gun at me,' somebody whispered. 'This is my home and I warn ye t' leave it er I'll do ye harm.'

Chapter 5

Here I shall quote you again from the diary of Uncle Eb. 'It was so dark I couldn't see a han' before me. "Don't p'int yer gun at me," the man whispered. Thought 'twas funny he could see me when I couldn't see him. Said 'twas his home an' we'd better leave. Tol him I was sick (rumatiz) an' couldn't stir. Said he was sorry an' come over near us. Tol' him I was an' ol' man goin' west with a small boy. Stopped in the rain. Got sick. Out o' purvisions. 'Bout ready t' die. Did'n know what t' do. Started t' stike a match an' the man said don't make no light cos I don't want to hev ye see my face. Never let nobody see my face. Said he never went out 'less 'twas a dark night until folks was abed. Said we looked like good folks. Scairt me a little cos we couldn't see a thing. Also he said don't be 'fraid of me. Do what I can fer ye.'

I remember the man crossed the creaking floor and sat down near us after he had parleyed with Uncle Eb awhile in whispers. Young as I was I keep a vivid impression of that night and, aided by the diary of Uncle Eb, I have made a record of what was said that is, in the main, accurate.

'Do you know where you are?' he enquired presently, whispering as he had done before.

'I've no idee,' said Uncle Eb.

'Well, down the hill is Paradise Valley in the township o' Faraway,' he continued. 'It's the end o' Paradise Road an' a purty country. Been settled a long time an' the farms are big an' prosperous—kind uv a land o' plenty. That big house at the foot o' the hill is Dave Brower's. He's the richest man in the valley.'

'How do you happen t' be livin' here?—if ye don't min' tellin' me,' Uncle Eb asked.

'Crazy,' said he; "fraid uv everybody an' everybody's 'fraid o' me. Lived a good long time in this way. Winters I go into the big woods. Got a camp in a big cave an' when I'm there I see a little daylight. Here 'n the clearin' I'm only up in the night-time. Thet's how I've come to see so well in the dark. It's give me cat's eyes.'

'Don't ye git lonesome?' Uncle Eb asked.

'Awful—sometimes,' he answered with a sad sigh, 'an' it seems good t' talk with somebody besides myself. I get enough to eat generally. There are deer in the woods an' cows in the fields, ye know, an' potatoes an' corn an' berries an' apples, an' all thet kind o' thing. Then I've got my traps in the woods where I ketch partridges, an' squirrels an' coons an' all the meat I need. I've got a place in the thick timber t' do my cookin'—all I want t' do—in the middle of the night Sometimes I come here an' spend a day in the garret if I'm caught in a storm or if I happen to stay a little too late in the valley. Once in a great while I meet a man somewhere in the open but he always gits away quick as he can. Guess they think I'm a ghost—dunno what I think o' them.'

Our host went on talking as if he were glad to tell the secrets of his heart to some creature of his own kind. I have often wondered at his frankness; but there was a fatherly tenderness, I remember in the voice of Uncle Eb, and I judge it tempted his confidence. Probably the love of companionship can never be so dead in a man but that the voice of kindness may call it back to life again.

'I'll bring you a bite t' eat before morning,' he said, presently, as he rose to go, 'leet me feel o' your han', mister.'

Uncle Eb gave him his hand and thanked him.

'Feels good. First I've hed hold of in a long time,' he whispered.

'What's the day o' the month?'

'The twenty-fifth.'

'I must remember. Where did you come from?'

Uncle Eb told him, briefly, the story of our going west

'Guess you'd never do me no harm—would ye?' the man asked. 'Not a bit,' Uncle Eb answered.

Then he bade us goodbye, crossed the creaking floor and went away in the darkness.

'Sing'lar character!' Uncle Eb muttered.

I was getting drowsy and that was the last I heard. In the morning we found a small pail of milk sitting near us, a roasted partridge, two fried fish and some boiled potatoes. It was more than enough to carry us through the day with a fair allowance for Fred. Uncle Eb was a bit better but very lame at that and kept to his bed the greater part of the day. The time went slow with me I remember. Uncle Eb was not cheerful and told me but one story and that had no life in it. At dusk he let me go out in the road to play awhile with Fred and the wagon, but came to the door and called us in shortly. I went to bed in a rather unhappy frame of mind. The dog roused me by barking in the middle of the right and I heard again the familiar whisper of the stranger.

'Sh-h-h! be still, dog,' he whispered; but I was up to my ears in sleep and went under shortly, so I have no knowledge of what passed that night. Uncle Eb tells in his diary that he had a talk with him lasting more than an hour, but goes no further and never seemed willing to talk much about that interview or others that followed it.

I only know the man had brought more milk and fish and fowl for us. We stayed another day in the old house, that went like the last, and the night man came again to see Uncle Eb. The next morning my companion was able to walk more freely, but Fred and I had to stop and wait for him very often going down the big hill. I was mighty glad when we were leaving the musty old house for good and had the dog hitched with all our traps in the wagon. It was a bright morning and the sunlight glimmered on the dew in the broad valley. The men were just coming from breakfast when we turned in at David Brower's. A barefooted little girl a bit older than I, with red cheeks and blue eyes and long curly hair, that shone like gold in the sunlight, came running out to meet us and led me up to the doorstep, highly amused at the sight of Fred and the wagon. I regarded her with curiosity and suspicion at first, while Uncle Eb was talking with the men. I shall never forget that moment when David Brower came and lifted me by the shoulders, high above his head, and shook me as if to test my mettle. He led me into the house then where his wife was working.

'What do you think of this small bit of a boy?' he asked.

She had already knelt on the floor and put her arms about my neck and kissed me.

'Am' no home,' said he. 'Come all the way from Vermont with an ol' man. They're worn out both uv 'em. Guess we'd better take 'em in awhile.'

'O yes, mother—please, mother,' put in the little girl who was holding my hand. 'He can sleep with me, mother. Please let him stay.'

She knelt beside me and put her arms around my little shoulders and drew me to her breast and spoke to me very tenderly.

'Please let him stay,' the girl pleaded again.

'David,' said the woman, 'I couldn't turn the little thing away. Won't ye hand me those cookies.'

And so our life began in Paradise Valley. Ten minutes later I was playing my first game of 'I spy' with little Hope Brower, among the fragrant stooks of wheat in the field back of the garden.

Chapter 6

The lone pine stood in Brower's pasture, just clear of the woods. When the sun rose, one could see its taper shadow stretching away to the foot of Woody Ledge, and at sunset it lay like a fallen mast athwart the cow-paths, its long top arm a flying pennant on the side of Bowman's Hill. In summer this bar of shadow moved like a clock-hand on the green dial of the pasture, and the help could tell the time by the slant of it. Lone Pine had a mighty girth at the bottom, and its bare body tapered into the sky as straight as an arrow. Uncle Eb used to say that its one long, naked branch that swung and creaked near the top of it, like a sign of hospitality on the highway of the birds, was two hundred feet above ground. There were a few stubs here and there upon its shaft—the roost of crows and owls and hen-hawks. It must have passed for a low resort in the feathered kingdom because it was only the robbers of the sky that halted on Lone Pine.

This towering shaft of dead timber commemorated the ancient forest through which the northern Yankees cut their trails in the beginning of the century. They were a tall, big fisted, brawny lot of men who came across the Adirondacks from Vermont, and began to break the green canopy that for ages had covered the valley of the St Lawrence. Generally they drove a cow with them, and such game as they could kill on the journey supplemented their diet of 'pudding and milk'. Some settled where the wagon broke or where they had buried a member of the family, and there they cleared the forests that once covered the smooth acres of today. Gradually the rough surface of the trail grew smoother until it became Paradise Road—the well-worn thoroughfare of the stagecoach with its 'inns and outs', as the drivers used to say—the inns where the 'men folks' sat in the firelight of the blazing logs after supper and told tales of adventure until bedtime, while the women sat with their knitting in the parlour, and the young men wrestled in the stableyard. The men of middle age had stooped and massive shoulders, and deep-furrowed brows: Tell one of them he was growing old and he might answer you by holding his whip in front of him and leaping over it between his hands.

There was a little clearing around that big pine tree when David Brower settled in the valley. Its shadows shifting in the light of sun and moon, like the arm of a compass, swept the spreading acres of his farm, and he built his house some forty rods from the foot of it on higher ground. David was the oldest of thirteen children. His father had died the year before he came to St Lawrence county, leaving him nothing but heavy responsibilities. Fortunately, his great strength and his kindly nature were equal to the burden. Mother and children were landed safely in their new home on Bowman's Hill the day that David was eighteen. I have heard the old folks of that country tell what a splendid figure of a man he was those days—six feet one in his stockings and broad at the shoulder. His eyes were grey and set under heavy brows. I have never forgotten the big man that laid hold of me and the broad clean-shaven serious face, that looked into mine the day I came to Paradise Valley. As I write I can see plainly his dimpled chin, his large nose, his firm mouth that was the key to his character. 'Open or shet,' I have heard the old folks say, 'it showed he was no fool.'

After two years David took a wife and settled in Paradise Valley. He prospered in a small way considered handsome thereabouts. In a few years he had cleared the rich acres of his farm to the sugar bush that was the north vestibule of the big forest; he had seen the clearing widen until he could discern the bare summits of the distant hills, and, far as he could see, were the neat white houses of the settlers. Children had come, three of them—the eldest a son who had left home and died in a far country long before we came to Paradise Valley—the youngest a baby.

I could not have enjoyed my new home more if I had been born in it. I had much need of a mother's tenderness, no doubt, for I remember with what a sense of peace and comfort I lay on the lap of Elizabeth Brower, that first evening, and heard her singing as she rocked. The little daughter stood at her knees, looking down at me and patting my bare toes or reaching over to feel my face.

'God sent him to us—didn't he, mother?' said she.

'Maybe,' Mrs Brower answered, 'we'll be good to him, anyway.'

Then that old query came into my mind. I asked them if it was heaven where we were.

'No,' they answered.

''Tain't anywhere near here, is it?' I went on.

Then she told me about the gate of death, and began sowing in me the seed of God's truth—as I know now the seed of many harvests. I slept with Uncle Eb in the garret, that night, and for long after we came to the Brower's. He continued to get better, and was shortly able to give his hand to the work of the farm.

There was room for all of us in that ample wilderness of his imagination, and the cry of the swift woke its echoes every evening for a time. Bears and panthers prowled in the deep thickets, but the swifts took a firmer grip on us, being bolder and more terrible. Uncle Eb became a great favourite in the family, and David Brower came to know soon that he was 'a good man to work' and could be trusted 'to look after things'. We had not been there long when I heard Elizabeth speak of Nehemiah—her lost son—and his name was often on the lips of others. He was a boy of sixteen when he went away, and I learned no more of him until long afterwards.

A month or more after we came to Faraway, I remember we went 'cross lots in a big box wagon to the orchard on the hill and gathered apples that fell in a shower when Uncle Eb went up to shake them down. Then cane the raw days of late October, when the crows went flying southward before the wind—a noisy pirate fleet that filled the sky at times—and when we all put on our mittens and went down the winding cow-paths to the grove of butternuts in the pasture. The great roof of the wilderness had turned red and faded into yellow. Soon its rafters began to show through, and then, in a day or two, they were all bare but for some patches of evergreen. Great, golden drifts of foliage lay higher than a man's head in the timber land about the clearing. We had our best fun then, playing 'I spy' in the groves.

In that fragrant deep of leaves one might lie undiscovered a long time. He could hear roaring like that of water at every move of the finder, wallowing nearer and nearer possibly, in his search. Old Fred came generally rooting his way to us in the deep drift with unerring accuracy.

And shortly winter came out of the north and, of a night, after rapping at the windows and howling in the chimney and roaring in the big woods, took possession of the earth. That was a time when hard cider flowed freely and recollection found a ready tongue among the older folk, and the young enjoyed many diversions, including measles and whooping cough.

Chapter 7

I had a lot of fun that first winter, but none that I can remember more gratefully than our trip in the sledgehouse—a tight little house fitted and fastened to a big sledge. Uncle Eb had to go to mill at Hillsborough, some twelve miles away, and Hope and I, after much coaxing and many family counsels, got leave to go with him. The sky was cloudless, and the frosty air was all aglow in the sunlight that morning we started. There was a little sheet iron stove in one corner of the sledgehouse, walled in with zinc and anchored with wires; a layer of hay covered the floor and over that we spread our furs and blankets. The house had an open front, and Uncle Eb sat on the doorstep, as it were, to drive, while we sat behind him on the blankets.

'I love you very much,' said Hope, embracing me, after we were seated. Her affection embarrassed me, I remember. It seemed unmanly to be petted like a doll.

'I hate to be kissed,' I said, pulling away from her, at which Uncle Eb laughed heartily.

The day came when I would have given half my life for the words I held so cheaply then.

'You'd better be good t' me,' she answered, 'for when mother dies I'm goin' t' take care o' you. Uncle Eb and Gran'ma Bisnette an' you an' everybody I love is goin' t' come an' live with me in a big, big house. An' I'm goin' t' put you t' bed nights an' hear ye say yer prayers an everything.'

'Who'll do the spankin?' Uncle Eb asked.

'My husban',' she answered, with a sigh at the thought of all the trouble that lay before her.

'An' I'll make him rub your back, too, Uncle Eb,' she added. 'Wall, I rather guess he'll object to that,' said he.

'Then you can give 'ins five cents, an' I guess he'll be glad t' do it,' she answered promptly.

'Poor man! He won't know whether he's runnin' a poorhouse er a hospital, will he?' said Uncle Eb. 'Look here, children,' he added, taking out his old leather wallet, as he held the reins between his knees. 'Here's tew shillin' apiece for ye, an' I want ye t' spend it jest eggsackly as ye please.' The last words were spoken slowly and with emphasis.

We took the two silver pieces that he handed to us and looked them all over and compared them.

'I know what I'll do,' said she, suddenly. 'I'm goin' t' buy my mother a new dress, or mebbe a beautiful ring,' she added thoughtfully.

For my own part I did not know what I should buy. I wanted a real gun most of all and my inclination oscillated between that and a red rocking horse. My mind was very busy while I sat in silence. Presently I rose and went to Uncle Eb and whispered in his ear.

'Do you think I could get a real rifle with two shilin'?' I enquired anxiously.

'No,' he answered in a low tone that seemed to respect my confidence. 'Bime by, when you're older, I'll buy ye a rifle—a real rip snorter, too, with a shiny barrel 'n a silver lock. When ye get down t, the village ye'll see lots o' things y'd rather hev, prob'ly. If I was you, children,' he added, in a louder tone, 'I wouldn't buy a thing but nuts 'n' raisins.'

'Nuts 'n' raisins!' Hope exclaimed, scornfully.

'Nuts 'n' raisins,' he repeated. 'They're cheap 'n' satisfyin'. If ye eat enough uv 'em you'll never want anything else in this world.'

I failed to see the irony in Uncle Eb's remark and the suggestion seemed to have a good deal of merit, the more I thought it over.

''T any rate,' said Uncle Eb, 'I'd git somethin' fer my own selves.'

'Well,' said Hope, 'You tell us a lot o' things we could buy.'

'Less see!' said Uncle Eb, looking very serious. 'There's bootjacks an' there's warmin' pans 'n' mustard plasters 'n' liver pads 'n' all them kind o' things.'

We both shook our heads very doubtfully.

'Then,' he added, 'there are jimmyjacks 'n' silver no nuthin's.'

There were many other suggestions but none of them were decisive.

The snow lay deep on either side of the way and there was a glimmer on every white hillside where Jack Frost had sown his diamonds. Here and there a fox track crossed the smooth level of the valley and dwindled on the distant hills like a seam in a great white robe. It grew warmer as the sun rose, and we were a jolly company behind the merry jingle of the sleigh bells. We had had a long spell of quiet weather and the road lay in two furrows worn as smooth as ice at the bottom.

'Consarn it!' said Uncle Eb looking up at the sky, after we had been on the road an hour or so. 'There's a sun dog. Wouldn't wonder if we got a snowstorm' fore night.

I was running behind the sledge and standing on the brake hooks going downhill. He made me get in when he saw the sun dog, and let our horse—a rat-tailed bay known as Old Doctor—go at a merry pace.

We were awed to silence when we came in sight of Hillsborough, with spires looming far into the sky, as it seemed to me then, and buildings that bullied me with their big bulk, so that I had no heart for the spending of the two shillings Uncle Eb had given me. Such sublimity of proportion I have never seen since; and yet it was all very small indeed. The stores had a smell about them that was like chloroform in its effect upon me; for, once in them, I fell into a kind of trance and had scarce sense enough to know my own mind. The smart clerks, who generally came and asked, 'Well, young man, what can I do for you?' I regarded with fear and suspicion. I clung the tighter to my coin always, and said nothing, although I saw many a trinket whose glitter went to my soul with a mighty fascination. We both stood staring silently at the show cases, our tongues helpless with awe and wonder. Finally, after a whispered conference, Hope asked for a 'silver no nothing', and provoked so much laughter that we both fled to the sidewalk. Uncle Eb had to do our buying for us in the end.

'Wall, what'll ye hev?' he said to me at length.

I tried to think-it was no easy thing to do after all I had seen.

'Guess I'll take a jacknife,' I whispered.

'Give this boy a knife,' he demanded. 'Wants t' be good 'n sharp. Might hev t' skin a swift with it sometime.'

'What ye want?' he asked, then turning to Hope.

'A doll,' she whispered.

'White or black?' said he.

'White,' said she, 'with dark eyes and hair.'

'Want a reel, splendid, firs'-class doll,' he said to the clerk. 'Thet one'll do, there, with the sky-blue dress 'n the pink apron.'

We were worn out with excitement when we left for home under lowering skies. We children lay side by side under the robes, the doll between us, and were soon asleep. It was growing dark when Uncle Eb woke us, and the snow was driving in at the doorway. The air was full of snow, I remember, and Old Doctor was wading to his knees in a drift. We were up in the hills and the wind whistled in our little chimney. Uncle Eb had a serious look in his face. The snow grew deeper and Old Doctor went slower every moment.

'Six mild from home,' Uncle Eb muttered, as he held up to rest a moment. 'Six mild from home. 'Fraid we're in fer a night uv it.'

We got to the top of Fadden's Hill about dark, and the snow lay so deep in the cut we all got out for fear the house would tip over. Old Doctor floundered along a bit further until he went down in the drift and lay between the shafts half buried. We had a shovel that always hung beside a small hatchet in the sledgehouse—for one might need much beside the grace of God of a winter's day in that country—and with it Uncle Eb began to uncover the horse. We children stood in the sledgehouse door watching him and holding the lantern. Old Doctor was on his feet in a few minutes.

''Tain' no use tryin',' said Uncle Eb, as he began to unhitch. 'Can't go no further t'night.'

Then he dug away the snow beside the sledgehouse, and hitched Old Doctor to the horseshoe that was nailed to the rear end of it. That done, he clambered up the side of the cut and took some rails off the fence and shoved them over on the roof of the house, so that one end rested there and the other on the high bank beside us. Then he cut a lot of hemlock boughs with the hatchet, and thatched the roof he had made over Old Doctor, binding them with the reins. Bringing more rails, he leaned them to the others on the windward side and nailed a big blanket over them, piecing it out with hemlock thatching, so it made a fairly comfortable shelter. We were under the wind in this deep cut on Fadden's Hill, and the snow piled in upon us rapidly. We had a warm blanket for Old Doctor and two big buffalo robes for our own use. We gave him a good feed of hay and oats, and then Uncle Eb cut up a fence rail with our hatchet and built a roaring fire in the stove. We had got a bit chilly wading in the snow, and the fire gave us a mighty sense of comfort.

'I thought somethin' might happen,' said Uncle Eb, as he hung his lantern to the ridge pole and took a big paper parcel out of his great coat pocket. 'I thought mebbe somethin' might happen, an' so I brought along a bite o' luncheon.'

He gave us dried herring and bread and butter and cheese.

"S a little dry,' he remarked, while we were eating, 'but it's drier where there's none.'

We had a pail of snow on top of the little stove and plenty of good drinking water for ourselves and the Old Doctor in a few minutes.

After supper Uncle Eb went up the side of the cut and brought back a lot of hemlock boughs and spread them under Old Doctor for bedding.

Then we all sat around the stove on the warm robes and listened to the wind howling above our little roof and the stories of Uncle Eb. The hissing of the snow as it beat upon the sledgehouse grew fainter by and by, and Uncle Eb said he guessed we were pretty well covered up. We fell asleep soon. I remember he stopped in the middle of a wolf story, and, seeing that our eyes were shut, pulled us back from the fire a little and covered us with one of the robes. It had been a mighty struggle between Sleep and Romance, and Sleep had won. I roused myself and begged him to go on with the story, but he only said, 'Hush, boy; it's bedtime,' and turned up the lantern and went out of doors. I woke once or twice in the night and saw him putting wood on the fire. He had put out the light. The gleam of the fire shone on his face when he opened the stove door.

'Gittin' a leetle cool here, Uncle Eb,' he was saying to himself.

We were up at daylight, and even then it was snowing and blowing fiercely. There were two feet of snow on the sledgehouse roof, and we were nearly buried in the bank. Uncle Eb had to do a lot of shoveling to get out of doors and into the stable. Old Doctor was quite out of the wind in a cave of snow and nickering for his breakfast. There was plenty for him, but we were on short rations. Uncle Eb put on the snow shoes, after we had eaten what there was left, and, cautioning us to keep in, set out for Fadden's across lots. He came back inside of an hour with a good supply of provisions in a basket on his shoulder. The wind had gone down and the air was milder. Big flakes of snow came fluttering slowly downward out of a dark sky. After dinner we went up on top of the sledgehouse and saw a big scraper coming in the valley below. Six teams of oxen were drawing it, and we could see the flying furrows on either side of the scraper as it ploughed in the deep drifts. Uncle Eb put on the snow shoes again, and, with Hope on his back and me clinging to his hand, he went down to meet them and to tell of our plight. The front team had wallowed to their ears, and the men were digging them out with shovels when we got to the scraper. A score of men and boys clung to the sides of that big, hollow wedge, and put their weight on it as the oxen pulled. We got on with the others, I remember, and I was swept off as soon as the scraper started by a roaring avalanche of snow that came down upon our heads and buried me completely. I was up again and had a fresh hold in a jiffy, and clung to my place until I was nearly smothered by the flying snow. It was great fun for me, and they were all shouting and hallooing as if it were a fine holiday. They made slow progress, however, and we left them shortly on their promise to try to reach us before night. If they failed to get through, one of them said he would drive over to Paradise Valley, if possible, and tell the Browers we were all right.

On our return, Uncle Eb began shoveling a tunnel in the cut. When we got through to the open late in the afternoon we saw the scraper party going back with their teams.

'Guess they've gi'n up fer t'day,' said he. 'Snow's powerful deep down there below the bridge. Mebbe we can get 'round to where the road's clear by goin' 'cross lots. I've a good mind t' try it.'

Then he went over in the field and picked a winding way down the hill toward the river, while we children stood watching him. He came back soon and took down a bit of the fence and harnessed Old Doctor and hitched him to the sledgehouse. The tunnel was just wide enough to let us through with a tight pinch here and there. The footing was rather soft' and the horse had hard pulling. We went in the field, struggling on afoot—we little people—while Uncle Eb led the horse. He had to stop frequently to tunnel through a snowdrift, and at dusk we had only got half-way to the bridge from our cave in the cut. Of a sudden Old Doctor went up to his neck in a wall of deep snow that seemed to cut us off completely. He struggled a moment, falling on his side and wrenching the shafts from the runners. Uncle Eb went to work vigorously with his shovel and had soon cut a narrow box stall in the deep snow around Old Doctor. Just beyond the hill dipped sharply and down the slope we could see the stubble sticking through the shallow snow. 'We'll hev t' stop right where we are until mornin',' he said. 'It's mos' dark now.

Our little house stood tilting forward about half-way down the hill, its runners buried in the snow. A few hundred yards below was a cliff where the shore fell to the river some thirty feet It had stopped snowing, and the air had grown warmer, but the sky was dark We put nearly all the hay in the sledgehouse under Old Doctor and gave him the last of the oats and a warm cover of blankets. Then Uncle Eb went away to the fence for more wood, while we spread the supper. He was very tired, I remember, and we all turned in for the night a short time after we had eaten. The little stove was roaring like a furnace when we spread our blankets on the sloping floor and lay down, our feet to the front, and drew the warm robes over us. Uncle Eb, who had had no sleep the night before, began to snore heavily before we children had stopped whispering. He was still snoring, and Hope sound asleep, when I woke in the night and heard the rain falling on our little roof and felt the warm breath of the south wind. The water dripping from the eaves and falling far and near upon the yielding snow had many voices. I was half-asleep when I heard a new noise under the sledge. Something struck the front corner of the sledgehouse—a heavy, muffled blow—and brushed the noisy boards. Then I heard the timbers creak and felt the runners leaping over the soft snow. I remember it was like a dream of falling. I raised myself and stared about me. We were slipping down the steep floor. The lantern, burning dimly under the roof, swung and rattled. Uncle Eb was up on his elbow staring wildly. I could feel the jar and rush of the runners and the rain that seemed to roar as it dashed into my face. Then, suddenly, the sledgehouse gave a great leap into the air and the grating of the runners ceased. The lantern went hard against the roof; there was a mighty roar in my ears; then we heard a noise like thunder and felt the shock of a blow that set my back aching, and cracked the roof above our heads. It was all still for a second; then we children began to cry, and Uncle Eb staggered to his feet and lit the lantern that had gone out and that had no globe, I remember, as he held it down to our faces.

'Hush! Are you hurt?' he said, as he knelt before us. 'Git up now, see if ye can stand.'

We got to our feet, neither of us much the worse for what had happened—My knuckles were cut a bit by a splinter, and Hope had been hit on the shins by the lantern globe as it fell.

'By the Lord Harry!' said Uncle Eb, when he saw we were not hurt. 'Wonder what hit us.'

We followed him outside while he was speaking.

'We've slid downhill,' he said. 'Went over the cliff. Went kerplunk in the deep snow, er there'd have been nuthin' left uv us. Snow's meltin' jest as if it was July.'

Uncle Eb helped us into our heavy coats, and then with a blanket over his arm led us into the wet snow. We came out upon clear ice in a moment and picked our way along the lowering shore. At length Uncle Eb clambered up, pulling us up after him, one by one. Then he whistled to Old Doctor, who whinnied a quick reply. He left us standing together, the blanket over our heads, and went away in the dark whistling as he had done before. We could hear Old Doctor answer as he came near, and presently Uncle Eb returned leading the horse by the halter. Then he put us both on Old Doctor's back, threw the blanket over our heads, and started slowly for the road. We clung to each other as the horse staggered in the soft snow, and kept our places with some aid from Uncle Eb. We crossed the fence presently, and then for a way it was hard going. We found fair footing after we had passed the big scraper, and, coming to a house a mile or so down the road called them out of bed. It was growing light and they made us comfortable around a big stove, and gave us breakfast. The good man of the house took us home in a big sleigh after the chores were done. We met David Brower coming after us, and if we'd been gone a year we couldn't have received a warmer welcome.

Chapter 8

Of all that long season of snow, I remember most pleasantly the days that were sweetened with the sugar-making. When the sun was lifting his course in the clearing sky, and March had got the temper of the lamb, and the frozen pulses of the forest had begun to stir, the great kettle was mounted in the yard and all gave a hand to the washing of spouts and buckets. Then came tapping time, in which I helped carry the buckets and tasted the sweet flow that followed the auger's wound. The woods were merry with our shouts, and, shortly, one could hear the heart-beat of the maples in the sounding bucket. It was the reveille of spring. Towering trees shook down the gathered storms of snow and felt for the sunlight. The arch and shanty were repaired, the great iron kettle was scoured and lifted to its place, and then came the boiling. It was a great, an inestimable privilege to sit on the robes of faded fur, in the shanty, and hear the fire roaring under the kettle and smell the sweet odour of the boiling sap. Uncle Eb minded the shanty and the fire and the woods rang with his merry songs. When I think of that phase of the sugaring, I am face to face with one of the greatest perils of my life. My foster father had consented to let me spend a night with Uncle Eb in the shanty, and I was to sleep on the robes, where he would be beside me when he was not tending the fire. It had been a mild, bright day, and David came up with our supper at sunset. He sat talking with Uncle Eb for an hour or so, and the woods were darkling when he went away.

When he started on the dark trail that led to the clearing, I wondered at his courage—it was so black beyond the firelight. While we sat alone I plead for a story, but the thoughts of Uncle Eb had gone to roost early in a sort of gloomy meditation.

'Be still, my boy,' said he, 'an' go t' sleep. I ain't agoin' t' tell no yarns an' git ye all stirred up. Ye go t' sleep. Come mornin' we'll go down t' the brook an' see if we can't find a mink or tew 'n the traps.'

I remember hearing a great crackling of twigs in the dark wood before I slept. As I lifted my head, Uncle Eb whispered, 'Hark!' and we both listened. A bent and aged figure came stalking into the firelight. His long white hair mingled with his beard and covered his coat collar behind.

'Don't be scairt,' said Uncle Eb. "Tain' no bear. It's nuthin' but a poet.'

I knew him for a man who wandered much and had a rhyme for everyone—a kindly man with a reputation for laziness and without any home.

'Bilin', eh?' said the poet

'Bilin',' said Uncle Eb.

'I'm bilin' over 'n the next bush,' said the poet, sitting down.

'How's everything in Jingleville?' Uncle Eb enquired.

Then the newcomer answered:

'Well, neighbour dear, in Jingleville

We live by faith but we eat our fill;

An' what w'u'd we do if it wa'n't fer prayer?

Fer we can't raise a thing but whiskers an' hair.'

'Cur'us how you can talk po'try,' said Uncle Eb. 'The only thing I've got agin you is them whiskers an' thet hair. 'Tain't Christian.'

"Tain't what's on the head, but what's in it—thet's the important thing,' said the poet. 'Did I ever tell ye what I wrote about the birds?'

'Don' know's ye ever did,' said Uncle Eb, stirring his fire.

'The boy'll like it, mebbe,' said he, taking a dirty piece of paper out of his pocket and holding it to the light.

The poem interested me, young as I was, not less than the strange figure of the old poet who lived unknown in the backwoods, and who died, I dare say, with many a finer song in his heart. I remember how he stood in the firelight and chanted the words in a sing-song tone. He gave us that rude copy of the poem, and here it is:

THE ROBIN'S WEDDING

Young robin red breast hed a beautiful nest an' he says to his love says he:

It's ready now on a rocking bough

In the top of a maple tree.

I've lined it with down an' the velvet brown on the waist of a bumble-bee.

They were married next day, in the land o' the hay, the lady bird an' he.

The bobolink came an' the wife o' the same

An' the lark an' the fiddle de dee.

An' the crow came down in a minister gown—there was nothing

that he didn't see.

He fluttered his wing as they ast him to sing an' he tried fer t' clear

out his throat;

He hemmed an' he hawed an' be hawked an' he cawed

But he couldn't deliver a note.

The swallow was there an' he ushered each pair with his linsey an'

claw hammer coat.

The bobolink tried fer t' flirt with the bride in a way thet was sassy

an' bold.

An' the notes that he took as he shivered an' shook

Hed a sound like the jingle of gold.

He sat on a briar an' laughed at the choir an' said thet the music was old.

The sexton he came—Mr Spider by name—a citizen hairy and grey.

His rope in a steeple, he called the good people

That live in the land o' the hay.

The ants an' the squgs an' the crickets an' bugs—came out in a

mighty array.

Some came down from Barleytown an' the neighbouring city o' Rye.

An' the little black people they climbed every steeple

An' sat looking up at the sky.

They came fer t' see what a wedding might be an' they

furnished the cake an' the pie.

I remember he turned to me when he had finished and took one of my small hands and held it in his hard palm and looked at it and then into my face.

'Ah, boy!' he said, 'your way shall lead you far from here, and you shall get learning and wealth and win—victories.'

'What nonsense are you talking, Jed Ferry?' said Uncle Eb.

'O, you all think I'm a fool an' a humbug, 'cos I look it. Why, Eben Holden, if you was what ye looked, ye'd be in the presidential chair. Folks here 'n the valley think o' nuthin' but hard work—most uv 'em, an' I tell ye now this boy ain't a goin' t' be wuth putty on a farm. Look a' them slender hands.

'There was a man come to me the other day an' wanted t' hev a poem 'bout his wife that hed jes' died. I ast him t' tell me all 'bout her.

'"Wall," said he, after he had scratched his head an' thought a minute, "she was a dretful good woman t' work."

'"Anything else?" I asked.

'He thought agin fer a minute.

'"Broke her leg once," he said, "an' was laid up fer more'n a year."

"Must o' suffered," said I.

'"Not then," he answered. "Ruther enjoyed it layin' abed an' readin' an' bein' rubbed, but 'twas hard on the children."

'"S'pose ye loved her," I said.

'Then the tears come into his eyes an' he couldn't speak fer a minute. Putty soon he whispered "Yes" kind o' confidential. 'Course he loved her, but these Yankees are ashamed o' their feelin's. They hev tender thoughts, but they hide 'em as careful as the wild goose hides her eggs. I wrote a poem t' please him, an' goin' home I made up one fer myself, an 'it run 'bout like this:

O give me more than a life, I beg,

That finds real joy in a broken leg.

Whose only thought is t' work an' save

An' whose only rest is in the grave.

Saving an' scrimping from day to day

While its best it has squandered an' flung away

Fer a life like that of which I tell

Would rob me quite o' the dread o' hell.

'Toil an' slave an' scrimp an' save—thet's 'bout all we think uv 'n this country. 'Tain't right, Holden.'

'No, 'tain't right,' said Uncle Eb.

'I know I'm a poor, mis'rable critter. Kind o' out o' tune with everybody I know. Alwus quarrelled with my own folks, an' now I ain't got any home. Someday I'm goin' t' die in the poorhouse er on the ground under these woods. But I tell ye'—here he spoke in a voice that grew loud with feeling—'mebbe I've been lazy, as they say, but I've got more out o' my life than any o' these fools. And someday God'll honour me far above them. When my wife an' I parted I wrote some lines that say well my meaning. It was only a log house we had, but this will show what I got out of it.' Then he spoke the lines, his voice trembling with emotion.

'O humble home! Thou hadst a secret door

Thro' which I looked, betimes, with wondering eye

On treasures that no palace ever wore

But now—goodbye!

In hallowed scenes what feet have trod thy stage!

The babe, the maiden, leaving home to wed

The young man going forth by duty led

And faltering age.

Thou hadst a magic window broad and high

The light and glory of the morning shone

Thro' it, however dark the day had grown,

Or bleak the sky.

'I know Dave Brower's folks hev got brains an' decency, but when thet boy is old enough t' take care uv himself, let him git out o' this country. I tell ye he'll never make a farmer, an' if he marries an' settles down here he'll git t' be a poet, mebbe, er some such shifless cuss, an' die in the poorhouse. Guess I better git back t' my bilin' now. Good-night,' he added, rising and buttoning his old coat as he walked away.

'Sing'lar man!' Uncle Eli exclaimed, thoughtfully, 'but anyone thet picks him up fer a fool'll find him a counterfeit.'

Young as I was, the rugged, elemental power of the old poet had somehow got to my heart and stirred my imagination. It all came not fully to my understanding until later. Little by little it grew upon me, and what an effect it had upon my thought and life ever after I should not dare to estimate. And soon I sought out the 'poet of the hills,' as they called him, and got to know and even to respect him in spite of his unlovely aspect.

Uncle Eb skimmed the boiling sap, put more wood on the fire and came and pulled off his boots and lay down beside me under the robe. And, hearing the boil of the sap and the crackle of the burning logs in the arch, I soon went asleep.

I remember feeling Uncle Eb's hand upon my cheek, and how I rose and stared about me in the fading shadows of a dream as he shook me gently.

'Wake up, my boy,' said he. 'Come, we mus' put fer home.'

The fire was out. The old man held a lantern as he stood before me, the blaze flickering. There was a fearsome darkness all around.

'Come, Willy, make haste,' he whispered, as I rubbed my eyes. 'Put on yer boots, an' here's yer little coat 'n' muffler.'

There was a mighty roar in the forest and icy puffs of snow came whistling in upon us. We stored the robes and pails and buckets and covered the big kettle.

The lofty tree-tops reeled and creaked above us, and a deep, sonorous moan was sweeping through the woods, as if the fingers of the wind had touched a mighty harp string in the timber. We could hear the crash and thunder of falling trees.

'Make haste! Make haste! It's resky here,' said Uncle Eb, and he held my hand and ran. We started through the brush and steered as straight as we could for the clearing. The little box of light he carried was soon sheathed in snow, and I remember how he stopped, half out of breath, often, and brushed it with his mittens to let out the light. We had made the scattering growth of little timber at the edge of the woods when the globe of the lantern snapped and fell. A moment later we stood in utter darkness. I knew, for the first time, then that we were in a bad fix.

'I guess God'll take care of us, Willy,' said Uncle Eb. 'If he don't, we'll never get there in this world never!'

It was a black and icy wall of night and storm on every side of us. I never saw a time when the light of God's heaven was so utterly extinguished; the cold never went to my bone as on that bitter night. My hands and feet were numb with aching, as the roar of the trees grew fainter in the open. I remember how I lagged, and how the old man urged me on, and how we toiled in the wind and darkness, straining our eyes for some familiar thing. Of a sudden we stumbled upon a wall that we had passed an hour or so before.

'Oh!' he groaned, and made that funny, deprecating cluck with his tongue, that I have heard so much from Yankee lips.

'God o' mercy!' said he, 'we've gone 'round in a half-circle. Now we'll take the wall an' mebbe it'll bring us home.'

I thought I couldn't keep my feet any longer, for an irresistible drowsiness had come over me. The voice of Uncle Eb seemed far away, and when I sank in the snow and shut my eyes to sleep he shook me as a terrier shakes a rat.

'Wake up, my boy,' said he, 'ye musn't sleep.'

Then he boxed my ears until I cried, and picked me up and ran with me along the side of the wall. I was but dimly conscious when he dropped me under a tree whose bare twigs lashed the air and stung my cheeks. I heard him tearing the branches savagely and muttering, 'Thanks to God, it's the blue beech.' I shall never forget how he turned and held to my hand and put the whip on me as I lay in the snow, and how the sting of it started my blood. Up I sprang in a jiffy and howled and danced. The stout rod bent and circled on me like a hoop of fire. Then I turned and tried to run while he clung to my coat tails, and every step I felt the stinging grab of the beech. There is a little seam across my cheek today that marks a footfall of one of those whips. In a moment I was as wide awake as Uncle Eb and needed no more stimulation.

The wall led us to the pasture lane, and there it was easy enough to make our way to the barnyard and up to the door of the house, which had a candle in every window, I remember. David was up and dressed to come after us, and I recall how he took Uncle Eb in his arms, when he fell fainting on the doorstep, and carried him to the lounge. I saw the blood on my face as I passed the mirror, and Elizabeth Brower came running and gave me one glance and rushed out of doors with the dipper. It was full of snow when she ran in and tore the wrappings off my neck and began to rub my ears and cheeks with the cold snow, calling loudly for Grandma Bisnette. She came in a moment and helped at the stripping of our feet and legs. I remember that she slit my trousers with the shears as I lay on the floor, while the others rubbed my feet with the snow. Our hands and ears were badly frosted, but in an hour the whiteness had gone out of them and the returning blood burnt like a fire.

'How queer he stares!' I heard them say when Uncle Eb first came to, and in a moment a roar of laughter broke from him.

'I'll never fergit,' said he presently, 'if I live a thousan' years, the lickin' I gin thet boy; but it hurt me worse'n it hurt him.'

Then he told the story of the blue beech.

The next day was that 'cold Friday' long remembered by those who felt its deadly chill—a day when water thrown in the magic air came down in clinking crystals, and sheaths of frost lay thick upon the windows. But that and the one before it were among the few days in that early period that lie, like a rock, under my character.

Chapter 9

Grandma Bisnette came from Canada to work for the Browers. She was a big, cheerful woman, with a dialect, an amiable disposition and a swarthy, wrinkled face. She had a loose front tooth that occupied all the leisure of her tongue. When she sat at her knitting this big tooth clicked incessantly. On every stitch her tongue went in and out across it' and I, standing often by her knees, regarded the process with great curiosity.

The reader may gather much from these frank and informing words of Grandma Bisnette. 'When I los' my man, Mon Dieu! I have two son. An' when I come across I bring him with me. Abe he rough; but den he no bad man.'

Abe was the butcher of the neighbourhood—that red-handed, stony-hearted, necessary man whom the Yankee farmer in that north country hires to do the cruel things that have to be done. He wore ragged, dirty clothes and had a voice like a steam whistle. His rough, black hair fell low and mingled with his scanty beard. His hands were stained too often with the blood of some creature we loved. I always crept under the bed in Mrs Brower's room when Abe came—he was such a terror to me with his bloody work and noisy oaths. Such men were the curse of the cleanly homes in that country. There was much to shock the ears and eyes of children in the life of the farm. It was a fashion among the help to decorate their speech with profanity for the mere sound of it' and the foul mouthings of low-minded men spread like a pestilence in the fields.

Abe came always with an old bay horse and a rickety buckboard. His one foot on the dash, as he rode, gave the picture a dare-devil finish. The lash of his bull-whip sang around him, and his great voice sent its blasts of noise ahead. When we heard a fearful yell and rumble in the distance, we knew Abe was coming.

'Abe he come,' said Grandma Bisnette. 'Mon Dieu! he make de leetle rock fly.'

It was like the coming of a locomotive with roar of wheel and whistle. In my childhood, as soon as I saw the cloud of dust, I put for the bed and from its friendly cover would peek out' often, but never venture far until the man of blood had gone.

To us children he was a marvel of wickedness. There were those who told how he had stood in the storm one night and dared the Almighty to send the lightning upon him.

The dog Fred had grown so old and infirm that one day they sent for Abe to come and put an end to his misery. Every man on the farm loved the old dog and not one of them would raise a hand to kill him. Hope and I heard what Abe was coming to do, and when the men had gone to the fields, that summer morning, we lifted Fred into the little wagon in which he had once drawn me and starting back of the barn stole away with him through the deep grass of the meadow until we came out upon the highroad far below. We had planned to take him to school and make him a nest in the woodshed where he could share our luncheon and be out of the way of peril. After a good deal of difficulty and heavy pulling we got to the road at last. The old dog, now blind and helpless, sat contentedly in the wagon while its wheels creaked and groaned beneath him. We had gone but a short way in the road when we heard the red bridge roar under rushing wheels and the familiar yell of Abe.

'We'd better run,' said Hope, "er we'll git swore at.'

I looked about me in a panic for some place to hide the party, but Abe was coming fast and there was only time to pick up clubs and stand our ground.

'Here!' the man shouted as he pulled up along side of us, 'where ye goin' with that dog?'

'Go 'way,' I answered, between anger and tears, lifting my club in a threatening manner.

He laughed then—a loud guffaw that rang in the near woods.

'What'll ye give me,' he asked leaning forward, his elbows on his knees, 'What'll ye give me if I don't kill him?'

I thought a moment. Then I put my hand in my pocket and presently took out my jack-knife—that treasure Uncle Eb had bought for me—and looked at it fondly.

Then I offered it to him.

Again he laughed loudly.

'Anything else?' he demanded while Hope sat hugging the old dog that was licking her hands.

'Got forty cents that I saved for the fair,' said I promptly.

Abe backed his horse and turned in the road.

'Wall boy,' he said, 'Tell 'em I've gone home.'

Then his great voice shouted, 'g'lang' the lash of his whip sang in the air and off he went.

We were first to arrive at the schoolhouse, that morning, and when the other children came we had Fred on a comfortable bed of grass in a corner of the woodshed. What with all the worry of that day I said my lessons poorly and went home with a load on my heart. Tomorrow would be Saturday; how were we to get food and water to the dog? They asked at home if we had seen old Fred and we both declared we had not—the first lie that ever laid its burden on my conscience. We both saved all our bread and butter and doughnuts next day, but we had so many chores to do it was impossible to go to the schoolhouse with them. So we agreed to steal away that night when all were asleep and take the food from its hiding place.

In the excitement of the day neither of us had eaten much. They thought we were ill and sent us to bed early. When Hope came into my room above stairs late in the evening we were both desperately hungry. We looked at our store of doughnuts and bread and butter under my bed. We counted it over.

'Won't you try one o' the doughnuts,' I whispered hoping that she would say yes so that I could try one also; for they did smell mighty good.

"Twouldn't be right,' said she regretfully. 'There ain't any more 'n he'll want now.

"Twouldn't be right,' I repeated with a sigh as I looked longingly at one of the big doughnuts. 'Couldn't bear t' do it—could you?'

'Don't seem as if I could,' she whispered, thoughtfully, her chin upon her hand.

Then she rose and went to the window.

'O my! how dark it is!' she whispered, looking out into the night.

'Purty dark!' I said, 'but you needn't be 'fraid. I'll take care o' you. If we should meet a bear I'll growl right back at him—that's what Uncle Eb tol' me t' do. I'm awful stout—most a man now! Can't nuthin' scare me.'

We could hear them talking below stairs and we went back to bed, intending to go forth later when the house was still. But' unfortunately for our adventure I fell asleep.

It was morning when I opened my eyes again. We children looked accusingly at each other while eating breakfast. Then we had to be washed and dressed in our best clothes to go to meeting. When the wagon was at the door and we were ready to start I had doughnuts and bread and butter in every pocket of my coat and trousers. I got in quickly and pulled the blanket over me so as to conceal the fullness of my pockets. We arrived so late I had no chance to go to the dog before we went into meeting. I was wearing boots that were too small for me, and when I entered with the others and sat down upon one of those straight backed seats of plain, unpainted pine my feet felt as if I had been caught in a bear trap. There was always such a silence in the room after the elder had sat down and adjusted his spectacles that I could hear the ticking of the watch he carried in the pocket of his broadcloth waistcoat. For my own part I know I looked with too much longing for the good of my soul on the great gold chain that spanned the broad convexity of his stomach. Presently I observed that a couple of young women were looking at me and whispering. Then suddenly I became aware that there were sundry protuberances on my person caused by bread and butter and doughnuts, and I felt very miserable indeed. Now and then as the elder spoke the loud, accusing neigh of some horse, tethered to the fence in the schoolyard, mingled with his thunder. After the good elder had been preaching an hour his big, fat body seemed to swim in my tears. When he had finished the choir sang. Their singing was a thing that appealed to the eye as well as the ear. Uncle Eb used to say it was a great comfort to see Elkenah Samson sing bass. His great mouth opened widely in this form of praise and his eyes had a wild stare in them when he aimed at the low notes.

Ransom Walker, a man of great dignity, with a bristling moustache, who had once been a schoolmaster, led the choir and carried the tenor part. It was no small privilege after the elder had announced the hymn, to see him rise and tap the desk with his tuning fork and hold it to his ear solemnly. Then he would seem to press his chin full hard upon his throat while he warbled a scale. Immediately, soprano, alto, bass and tenor launched forth upon the sea of song. The parts were like the treacherous and conflicting currents of a tide that tossed them roughly and sometimes overturned their craft. And Ransom Walker showed always a proper sense of danger and responsibility. Generally they got to port safely on these brief excursions, though exhausted. He had a way of beating time with his head while singing and I have no doubt it was a great help to him.

The elder came over to me after meeting, having taken my tears for a sign of conviction.

'May the Lord bless and comfort you, my boy!' said he.

I got away shortly and made for the door. Uncle Eb stopped me.

'My stars, Willie!' said he putting his hand on my upper coat pocket' 'what ye got in there?'

'Doughnuts,' I answered.

'An' what's this?' he asked touching one of my side pockets.

'Doughnuts,' I repeated.

'An' this,' touching another.

'That's doughnuts too,' I said.

'An' this,' he continued going down to my trousers pocket.

'Bread an' butter,' I answered, shamefacedly, and on the verge of tears.

'Jerusalem!' he exclaimed, 'must a 'spected a purty long sermon.

'Brought 'em fer ol' Fred,' I replied.

'Ol' Fred!' he whispered, 'where's he?'

I told my secret then and we both went out with Hope to where we had left him. He lay with his head between his paws on the bed of grass just as I had seen him lie many a time when his legs were weary with travel on Paradise Road, and when his days were yet full of pleasure. We called to him and Uncle Eb knelt and touched his head. Then he lifted the dog's nose, looked a moment into the sightless eyes and let it fall again.

'Fred's gone,' said he in a low tone as he turned away. 'Got there ahead uv us, Willy.'

Hope and I sat down by the old dog and wept bitterly.

Chapter 10

Uncle Eb was a born lover of fun. But he had a solemn way of fishing that was no credit to a cheerful man. It was the same when he played the bass viol, but that was also a kind of fishing at which he tried his luck in a roaring torrent of sound. Both forms of dissipation gave him a serious look and manner, that came near severity. They brought on his face only the light of hope and anticipation or the shadow of disappointment.

We had finished our stent early the day of which I am writing. When we had dug our worms and were on our way to the brook with pole and line a squint of elation had hold of Uncle Eb's face. Long wrinkles deepened as he looked into the sky for a sign of the weather, and then relaxed a bit as he turned his eyes upon the smooth sward. It was no time for idle talk. We tiptoed over the leafy carpet of the woods. Soon as I spoke he lifted his hand with a warning 'Sh—h!' The murmur of the stream was in our ears. Kneeling on a mossy knoll we baited the hooks; then Uncle Eb beckoned to me.

I came to him on tiptoe.

'See thet there foam 'long side o' the big log?' he whispered, pointing with his finger.

I nodded.

'Cre-e-ep up jest as ca-a-areful as ye can,' he went on whispering. 'Drop in a leetle above an' let 'er float down.'

Then he went on, below me, lifting his feet in slow and stealthy strides.

He halted by a bit of driftwood and cautiously threw in, his arm extended, his figure alert. The squint on his face took a firmer grip. Suddenly his pole gave a leap, the water splashed, his line sang in the air and a fish went up like a rocket. As we were looking into the treetops it thumped the shore beside him, quivered a moment and flopped down the bank He scrambled after it and went to his knees in the brook coming up empty-handed. The water was slopping out of his boot legs.

'Whew!' said he, panting with excitement, as I came over to him. 'Reg'lar ol' he one,' he added, looking down at his boots. 'Got away from me—consarn him! Hed a leetle too much power in the arm.'

He emptied his boots, baited up and went back to his fishing. As I looked up at him he stood leaning over the stream jiggling his hook. In a moment I saw a tug at the line. The end of his pole went under water like a flash. It bent double as Uncle Eb gave it a lift. The fish began to dive and rush. The line cut the water in a broad semicircle and then went far and near with long, quick slashes. The pole nodded and writhed like a thing of life. Then Uncle Eb had a look on him that is one of the treasures of my memory. In a moment the fish went away with such a violent rush, to save him, he had to throw his pole into the water.

'Heavens an' airth!' he shouted, 'the ol' settler!'

The pole turned quickly and went lengthwise into the rapids. He ran down the bank and I after him. The pole was speeding through the swift water. We scrambled over logs and through bushes, but the pole went faster than we. Presently it stopped and swung around. Uncle Eb went splashing into the brook. Almost within reach of the pole he dashed his foot upon a stone, falling headlong in the current. I was close upon his heels and gave him a hand. He rose hatless, dripping from head to foot and pressed on. He lifted his pole. The line clung to a snag and then gave way; the tackle was missing. He looked at it silently, tilting his head. We walked slowly to the shore. Neither spoke for a moment.

'Must have been a big fish,' I remarked.

'Powerful!' said he, chewing vigorously on his quid of tobacco as he shook his head and looked down at his wet clothing. 'In a desp'rit fix, ain't I?'

'Too bad!' I exclaimed.

'Seldom ever hed sech a disapp'intment,' he said. 'Ruther counted on ketchin' thet fish—he was s' well hooked.'

He looked longingly at the water a moment 'If I don't go hum,' said he, 'an' keep my mouth shet I'll say sumthin' I'll be sorry fer.'

He was never quite the same after that. He told often of his struggle with this unseen, mysterious fish and I imagined he was a bit more given to reflection. He had had hold of the 'ol' settler of Deep Hole'—a fish of great influence and renown there in Faraway. Most of the local fishermen had felt him tug at the line one time or another. No man had ever seen him for the water was black in Deep Hole. No fish had ever exerted a greater influence on the thought, the imagination, the manners or the moral character of his contemporaries. Tip Taylor always took off his hat and sighed when he spoke of the 'ol' settler'. Ransom Walker said he had once seen his top fin and thought it longer than a razor. Ransom took to idleness and chewing tobacco immediately after his encounter with the big fish, and both vices stuck to him as long as he lived. Everyone had his theory of the 'ol' settler'. Most agreed he was a very heavy trout. Tip Taylor used to say that in his opinion "twas nuthin' more'n a plain, overgrown, common sucker,' but Tip came from the Sucker Brook country where suckers lived in colder water and were more entitled to respect.

Mose Tupper had never had his hook in the 'ol' settler' and would believe none of the many stories of adventure at Deep Hole that had thrilled the township.

'Thet fish hes made s' many liars 'round here ye dimno who t' b'lieve,' he had said at the corners one day, after Uncle Eb had told his story of the big fish. 'Somebody 't knows how t' fish hed oughter go 'n ketch him fer the good o' the town—thet's what I think.'

Now Mr Tupper was an excellent man but his incredulity was always too bluntly put. It had even led to some ill feeling.

He came in at our place one evening with a big hook and line from 'down east'—the kind of tackle used in salt water.

'What ye goin' t' dew with it?' Uncle Eb enquired.

'Ketch thet fish ye talk s' much about—goin' t' put him out o' the way.'

''Tain't fair,' said Uncle Eb, 'its reedic'lous. Like leading a pup with a log chain.'

'Don't care,' said Mose, 'I'm goin' t' go fishin t'morrer. If there reely is any sech fish—which I don't believe there is—I'm goin' t' rassle with him an' mebbe tek him out o' the river. Thet fish is sp'llin' the moral character o' this town. He oughter be rode on a rail—thet fish hed.'

How he would punish a trout in that manner Mr Tupper failed to explain, but his metaphor was always a worse fit than his trousers and that was bad enough.

It was just before haying and, there being little to do, we had also planned to try our luck in the morning. When, at sunrise, we were walking down the cow-path to the woods I saw Uncle Eb had a coil of bed cord on his shoulder.

'What's that for?' I asked.

'Wall,' said he, 'goin' t' hev fun anyway. If we can't ketch one thing we'll try another.'

We had great luck that morning and when our basket was near full we came to Deep Hole and made ready for a swim in the water above it. Uncle Eb had looped an end of the bed cord and tied a few pebbles on it with bits of string.

'Now,' said he presently, 'I want t' sink this loop t' the bottom an' pass the end o' the cord under the driftwood so 't we can fetch it 'crost under water.'

There was a big stump, just opposite, with roots running down the bank into the stream. I shoved the line under the drift with a pole and then hauled it across where Uncle Eb drew it up the bank under the stump roots.

'In 'bout half an hour I cal'late Mose Tupper'll be 'long,' he whispered. 'Wisht ye'd put on yer clo's an' lay here back o' the stump an' hold on t' the cord. When ye feel a bite give a yank er two an' haul in like Sam Hill—fifteen feet er more quicker'n scat. Snatch his pole right away from him. Then lay still.'

Uncle Eb left me, shortly, going up stream. It was near an hour before I heard them coming. Uncle Eb was talking in a low tone as they came down the other bank.

'Drop right in there,' he was saying, 'an' let her drag down, through the deep water, deliberate like. Git clus t' the bottom.'

Peering through a screen of bushes I could see an eager look on the unlovely face of Moses. He stood leaning toward the water and jiggling his hook along the bottom. Suddenly I saw Mose jerk and felt the cord move. I gave it a double twitch and began to pull. He held hard for a jiffy and then stumbled and let go yelling like mad. The pole hit the water with a splash and went out of sight like a diving frog. I brought it well under the foam and driftwood. Deep Hole resumed its calm, unruffled aspect. Mose went running toward Uncle Eb.

''S a whale!' he shouted. 'Ripped the pole away quicker'n lightnin'.'

'Where is it?' Uncle Eb asked.

'Tuk it away f'm me,' said Moses. 'Grabbed it jes' like thet,' he added with a violent jerk of his hand.

'What d' he dew with it?' Uncle Eb enquired.

Mose looked thoughtfully at the water and scratched his head, his features all a tremble.

'Dunno,' said he. 'Swallered it mebbe.'

'Mean t' say ye lost hook, line, sinker 'n pole?'

'Hook, line, sinker 'n pole,' he answered mournfully. 'Come nigh haulin' me in tew.'

''Tain't possible,' said Uncle Eb.

Mose expectorated, his hands upon his hips, looking down at the water.

'Wouldn't eggzac'ly say 'twas possible,' he drawled, 'but 'twas a fact.'

'Yer mistaken,' said Uncle Eb.

'No I hain't,' was the answer, 'I tell ye I see it.'

'Then if ye see it the nex' thing ye orter see 's a doctor. There's sumthin' wrong with you sumwheres.'

'Only one thing the matter o' me,' said Mose with a little twinge of remorse. 'I'm jest a natural born perfec' dum fool. Never c'u'd b'lieve there was any sech fish.'

'Nobody ever said there was any sech fish,' said Uncle Eb. 'He's done more t' you 'n he ever done t' me. Never served me no sech trick as thet. If I was you I'd never ask nobody t' b'lieve it 'S a leetle tew much.'

Mose went slowly and picked up his hat. Then he returned to the bank and looked regretfully at the water.

'Never see the beat o' thet,' he went on. 'Never see sech power 'n a fish. Knocks the spots off any fish I ever hearn of.'

'Ye riled him with that big tackle o' yourn,' said Uncle Eb. 'He wouldn't stan' it.'

'Feel jest as if I'd hed holt uv a wil' cat,' said Mose. 'Tuk the hull thing—pole an' all—quicker 'n lightnin'. Nice a bit o' hickory as a man ever see. Gol' durned if I ever heern o' the like o' that, ever.'

He sat down a moment on the bank.

'Got t' rest a minute,' he remarked. 'Feel kind o' wopsy after thet squabble.'

They soon went away. And when Mose told the story of 'the swallered pole' he got the same sort of reputation he had given to others. Only it was real and large and lasting.

'Wha' d' ye think uv it?' he asked, when he had finished.

'Wall,' said Ransom Walker, 'wouldn't want t' say right out plain t' yer face.'

"Twouldn't he p'lite,' said Uncle Eb soberly.

'Sound a leetle ha'sh,' Tip Taylor added.

'Thet fish has jerked the fear o' God out o' ye—thet's the way it looks t' me,' said Carlyle Barber.

'Yer up 'n the air, Mose,' said another. 'Need a sinker on ye.' They bullied him—they talked him down, demurring mildly, but firmly.

'Tell ye what I'll do,' said Mose sheepishly, 'I'll b'lieve you fellers if you'll b'lieve me.'

'What, swop even? Not much!' said one, with emphasis. "Twouldn't be fair. Ye've ast us t' b'lieve a genuwine out 'n out impossibility.'

Mose lifted his hat and scratched his head thoughtfully. There was a look of embarrassment in his face.

'Might a ben dreamin',' said he slowly. 'I swear it's gittin' so here 'n this town a feller can't hardly b'lieve himself.'

'Fur 's my experience goes,' said Ransom Walker, 'he'd be a fool 'f he did.'

"Minds me o' the time I went fishin' with Ab Thomas,' said Uncle Eb. 'He ketched an ol' socker the fast thing. I went off by myself 'n got a good sized fish, but 'twant s' big 's hisn. So I tuk 'n opened his mouth n poured in a lot o' fine shot. When I come back Ab he looked at my fish 'n begun t' brag. When we weighed 'em mine was a leetle heavier.

'"What!" says he. "'Tain't possible thet leetle cuss uv a trout 's heavier 'n mine."

"Tis sarrin,' I said.

'"Dummed deceivin' business," said he as he hefted 'em both. "Gittin' so ye can't hardly b'lieve the stillyards."'

Chapter 11

The fifth summer was passing since we came down Paradise Road—the dog, Uncle Eb and I. Times innumerable I had heard my good old friend tell the story of our coming west until its every incident was familiar to me as the alphabet. Else I fear my youthful memory would have served me poorly for a chronicle of my childhood so exact and so extended as this I have written. Uncle Eb's hair was white now and the voices of the swift and the panther had grown mild and tremulous and unsatisfactory and even absurd. Time had tamed the monsters of that imaginary wilderness and I had begun to lose my respect for them. But one fear had remained with me as I grew older—the fear of the night man. Every boy and girl in the valley trembled at the mention of him. Many a time I had held awake in the late evening to hear the men talk of him before they went asleep—Uncle Eb and Tip Taylor. I remember a night when Tip said, in a low awesome tone, that he was a ghost. The word carried into my soul the first thought of its great and fearful mystery.

'Years and years ago,' said he, 'there was a boy by the name of Nehemiah Brower. An' he killed another boy, once, by accident an' run away an' was drownded.'

'Drownded!' said Uncle Eb. 'How?'

'In the ocean,' the first answered gaping. 'Went away off 'round the world an' they got a letter that said he was drownded on his way to Van Dieman's Land.'

'To Van Dieman's Land!'

'Yes, an some say the night man is the ghost o' the one he killed.'

I remember waking that night and hearing excited whispers at the window near my bed. It was very dark in the room and at first I could not tell who was there.

'Don't you see him?' Tip whispered.

'Where?' I heard Uncle Be ask

'Under the pine trees—see him move.'

At that I was up at the window myself and could plainly see the dark figure of a man standing under the little pine below us.

'The night man, I guess,' said Uncle Be, 'but he won't do no harm. Let him alone; he's going' away now.'

We saw him disappear behind the trees and then we got back into our beds again. I covered my head with the bedclothes and said a small prayer for the poor night man.

And in this atmosphere of mystery and adventure, among the plain folk of Faraway, whose care of me when I was in great need, and whose love of me always, I count among the priceless treasures of God's providence, my childhood passed. And the day came near when I was to begin to play my poor part in the world.

BOOK TWO

Chapter 12

It was a time of new things—that winter when I saw the end of my fifteenth year. Then I began to enjoy the finer humours of life in Faraway—to see with understanding; and by God's grace—to feel.

The land of play and fear and fable was now far behind me and I had begun to feel the infinite in the ancient forest' in the everlasting hills, in the deep of heaven, in all the ways of men. Hope Brower was now near woman grown. She had a beauty of face and form that was the talk of the countryside. I have travelled far and seen many a fair face hut never one more to my eye. I have heard men say she was like a girl out of a story-book those days.

Late years something had come between us. Long ago we had fallen out of each other's confidence, and ever since she had seemed to shun me. It was the trip in the sledgehouse that' years after, came up between us and broke our childish intimacy. Uncle Be had told, before company, how she had kissed me that day and bespoke me for a husband, and while the others laughed loudly she had gone out of the room crying. She would have little to say to me then. I began to play with boys and she with girls. And it made me miserable to hear the boys a bit older than I gossip of her beauty and accuse each other of the sweet disgrace of love.

But I must hasten to those events in Faraway that shaped our destinies. And first comes that memorable night when I had the privilege of escorting Hope to the school lyceum where the argument of Jed Feary—poet of the hills—fired my soul with an ambition that has remained with me always.

Uncle Be suggested that I ask Hope to go with me.

'Prance right up to her,' he said, 'an' say you'd be glad of the pleasure of her company.

It seemed to me a very dubious thing to do. I looked thoughtful and turned red in the face.

'Young man,' he continued, 'the boy thet's 'fraid o' women'll never hev whiskers.'

'How's that?' I enquired.

'Be scairt t' death,' he answered,' 'fore they've hed time t' start Ye want t' step right up t' the rack jes' if ye'd bought an' paid fer yerself an' was proud o' yer bargain.'

I took his advice and when I found Hope alone in the parlour I came and asked her, very awkwardly as I now remember, to go with me.

She looked at me, blushing, and said she would ask her mother.

And she did, and we walked to the schoolhouse together that evening, her hand holding my arm, timidly, the most serious pair that ever struggled with the problem of deportment on such an occasion. I was oppressed with a heavy sense of responsibility in every word I uttered.

Ann Jane Foster, known as 'Scooter Jane', for her rapid walk and stiff carriage, met us at the corners on her way to the schoolhouse.

'Big turn out I guess,' said she. 'Jed Feary 'n' Squire Town is comin' over from Jingleville an' all the big guns'll be there. I love t' hear Jed Feary speak, he's so techin'.'

Ann Jane was always looking around for some event likely to touch her feelings. She went to every funeral in Faraway and, when sorrow was scarce in her own vicinity, journeyed far in quest of it.

'Wouldn't wonder 'f the fur flew when they git t' going',' she remarked, and then hurried on, her head erect, her body motionless, her legs flying. Such energy as she gave to the pursuit of mourning I have never seen equalled in any other form of dissipation.

The schoolhouse was nearly full of people when we came in. The big boys were wrestling in the yard; men were lounging on the rude seats, inside, idly discussing crops and cattle and lapsing into silence, frequently, that bore the signs both of expectancy and reflection. Young men and young women sat together on one side of the house whispering and giggling. Alone among them was the big and eccentric granddaughter of Mrs Bisnette, who was always slapping some youngster for impertinence. Jed Feary and Squire Town sat together behind a pile of books, both looking very serious. The long hair and beard of the old poet were now white and his form bent with age. He came over and spoke to us and took a curl of Hope's hair in his stiffened fingers and held it to the lamplight.

'What silky gold!' he whispered.' 'S a skein o' fate, my dear girl!'

Suddenly the schoolteacher rapped on the desk and bade us come to order and Ransom Walker was called to the chair.

'Thet there is talent in Faraway township,' he said, having reluctantly come to the platform, 'and talent of the very highest order, no one can deny who has ever attended a lyceum at the Howard schoolhouse. I see evidences of talent in every face before me. And I wish to ask what are the two great talents of the Yankee—talents that made our forefathers famous the world over? I pause for an answer.'

He had once been a schoolmaster and that accounted for his didactic style.

'What are the two great talents of the Yankee?' he repeated, his hands clasped before him.

'Doughnuts an' pie,' said Uncle Be who sat in a far corner.

'No sir,' Mr Walker answered, 'there's some hev a talent fer sawin' wood, but we don't count that. It's war an' speakin', they are the two great talents of the Yankee. But his greatest talent is the gift o' gab. Give him a chance t' talk it over with his enemy an' he'll lick 'im without a fight. An' when his enemy is another Yankee—why, they both git licked, jest as it was in the case of the man thet sold me lightnin' rods. He was sorry he done it before I got through with him. If we did not encourage this talent in our sons they would be talked to death by our daughters. Ladies and gentlemen, it gives me pleasure t' say that the best speakers in Faraway township have come here t' discuss the important question:

'Resolved, that intemperance has caused more misery than war?

'I call upon Moses Tupper to open for the affirmative.'

Moses, as I have remarked, had a most unlovely face with a thin and bristling growth of whiskers. In giving him features Nature had been generous to a fault. He had a large red nose, and a mouth vastly too big for any proper use. It was a mouth fashioned for odd sayings. He was well to do and boasted often that he was a self-made man. Uncle Be used to say that if Mose Tupper had had the 'makin' uv himself he'd oughter done it more careful.'

I remember not much of the speech he made, but the picture of him, as he rose on tiptoe and swung his arms like a man fighting bees, and his drawling tones are as familiar as the things of yesterday.

'Gentlemen an' ladies,' said he presently, 'let me show you a pictur'. It is the drunkard's child. It is hungry an' there ain't no food in its home. The child is poorer'n a straw-fed hoss. 'Tain't hed a thing t' eat since day before yistiddy. Pictur' it to yourselves as it comes cryin' to its mother an' says:

'"Ma! Gi' me a piece o' bread an' butter."

'She covers her face with her apron an' says she, "There am none left, my child."

'An' bime bye the child comes agin' an' holds up its poor little han's an' says: "Ma! please gi' me a piece O' cake."

'An' she goes an' looks out O' the winder, er mebbe pokes the fire, an' says: "There am' none left, my child."

'An' bime bye it comes agin' an' it says: "Please gi' me a little piece O' pie."

'An' she mebbe flops into a chair an' says, sobbin', "There ain' none left, my child."

'No pie! Now, Mr Chairman!' exclaimed the orator, as he lifted both hands high above his head, 'If this ain't misery, in God's name, what is it?

'Years ago, when I was a young man, Mr President, I went to a dance one night at the village of Migleyville. I got a toothache, an' the Devil tempted me with whiskey, an' I tuk one glass an' then another an' purty soon I began t' thank I was a mighty hefty sort of a character, I did, an' I stud on a corner an' stumped everybody t' fight with me, an' bime bye an accomanodatin' kind of a chap come along, an' that's all I remember O' what happened. When I come to, my coat tails had been tore off, I'd lost one leg O' my trousers, a bran new silver watch, tew dollars in money, an a pair O' spectacles. When I stud up an' tried t' realise what hed happened I felt jes' like a blind rooster with only one leg an' no tail feathers.'

A roar of laughter followed these frank remarks of Mr Tupper and broke into a storm of merriment when Uncle Eb rose and said:

'Mr President, I hope you see that the misfortunes of our friend was due t' war, an' not to intemperance.'

Mr Tupper was unhorsed. For some minutes he stood helpless or shaking with the emotion that possessed all. Then he finished lamely and sat down.

The narrowness of the man that saw so much where there was so little in his own experience and in the trivial events of his own township was what I now recognise as most valuable to the purpose of this history. It was a narrowness that covered a multitude of people in St Lawrence county in those days.

Jed Feary was greeted with applause and then by respectful silence when he rose to speak. The fame of his verse and his learning had gone far beyond the narrow boundaries of the township in which he lived. It was the biggest thing in the county. Many a poor sinner who had gone out of Faraway to his long home got his first praise in the obituary poem by Jed Feary. These tributes were generally published in the county paper and paid for by the relatives of the deceased at the rate of a dollar a day for the time spent on them, or by a few days of board and lodging glory and consolation that was, alas! too cheap, as one might see by a glance at his forlorn figure. I shall never forget the courtly manner, so strangely in contrast with the rude deportment of other men in that place, with which he addressed the chairman and the people. The drawling dialect of the vicinity that flavoured his conversation fell from him like a mantle as he spoke and the light in his soul shone upon that little company a great light, as I now remember, that filled me with burning thoughts of the world and its mighty theatre of action. The way of my life lay clear before me, as I listened, and its days of toil and the sweet success my God has given me, although I take it humbly and hold it infinitely above my merit. I was to get learning and seek some way of expressing what was in me.

It would ill become me to try to repeat the words of this venerable seer, but he showed that intemperance was an individual sin, while war was a national evil. That one meant often the ruin of a race; the other the ruin of a family; that one was as the ocean, the other as a single drop in its waters. And he told us of the fall of empires and the millions that had suffered the oppression of the conqueror and perished by the sword since Agamemnon.

After the debate a young lady read a literary paper full of clumsy wit, rude chronicles of the countryside, essays on 'Spring', and like topics—the work of the best talent of Faraway. Then came the decision, after which the meeting adjourned.

At the door some other boys tried 'to cut me out'. I came through the noisy crowd, however, with Hope on my arm and my heart full of a great happiness.

'Did you like it?' she asked.

'Very much,' I answered.

'What did you enjoy most?'

'Your company,' I said, with a fine air of gallantry.

'Honestly?'

'Honestly. I want to take you to Rickard's sometime?'

That was indeed a long cherished hope.

'Maybe I won't let you,' she said.

'Wouldn't you?'

'You'd better ask me sometime and see.'

'I shall. I wouldn't ask any other girl.'

'Well,' she added, with a sigh, 'if a boy likes one girl I don't think he ought to have anything to do with other girls. I hate a flirt.'

I happened to hear a footfall in the snow behind us, and looking back saw Ann Jane Foster going slow in easy hearing. She knew all, as we soon found out.

'I dew jes love t' see young folks enjoy themselves,' said she, 'it's entrancin'.'

Coming in at our gate I saw a man going over the wall back of the big stables. The house was dark.

'Did you see the night man?' Elizabeth Brower whispered as I lit the lamp. 'Went through the garden just now. I've been watching him here at the window.'

Chapter 13

The love of labour was counted a great virtue there in Faraway. As for myself I could never put my heart in a hoe handle or in any like tool of toil. They made a blister upon my spirit as well as upon my hands. I tried to find in the sweat of my brow that exalted pleasure of which Mr Greeley had visions in his comfortable retreat on Printing House Square. But unfortunately I had not his point of view.

Hanging in my library, where I may see it as I write, is the old sickle of Uncle Eb. The hard hickory of its handle is worn thin by the grip of his hand. It becomes a melancholy symbol when I remember how also the hickory had worn him thin and bent him low, and how infinitely better than all the harvesting of the sickle was the strength of that man, diminishing as it wore the wood. I cannot help smiling when I look at the sickle and thank of the soft hands and tender amplitude of Mr Greeley.

The great editor had been a playmate of David Brower when they were boys, and his paper was read with much reverence in our home.

'How quick ye can plough a ten-acre lot with a pen,' Uncle Eb used to say when we had gone up to bed after father had been reading aloud from his Tribune.

Such was the power of the press in that country one had but to say of any doubtful thing, 'Seen it in print,' to stop all argument. If there were any further doubt he had only to say that he had read it either in the Tribune or the Bible, and couldn't remember which. Then it was a mere question of veracity in the speaker. Books and other reading were carefully put away for an improbable time of leisure.

'I might break my leg sometime,' said David Brower, 'then they'll come handy.' But the Tribune was read carefully every week.

I have seen David Brower stop and look at me while I have been digging potatoes, with a sober grin such as came to him always after he had swapped 'hosses' and got the worst of it. Then he would show me again, with a little impatience in his manner, how to hold the handle and straddle the row. He would watch me for a moment, turn to Uncle Eb, laugh hopelessly and say: 'Thet boy'll hev to be a minister. He can't work.'

But for Elizabeth Brower it might have gone hard with me those days. My mind was always on my books or my last talk with Jed Feary, and she shared my confidence and fed my hopes and shielded me as much as possible from the heavy work. Hope had a better head for mathematics than I, and had always helped me with my sums, but I had a better memory and an aptitude in other things that kept me at the head of most of my classes. Best of all at school I enjoyed the 'compositions'—I had many thoughts, such as they were, and some facility of expression, I doubt not, for a child. Many chronicles of the countryside came off my pen—sketches of odd events and characters there in Faraway. These were read to the assembled household. Elizabeth Brower would sit looking gravely down at me, as I stood by her knees reading, in those days of my early boyhood. Uncle Eb listened with his head turned curiously, as if his ear were cocked for coons. Sometimes he and David Brower would slap their knees and laugh heartily, whereat my foster mother would give them a quick glance and shake her head. For she was always fearful of the day when she should see in her children the birth of vanity, and sought to put it off as far as might be. Sometimes she would cover her mouth to hide a smile, and, when I had finished, look warningly at the rest, and say it was good, for a little boy. Her praise never went further, and indeed all those people hated flattery as they did the devil and frowned upon conceit She said that when the love of flattery got hold of one he would lie to gain it.

I can see this slender, blue-eyed woman as I write. She is walking up and down beside her spinning-wheel. I can hear the dreary buz-z-z-z of the spindle as she feeds it with the fleecy ropes. That loud crescendo echoes in the still house of memory. I can hear her singing as she steps forward and slows the wheel and swings the cradle with her foot:

'On the other side of Jordan,

In the sweet fields of Eden,

Where the tree of Life is blooming,

There is rest for you.

She lays her hand to the spokes again and the roar of the spindle drowns her voice.

All day, from the breakfast hour to supper time, I have heard the dismal sound of the spinning as she walked the floor, content to sing of rest but never taking it.

Her home was almost a miracle of neatness. She could work with no peace of mind until the house had been swept and dusted. A fly speck on the window was enough to cloud her day. She went to town with David now and then—not oftener than once a quarter—and came back ill and exhausted. If she sat in a store waiting for David, while he went to mill or smithy, her imagination gave her no rest. That dirt abhorring mind of hers would begin to clean the windows, and when that was finished it would sweep the floor and dust the counters. In due course it would lower the big chandelier and take out all the lamps and wash the chimneys with soap and water and rub them till they shone. Then, if David had not come, it would put in the rest of its time on the woodwork. With all her cleaning I am sure the good woman kept her soul spotless. Elizabeth Brower believed in goodness and the love of God, and knew no fear. Uncle Eb used to say that wherever Elizabeth Brower went hereafter it would have to be clean and comfortable.

Elder Whitmarsh came often to dinner of a Sunday, when he and Mrs Brower talked volubly about the Scriptures, he taking a sterner view of God than she would allow. He was an Englishman by birth, who had settled in Faraway because there he had found relief for a serious affliction of asthma.

He came over one noon in the early summer, that followed the event of our last chapter, to tell us of a strawberry party that evening at the White Church.

'I've had a wonderful experience,' said he as he took a seat on the piazza, while Mrs Brower came and sat near him. 'I've discovered a great genius—a wandering fiddler, and I shall try to bring him to play for us.'

'A fiddler! why, Elder!' said she, 'you astonish me!'

'Nothing but sacred music,' he said, lifting his hand. 'I heard him play all the grand things today—"Rock of Ages", "Nearer My God, to Thee", "The Marseillaise" and "Home, Sweet Home". Lifted me off my feet! I've heard the great masters in New York and London, but no greater player than this man.'

'Where is he and where did he come from?'

'He's at my house now,' said the good man. 'I found him this morning. He stood under a tree by the road side, above Northrup's. As I came near I heard the strains of "The Marseillaise". For more than an hour I sat there listening. It was wonderful, Mrs Brower, wonderful! The poor fellow is eccentric. He never spoke to me. His clothes were dusty and worn. But his music went to my heart like a voice from Heaven. When he had finished I took him home with me, gave him food and a new coat, and left him sleeping. I want you to come over, and be sure to bring Hope. She must sing for us.'

'Mr Brower will be tired out, but perhaps the young people may go,' she said, looking at Hope and me.

My heart gave a leap as I saw in Hope's eyes a reflection of my own joy. In a moment she came and gave her mother a sounding kiss and asked her what she should wear.

'I must look my best, mother,' she said.

'My child,' said the elder, 'it's what you do and not what you wear that's important.'

'They're both important, Elder,' said my foster mother. You should teach your people the duty of comeliness. They honour their Maker when they look their best.'

The spirit of liberalism was abroad in the sons of the Puritans. In Elizabeth Brower the ardent austerity of her race had been freely diluted with humour and cheerfulness and human sympathy. It used to be said of Deacon Hospur, a good but lazy man, that he was given both to prayer and profanity. Uncle Eb, who had once heard the deacon swear, when the latter had been bruised by a kicking cow, said that, so far as he knew, the deacon never swore except when 'twas necessary. Indeed, most of those men had, I doubt not, too little of that fear of God in them that characterised their fathers. And yet, as shall appear, there were in Faraway some relics of a stern faith.

Hope came out in fine feather, and although I have seen many grand ladles, gowned for the eyes of kings, I have never seen a lovelier figure than when, that evening, she came tripping down to the buggy. It was three miles to the white Church, and riding over in the twilight I laid the plan of my life before her. She sat a moment in silence after I had finished.

'I am going away, too,' she remarked, with a sigh.

'Going away!' I said with some surprise, for in all my plans I had secretly counted on returning in grand style to take her back with me.

'Going away,' said she decisively.

'It isn't nice for girls to go away from home,' I said.

'It isn't nice for boys, either,' said she.

We had come to the church, its open doors and windows all aglow with light. I helped her out at the steps, and hitched my horse under the long shed. We entered together and made our way through the chattering crowd to the little cloakroom in one corner. Elder Whitmarsh arrived in a moment and the fiddler, a short, stout, stupid-looking man, his fiddle in a black box under his arm, followed him to the platform that had been cleared of its pulpit The stranger stood staring vacantly at the crowd until the elder motioned him to a chair, when he obeyed with the hesitating, blind obedience of a dog. Then the elder made a brief prayer, and after a few remarks flavoured with puns, sacred and immemorial as the pulpit itself, started a brief programme of entertainment. A broad smile marked the beginning of his lighter mood. His manner seemed to say: 'Now, ladies and gentlemen, if you will give good heed, you shall see I can be witty on occasion.'

Then a young man came to the platform and recited, after which Hope went forward and sang 'The Land o' the Leal' with such spirit that I can feel my blood go faster even now as I thank of it, and of that girlish figure crowned with a glory of fair curls that fell low upon her waist and mingled with the wild pink roses at her bosom. The fiddler sat quietly as if he heard nothing until she began to sing, when he turned to look at her. The elder announced, after the ballad, that he had brought with him a wonderful musician who would favour them with some sacred music. He used the word 'sacred' because he had observed, I suppose, that certain of the 'hardshells' were looking askance at the fiddle. There was an awkward moment in which the fiddler made no move or sign of intelligence. The elder stepped near him and whispered. Getting no response, he returned to the front of the platform and said: 'We shall first resign ourselves to social intercourse and the good things the ladies have provided.'

Mountains of frosted cake reared their snowy summits on a long table, and the strawberries, heaped in saucers around them, were like red foothills. I remember that while they were serving us Hope and I were introduced to one Robert Livingstone—a young New Yorker, stopping at the inn near by, on his way to the big woods. He was a handsome fellow, with such a fine air of gallantry and so prig in fashionable clothes that he made me feel awkward and uncomfortable.

'I have never heard anything more delightful than that ballad,' he said to Hope. 'You must have your voice trained—you really must. It will make a great name for you.'

I wondered then why his words hurt me to the soul. The castle of my dreams had fallen as he spoke. A new light came into her face—I did not know then what it meant.

'Will you let me call upon you before I leave—may I?' He turned to me while she stood silent. 'I wish to see your father,' he added.

'Certainly,' she answered, blushing, 'you may come—if you care to come.

The musician had begun to thrum the strings of his violin. We turned to look at him. He still sat in his chair, his ear bent to the echoing chamber of the violin. Soon he laid his bow to the strings and a great chord hushed every whisper and died into a sweet, low melody, in which his thought seemed to be feeling its way through sombre paths of sound. The music brightened, the bow went faster, and suddenly 'The Girl I Left Behind Me' came rushing off the strings. A look of amazement gathered on the elder's face and deepened into horror. It went from one to another as if it had been a dish of ipecac. Ann Jane Foster went directly for her things, and with a most unchristian look hurried out into the night. Half a dozen others followed her, while the unholy music went on, its merry echoes rioting in that sacred room, hallowed with memories of the hour of conviction, of the day of mourning, of the coming of the bride in her beauty.

Deacon Hospur rose and began to drawl a sort of apology, when the player stopped suddenly and shot an oath at him. The deacon staggered under the shock of it. His whiskers seemed to lift a bit like the hair of a cat under provocation. Then he tried to speak, but only stuttered helplessly a moment as if his tongue were oscillating between silence and profanity, and was finally pulled down by his wife, who had laid hold of his coat tails. If it had been any other man than Deacon Hospur it would have gone badly with the musician then and there, but we boys saw his discomfiture with positive gratitude. In a moment all rose, the dishes were gathered up, and many hurried away with indignant glances at the poor elder, who was busy taking counsel with some of the brethren.

I have never seen a more pathetic figure than that of poor Nick Goodall as he sat there thrumming the strings of which he was a Heaven-born master. I saw him often after that night—a poor, halfwitted creature, who wandered from inn to inn there in the north country, trading music for hospitality. A thoroughly intelligible sentence never passed his lips, but he had a great gift of eloquence in music. Nobody knew whence he had come or any particular of his birth or training or family. But for his sullen temper, that broke into wild, unmeaning profanity at times, Nick Goodall would have made fame and fortune.

He stared at the thinning crowd as if he had begun dimly to comprehend the havoc he had wrought. Then he put on his hat, came down off the platform, and shuffled out of the open door, his violin in one hand, its box in the other. There were not more than a dozen of us who followed him into the little churchyard. The moon was rising, and the shadows of lilac and rose bush, of slab and monument lay long across the green mounds. Standing there between the graves of the dead he began to play. I shall never forget that solemn calling of the silver string:

'Come ye disconsolate where'er ye languish.'

It was a new voice, a revelation, a light where darkness had been, to Hope and to me. We stood listening far into the night, forgetful of everything, even the swift flight of the hours.

Loud, impassioned chords rose into the moonlit sky and sank to a faint whisper of melody, when we could hear the gossip of the birds in the belfry and under the eaves; trembling tones of supplication, wailing notes of longing and regret swept through the silent avenues of the churchyard, thrilling us with their eloquence. For the first time we heard the music of Handel, of Mendelssohn, of Paganini, and felt its power, then knowing neither name nor theme. Hour by hour he played on for the mere joy of it. When we shook hands with the elder and tiptoed to the buggy he was still playing. We drove slowly and listened a long way down the road. I could hear the strains of that ballad, then new to me, but now familiar, growing fainter in the distance:

O ye'll tak' the high road an' I'll tak' the low road An' I'll be in Scotland afore ye; But me an' me true love will never meet again On the bonnie, bonnie banks o' Loch Lomond.

what connection it may have had with the history of poor Nick Goodall [*1] I have often wondered.

*[*1] Poor Nick Coodall died in the almshouse of Jefferson*

County some thirty years ago. A better account of this

incident was widely printed at that time.

As the last note died into silence I turned to Hope, and she was crying.

'Why are you crying?' I asked, in as miserable a moment as I have ever known.

'It's the music,' she said.

We both sat in silence, then, hearing only the creak of the buggy as it sped over the sandy road. Well ahead of us I saw a man who suddenly turned aside, vaulting over the fence and running into the near woods.

'The night man!' I exclaimed, pulling up a moment to observe him.

Then a buggy came in sight, and presently we heard a loud 'hello' from David Brower, who, worried by our long stay, had come out in quest of us.

Chapter 14

Hope's love of music became a passion after that night. Young Mr Livingstone, 'the city chap' we had met at the church, came over next day. His enthusiasm for her voice gave us all great hope of it. David Brower said he would take her away to the big city when she was older. They soon decided to send her in September to the big school in Hillsborough.

'She's got t' be a lady,' said David Brower, as he drew her into his lap the day we had all discussed the matter. 'She's learnt everything in the 'rithinetic an' geography an' speller. I want her t' learn somethin' more scientific.'

'Now you're talkin',' said Uncle Eb. 'There's lots o' things ye can't learn by cipherin'. Nuthin's too good fer Hope.'

'I'd like t' know what you men expect of her anyway,' said Elizabeth Brower.

'A high stepper,' said Uncle Eb. 'We want a slick coat, a kind uv a toppy head, an a lot O' ginger. So't when we hitch 'er t' the pole bime bye we shan't be 'shamed o' her.'

'Eggzac'ly,' said David Brower, laughing. 'An' then she shall have the best harness in the market.'

Hope did not seem to comprehend all the rustic metaphors that had been applied to her. A look of puzzled amusement came over her face, and then she ran away into the garden, her hair streaming from under her white sun-bonnet.

'Never see sech a beauty! Beats the world,' said Uncle Eb in a whisper, whereat both David and Elizabeth shook their heads.

'Lord o' mercy! Don't let her know it,' Elizabeth answered, in a low tone. 'She's beginning to have-'

Just then Hope came by us leading her pet filly that had been born within the month. Immediately Mrs Brower changed the subject.

'To have what?' David enquired as soon as the girl was out of hearing.

'Suspicions,' said Elizabeth mournfully. 'Spends a good deal of her time at the looking-glass. I think the other girls tell her and then that young Livingstone has been turning her head.'

'Turning her head!' he exclaimed.

'Turning her head,' she answered. 'He sat here the other day and deliberately told her that he had never seen such a complexion and such lovely hair.'

Elizabeth Brower mocked his accent with a show of contempt that feebly echoed my own emotions.

'That's the way o' city folks, mother,' said David.

'It's a bad way,' she answered. 'I do not thank he ought to come here. Hope's a child yet, and we mustn't let her get notions.'

'I'll tell him not t' come any more,' said David, as he and Uncle Eb rose to go to their work.'

'I'm 'fraid she ought not to go away to school for a year yet,' said Elizabeth, a troubled look in her face.

'Pshaw, mother! Ye can't keep her under yer wing alwus,' said he. 'Well, David, you know she is very young and uncommonly—' she hesitated.

'Han'some,' said he, 'we might as well own up if she is our child.'

'If she goes away,' continued Elizabeth, 'some of us ought t' go with her.'

Then Uncle Eb and David went to their work in the fields and I to my own task That very evening they began to talk of renting the farm and going to town with the children.

I had a stent of cording wood that day and finished it before two o'clock Then I got my pole of mountain ash, made hook and line ready, dug some worms and went fishing. I cared not so much for the fishing as for the solitude of the woods. I had a bit of think to do. In the thick timber there was a place where Tinkle brook began to hurry and break into murmurs on a pebble bar, as if its feet were tickled. A few more steps and it burst into a peal of laughter that lasted half the year as it tumbled over narrow shelves of rock into a foamy pool. Many a day I had sat fishing for hours at the little fall under a birch tree, among the brakes and moss. No ray of sunlight ever got to the dark water below me—the lair of many a big fish that had yielded to the temptation of my bait. Here I lay in the cool shade while a singular sort of heart sickness came over me. A wild partridge was beating his gong in the near woods all the afternoon. The sound of the water seemed to break in the tree-tops and fall back upon me. I had lain there thinking an hour or more when I caught the jar of approaching footsteps. Looking up I saw Jed Feary coming through the bushes, pole in hand.

'Fishin'?' he asked.

'Only thinking,' I answered.

'Couldn't be in better business,' said he as he sat down beside me.

More than once he had been my father confessor and I was glad he had come.

'In love?' he asked. 'No boy ever thinks unless he's in love.'

'In trouble,' said I.

'Same thing,' he answered, lighting his pipe. 'Love is trouble with a bit of sugar in it—the sweetest trouble a man can have. What's the matter?'

'It's a great secret,' I said, 'I have never told it. I am in love.'

'Knew it,' he said, puffing at his pipe and smiling in a kindly way. 'Now let's put in the trouble.'

'She does not love me,' I answered.

'Glad of it,' he remarked. 'I've got a secret t, tell you.'

'What's that?' I enquired.

'Wouldn't tell anybody else for the world, my boy,' he said, 'it's between you an' me.'

'Between you an' me,' I repeated.

'Well,' he said, you're a fool.'

'That's no secret,' I answered much embarrassed.

'Yes it is,' he insisted, 'you're smart enough an' ye can have most anything in this world if ye take the right road. Ye've grown t' be a great big strapping fellow but you're only—sixteen?'

'That's all,' I said mournfully.

'Ye're as big a fool to go falling in love as I'd be. Ye're too young an' I'm too old. I say to you, wait. Ye've got to go t' college.'

'College!' I exclaimed, incredulously.

'Yes! an' thet's another secret,' said he. I tol' David Brower what I thought o' your writing thet essay on bugs in pertickier—an' I tol' 'im what people were sayin' o' your work in school.'

'What d' he say?' I asked.

'Said Hope had tol' him all about it—that she was as proud o' you as she was uv her curls, an' I believe it. "Well," says I, "y' oughter sen' that boy t' college." "Goin' to," says he. "He'll go t' the 'Cademy this fall if he wants to. Then he can go t' college soon's he's ready." Threw up my hat an' shouted I was that glad.'

As he spoke the old man's face kindled with enthusiasm. In me he had one who understood him, who saw truth in his thought, music in his verse, a noble simplicity in his soul. I took his hand in mine and thanked him heartily. Then we rose and came away together.

'Remember,' he said, as we parted at the corner, 'there's a way laid out fer you. In God's time it will lead to every good thing you desire. Don't jump over the fence. Don't try t' pass any milestun 'fore ye've come to it. Don't mope. Keep yer head cool with philosophy, yer feet warm with travel an' don't worry bout yer heart. It won't turn t' stun if ye do keep it awhile. Allwus hev enough of it about ye t' do business with. Goodbye!'

Chapter 15

Gerald Brower, who was a baby when I came to live at Faraway, and was now eleven, had caught a cold in seed time, and he had never quite recovered. His coughing had begun to keep him awake, and one night it brought alarm to the whole household. Elizabeth Brower was up early in the morning and called Uncle Eb, who went away for the doctor as soon as light came. We ate our breakfast in silence. Father and mother and Grandma Bisnette spoke only in low tones and somehow the anxiety in their faces went to my heart. Uncle Eb returned about eight o'clock and said the doctor was coming. Old Doctor Bigsby was a very great man in that country. Other physicians called him far and wide for consultation. I had always regarded him with a kind of awe intensified by the aroma of his drugs and the gleam of his lancet. Once I had been his patient and then I had trembled at his approach. When he took my little wrist in his big hand, I remember with what reluctance I stuck out my quivering tongue, black, as I feared with evidences of prevarication.

He was a picture for a painter man as he came that morning erect in his gig. Who could forget the hoary majesty of his head—his 'stovepipe' tilted back, his white locks flying about his ears? He had a long nose, a smooth-shaven face and a left eye that was a trifle turned. His thoughts were generally one day behind the calendar. Today he seemed to be digesting the affairs of yesterday. He was, therefore, absentminded, to a degree that made no end of gossip. If he came out one day with shoe-strings flying, in his remorse the next he would forget his collar; if one told him a good joke today, he might not seem to hear it, but tomorrow he would take it up in its turn and shake with laughter.

I remember how, that morning after noting the symptoms of his patient, he sat a little in silent reflection. He knew that colour in the cheek, that look in the eye—he had seen so much of it. His legs were crossed and one elbow thrown carelessly over the back of his chair. We all sat looking at him anxiously. In a moment he began chewing hard on his quid of tobacco. Uncle Eb pushed the cuspidor a bit nearer. The doctor expectorated freely and resumed his attitude of reflection. The clock ticked loudly, the patient sighed, our anxiety increased. Uncle Eb spoke to father, in a low tone, whereupon the doctor turned suddenly, with a little grunt of enquiry, and seeing he was not addressed, sank again into thoughtful repose. I had begun to fear the worst when suddenly the hand of the doctor swept the bald peak of benevolence at the top of his head. Then a smile began to spread over his face. It was as if some feather of thought had begun to tickle him. In a moment his head was nodding with laughter that brought a great sense of relief to all of us. In a slow, deliberate tone he began to speak:

'I was over t' Rat Tupper's t'other day,' said he, 'Rat was sitting with me in the door yard. Purty soon a young chap came in, with a scythe, and asked if he might use the grindstun. He was a new hired man from somewhere near. He didn't know Rat, an' Rat didn't know him. So Rat o' course had t' crack one o' his jokes.

'"May I use yer grindstun?" said the young feller.

'"Dunno," said Rat, "I'm only the hired man here. Go an' ask Mis' Tupper."

'The ol' lady had overheard him an' so she says t' the young feller, "Yes—ye can use the grindstun. The hired man out there'll turn it fer ye."

'Rat see he was trapped, an' so he went out under the plum tree, where the stun was, an' begun t' turn. The scythe was dull an' the young feller bore on harder'n wuz reely decent fer a long time. Rat begun t' git very sober lookin'.

'"Ain't ye 'bout done," said he.

'"Putty nigh," said the young feller bearin' down a leetle harder all the time.

'Rat made the stun go faster. Putty soon he asked agin, "Ain't ye done yit?"

'"Putty nigh!" says the other, feeling o' the edge.

'"I'm done," said Rat, an' he let go o' the handle. "I dunno 'bout the scythe but I'm a good deal sharper'n I wuz."

'"You're the hired man here ain't ye?" said the young feller.

'"No, I ain't," said Rat. "'D rather own up t' bein' a liar than turn that stun another minnit."

As soon as he was fairly started with this droll narrative the strain of the situation was relieved. We were all laughing as much at his deliberate way of narration as at the story itself.

Suddenly he turned to Elizabeth Brower and said, very soberly, 'Will you bring me some water in a glass?'

Then he opened his chest of medicine, made some powders and told us how to give them.

'In a few days I would take him into the big woods for a while,' he said. 'See how it agrees with him.'

Then he gathered up his things and mother went with him to the gig.

Humour was one of the specifics of Doctor Bigsby. He was always a poor man. He had a way of lumping his bills, at about so much, in settlement and probably never kept books. A side of pork paid for many a long journey. He came to his death riding over the hills one bitter day not long after the time of which I write, to reach a patient.

The haying over, we made ready for our trip into the woods. Uncle Eb and Tip Taylor, who knew the forest, and myself, were to go with Gerald to Blueberry Lake. We loaded our wagon with provisions one evening and made ready to be off at the break of day.

Chapter 16

I remember how hopefully we started that morning with Elizabeth Brower and Hope waving their handkerchiefs on the porch and David near them whittling. They had told us what to do and what not to do over and over again. I sat with Gerald on blankets that were spread over a thick mat of hay. The morning air was sweet with the odour of new hay and the music of the bobolink. Uncle Eb and Tip Taylor sang merrily as we rode over the hills.

When we entered the shade of the big forest Uncle Eb got out his rifle and loaded it. He sat a long time whispering and looking eagerly for game to right and left. He was still a boy. One could see evidences of age only in his white hair and beard and wrinkled brow. He retained the little tufts in front of his ears, and lately had grown a silver crescent of thin and silky hair that circled his throat under a bare chin. Young as I was I had no keener relish for a holiday than he. At noon we halted beside a brook and unhitched our horses. Then we caught some fish, built a fire and cooked them, and brewed our tea. At sunset we halted at Tuley Pond, looking along its reedy margin, under purple tamaracks, for deer. There was a great silence, here in the deep of the woods, and Tip Taylor's axe, while he peeled the bark for our camp, seemed to fill the wilderness with echoes. It was after dark when the shanty was covered and we lay on its fragrant mow of balsam and hemlock. The great logs that we had rolled in front of our shanty were set afire and shortly supper was cooking.

Gerald had stood the journey well. Uncle Eb and he stayed in while Tip and I got our jack ready and went off in quest of a dugout He said Bill Ellsworth had one hid in a thicket on the south side of Tuley. We found it after an hour's tramp near by. It needed a little repairing but we soon made it water worthy, and then took our seats, he in the stern, with the paddle, and I in the bow with the gun. Slowly and silently we clove a way through the star-sown shadows. It was like the hushed and mystic movement of a dream. We seemed to be above the deep of heaven, the stars below us. The shadow of the forest in the still water looked like the wall of some mighty castle with towers and battlements and myriads of windows lighted for a fete. Once the groan of a nighthawk fell out of the upper air with a sound like that of a stone striking in water. I thought little of the deer Tip was after. His only aim in life was the one he got with a gun barrel. I had forgotten all but the beauty of the scene. Suddenly Tip roused me by laying his hand to the gunwale and gently shaking the dugout. In the dark distance, ahead of us, I could hear the faint tinkle of dripping water. Then I knew a deer was feeding not far away and that the water was falling from his muzzle. When I opened my jack we were close upon him. His eyes gleamed. I shot high above the deer that went splashing ashore before I had pulled my trigger. After the roar of the gun had got away, in the distant timber, Tip mentioned a place abhorred of all men, turned and paddled for the landing.

'Could 'a killed 'im with a club,' said he snickering. 'Guess he must a looked putty tall didn't he?'

'Why?' I asked.

'Cos ye aimed into the sky,' said he. 'Mebbe ye thought he was a bird.'

'My hand trembled a little,' said I.

"Minds me of Bill Barber,' he said in a half-whisper, as he worked his paddle, chuckling with amusement.

'How's that?' I asked.

'Nothin' safe but the thing he shoots at,' said he. 'Terrible bad shot. Kills a cow every time he goes huntin'.'

Uncle Eb was stirring the fire when we came whispering into camp, and Gerald lay asleep under the blankets.

'Willie couldn't hit the broadside of a bam,' said Tip. 'He don't take to it nat'ral.'

'Killin' an' book learnin' don't often go together,' said Uncle Eb.

I turned in by the side of Gerald and Uncle Eb went off with Tip for another trip in the dugout. The night was chilly but the fire flooded our shanty with its warm glow. What with the light, and the boughs under us, and the strangeness of the black forest we got little sleep. I heard the gun roar late in the night, and when I woke again Uncle Eb and Tip Taylor were standing over the fire in the chilly grey of the morning. A dead deer hung on the limb of a tree near by. They began dressing it while Gerald and I went to the spring for water, peeled potatoes, and got the pots boiling. After a hearty breakfast we packed up, and were soon on the road again, reaching Blueberry Lake before noon. There we hired a boat of the lonely keeper of the reservoir, found an abandoned camp with an excellent bark shanty and made ourselves at home.

That evening in camp was one to be remembered. An Thomas, the guide who tended the reservoir, came over and sat beside our fire until bedtime. He had spent years in the wilderness going out for nothing less important than an annual spree at circus time. He eyed us over, each in turn, as if he thought us all very rare and interesting.

'Many bears here?' Uncle Eb enquired.

'More plenty 'n human bein's,' he answered, puffing lazily at his pipe with a dead calm in his voice and manner that I have never seen equalled except in a tropic sea.

'See 'em often?' I asked.

He emptied his pipe, striking it on his palm until the bowl rang, without answering. Then he blew into the stem with great violence.

'Three or four 'n a summer, mebbe,' he said at length.

'Ever git sassy?' Uncle Eb asked.

He whipped a coal out of the ashes then and lifted it in his fingers to the bowl of his pipe.

'Never real sassy,' he said between vigourous puffs. 'One stole a ham off my pyazz las' summer; Al Fifield brought 't in fer me one day—smelt good too! I kep' savin' uv it thinkin' I'd enjoy it all the more when I did hev it. One day I went off cuttin' timber an' stayed 'til mos' night. Comin' home I got t' thinkin' o' thet ham, an' made up my mind I'd hev some fer supper. The more I thought uv it the faster I hurried an' when I got hum I was hungrier'n I'd been fer a year. When I see the ol' bear's tracks an' the empty peg where the ham had hung I went t' work an' got mad. Then I started after thet bear. Tracked 'im over yender, up Cat Mountin'.'

Here Ab paused. He had a way of stopping always at the most interesting point to puff at his pipe. It looked as if he were getting up steam for another sentence and these delays had the effect of 'continued in our next'.

'Kill 'im?' Uncle Eb asked.

'Licked him,' he said.

'Huh!' we remarked incredulously.

'Licked 'im,' he repeated chucking. 'Went into his cave with a sledge stake an' whaled 'im—whaled 'im 'til he run fer his life.'

Whether it was true or not I have never been sure, even to this day, but Ab's manner was at once modest and convincing.

'Should 'a thought he'd 'a rassled with ye,' Uncle Eb remarked.

'Didn't give 'im time,' said Ab, as he took out his knife and began slowly to sharpen a stick.

'Don't never wan' t' rassle with no bear,' he added, 'but hams is too scurce here 'n the woods t' hev 'em tuk away 'fore ye know the taste uv 'em. I ain't never been hard on bears. Don't seldom ever set no traps an' I ain't shot a bear fer mor'n 'n ten year. But they've got t' be decent. If any bear steals my vittles he's goin' t' git cuffed bard.'

Ab's tongue had limbered up at last. His pipe was going well and he seemed to have struck an easy grade. There was a tone of injury and aggrievement in his talk of the bear's ingratitude. He snailed over his whittling as we laughed heartily at the droll effect of it all.

'D'ye ever hear o' the wild man 'at roams 'round'n these woods?' he asked.

'Never did,' said Uncle Eb.

'I've seen 'im more times 'n ye could shake a stick at,' said Ab crossing his legs comfortably and spitting into the fire. 'Kind o' thank he's the same man folks tells uv down 'n Paradise Valley there—'at goes 'round 'n the clearin' after bedtime.'

'The night man!' I exclaimed.

'Guess thet's what they call 'im,' said Ab. 'Curus man! Sometimes I've hed a good squint at 'im off 'n the woods. He's wilder 'n a deer an' I've seen 'im jump over logs, half as high as this shanty, jest as easy as ye 'd hop a twig. Tried t' foller 'im once er twice but tain' no use. He's quicker 'n a wil' cat.'

'What kind of a lookin' man is he?' Tip Taylor asked.

'Great, big, broad-shouldered feller,' said Ab. 'Six feet tall if he's an inch. Hed a kind of a deerskin jacket on when I seen 'im an' breeches an' moccasins made o' some kind o' hide. I recollec' one day I was over on the ridge two mile er more from the Stillwater goin' south. I seen 'im gittin' a drink at the spring there 'n the burnt timber. An' if I ain't mistaken there was a real live panther playin' 'round 'im. If 't wa'n't a panther 'twas pesky nigh it I can tell ye. The critter see me fast an' drew up 'is back. Then the man got up quickerin' a flash. Soon 'she see me—Jeemimey! didn't they move. Never see no human critter run as he did! A big tree hed fell 'cross a lot o' bush right 'n his path. I'll be gol dummed if 'twan't higher 'n my head! But he cleared it—jest as easy as a grasshopper'd go over a straw. I'd like t' know wher he comes from, gol dummed if I wouldn't. He's the consarndest queerest animal 'n these woods.'

Ab emphasised this lucid view of the night man by an animated movement of his fist that held the big hunting knife with which he whittled. Then he emptied his pipe and began cutting more tobacco.

'Some says 'e 's a ghost,' said Tip Taylor, splitting his sentence with a yawn, as he lay on a buffalo robe in the shanty.

'Shucks an' shoestrings!' said Ab, 'he looks too nat'ral. Don't believe no ghost ever wore whiskers an' long hair like his'n. Thet don't hol' t' reason.'

This remark was followed by dead silence. Tip seemed to lack both courage and information with which to prolong the argument.

Gerald had long been asleep and we were all worn out with uphill travelling and the lack of rest. Uncle Eb went out to look after the horses that were tethered near us. Ab rose, looked up through the tree-tops, ventured a guess about the weather, and strode off into the darkness.

We were five days in camp, hunting, fishing, fighting files and picking blueberries. Gerald's cough had not improved at all—it was, if anything, a bit worse than it had been and the worry of that had clouded our holiday. We were not in high spirits when, finally, we decided to break camp the next afternoon.

The morning of our fourth day at Blueberry Uncle Eb and I crossed the lake, at daylight, to fish awhile in Soda Brook and gather orchids then abundant and beautiful in that part of the woods. We headed for camp at noon and were well away from shore when a wild yell rang in the dead timber that choked the wide inlet behind us. I was rowing and stopped the oars while we both looked back at the naked trees, belly deep in the water.

But for the dry limbs, here and there, they would have looked like masts of sunken ships. In a moment another wild whoop came rushing over the water. Thinking it might be somebody in trouble we worked about and pulled for the mouth of the inlet. Suddenly I saw a boat coming in the dead timber. There were three men in it, two of whom were paddling. They yelled like mad men as they caught sight of us, and one of them waved a bottle in the air.

'They're Indians,' said Uncle Eb. 'Drunk as lords. Guess we'd better git out o' the way.'

I put about and with a hearty pull made for the other side of the lake, three miles away. The Indians came after us, their yells echoing in the far forest. Suddenly one of them lifted his rifle, as if taking aim at us, and, bang it went the ball ricocheting across our bows.

'Crazy drunk,' said Uncle Eb, 'an' they're in fer trouble. Pull with all yer might.'

I did that same putting my arms so stiffly to their task I feared the oars would break.

In a moment another ball came splintering the gunwales right between us, but fortunately, well above the water line. Being half a mile from shore I saw we were in great peril. Uncle Eb reached for his rifle, his hand trembling.

'Sink 'em,' I shouted, 'an' do it quick or they'll sink us.'

My old companion took careful aim and his ball hit them right on the starboard bow below the water line. A splash told where it had landed. They stopped yelling. The man in the bow clapped his hat against the side of the boat.

'Guess we've gin 'em a little business t' ten' to,' said Uncle Eb as he made haste to load his rifle.

The Indian at the bow was lifting his rifle again. He seemed to reel as he took aim. He was very slow about it. I kept pulling as I watched him. I saw that their boat was slowly sinking. I had a strange fear that he would hit me in the stomach. I dodged when I saw the flash of his rifle. His ball struck the water, ten feet away from us, and threw a spray into my face.

Uncle Eb had lifted his rifle to shoot again. Suddenly the Indian, who had shot at us, went overboard. In a second they were all in the water, their boat bottom up.

'Now take yer time,' said Uncle Eb coolly, a frown upon his face.

'They'll drown,' said I.

'Don't care if they do, consam 'em,' he answered. 'They're some o' them St Regis devils, an' when they git whisky in 'em they'd jes' soon kill ye as look at ye. They am' no better 'n rats.'

We kept on our way and by and by a wind came up that gave us both some comfort, for we knew it would soon blow them ashore. Ab Thomas had come to our camp and sat with Tip and Gerald when we got there. We told of our adventure and then Ab gave us a bad turn, and a proper appreciation of our luck, by telling us that they were a gang of cut-throats—the worst in the wilderness.

'They'd a robbed ye sure,' he said. 'It's the same gang 'at killed a man on Cat Mountain las' summer, an' I'll bet a dollar on it.'

Tip had everything ready for our journey home. Each day Gerald had grown paler and thinner. As we wrapped him in a shawl and tenderly helped him into the wagon I read his doom in his face. We saw so much of that kind of thing in our stern climate we knew what it meant. Our fun was over. We sat in silence, speeding down the long hills in the fading light of the afternoon. Those few solemn hours in which I heard only the wagon's rumble and the sweet calls of the whip-poor-will-waves of music on a sea of silence-started me in a way of thought which has led me high and low these many years and still invites me. The day was near its end when we got to the first big clearing. From the top of a high hill we could see above the far forest, the red rim of the setting sun, big with winding from the skein of day, that was now flying off the tree-tops in the west.

We stopped to feed the horses and to take a bite of jerked venison, wrapped ourselves warmer, for it was now dunk and chilly, and went on again. The road went mostly downhill, going out of the woods, and we could make good time. It was near midnight when we drove in at our gate. There was a light in the sitting-room and Uncle Eb and I went in with Gerald at once. Elizabeth Brower knelt at the feet of her son, unbuttoned his coat and took off his muffler. Then she put her arms about his neck while neither spoke nor uttered any sound. Both mother and son felt and understood and were silent. The ancient law of God, that rends asunder and makes havoc of our plans, bore heavy on them in that moment, I have no doubt, but neither murmured. Uncle Eb began to pump vigorously at the cistern while David fussed with the fire. We were all quaking inwardly but neither betrayed a sign of it. It is a way the Puritan has of suffering. His emotions are like the deep undercurrents of the sea.

Chapter 17

If I were writing a novel merely I should try to fill it with merriment and good cheer. I should thrust no sorrow upon the reader save that he might feel for having wasted his time. We have small need of manufactured sorrow when, truly, there is so much of the real thing on every side of us. But this book is nothing more nor less than a history, and by the same token it cannot be all as I would have wished it. In October following the events of the last chapter, Gerald died of consumption, having borne a lingering illness with great fortitude. I, who had come there a homeless orphan in a basket, and who, with the God-given eloquence of childhood had brought them to take me to their hearts and the old man that was with me as well, was now the only son left to Elizabeth and David Brower. There were those who called it folly at the time they took us in, I have heard, but he who shall read this history to the end shall see how that kind of folly may profit one or even many here in this hard world.

It was a gloomy summer for all of us. The industry and patience with which Hope bore her trial, night and day, is the sweetest recollection of my youth. It brought to her young face a tender soberness of womanhood—a subtle change of expression that made her all the more dear to me. Every day, rain or shine, the old doctor had come to visit his patient, sometimes sitting an hour and gazing thoughtfully in his face, occasionally asking a question, or telling a quaint anecdote. And then came the end.

The sky was cold and grey in the late autumn and the leaves were drifted deep in the edge of the woodlands when Hope and I went away to school together at Hillsborough. Uncle Eb drove us to our boarding place in town. When we bade him goodbye and saw him driving away, alone in the wagon, we hardly dared look at each other for the tears in our eyes.

David Brower had taken board for us at the house of one Solomon Rollin—universally known as 'Cooky' Rollin; that was one of the first things I learned at the Academy. It seemed that many years ago he had taken his girl to a dance and offered her, in lieu of supper, cookies that he had thoughtfully brought with him. Thus cheaply he had come to life-long distinction.

'You know Rollin's Ancient History, don't you?' the young man asked who sat with me at school that first day.

'Have it at home,' I answered, 'It's in five volumes.'

'I mean the history of Sol Rollin, the man you are boarding with,' said he smiling at me and then he told the story of the cookies.

The principal of the Hillsborough Academy was a big, brawny bachelor of Scotch descent, with a stem face and cold, grey, glaring eyes. When he stood towering above us on his platform in the main room of the building where I sat, there was an alertness in his figure, and a look of responsibility in his face, that reminded me of the pictures of Napoleon at Waterloo. He always carried a stout ruler that had blistered a shank of every mischievous boy in school. As he stood by the line, that came marching into prayers every morning he would frequently pull out a boy, administer a loud whack or two, shake him violently and force him into a seat. The day I began my studies at the Academy I saw him put two dents in the wall with the heels of a young man who had failed in his algebra. To a bashful and sensitive youth, just out of a country home, the sight of such violence was appalling. My first talk with him, however, renewed my courage. He had heard I was a good scholar and talked with me in a friendly way about my plans. Both Hope and I were under him in algebra and Latin. I well remember my first error in his class. I had misconstrued a Latin sentence. He looked at me, a smile and a sneer crowding each other for possession of his face. In a loud, jeering tone he cried: 'Mirabile dictu!'

I looked at him in doubt of his meaning.

'Mirabile dictu!' he shouted, his tongue trilling the r.

I corrected my error.

'Perfect!' he cried again. 'Puer pulchre! Next!'

He never went further than that with me in the way of correction. My size and my skill as a wrestler, that shortly ensured for me the respect of the boys, helped me to win the esteem of the master. I learned my lessons and kept out of mischief. But others of equal proficiency were not so fortunate. He was apt to be hard on a light man who could be handled without over-exertion.

Uncle Eb came in to see me one day and sat awhile with me in my seat. While he was there the master took a boy by the collar and almost literally wiped the blackboard with him. There was a great clatter of heels for a moment. Uncle Eb went away shortly and was at Sol Rollin's when I came to dinner.

'Powerful man ain't he?' said Uncle Eb.

'Rather,' I said.

'Turned that boy into a reg'lar horse fiddle,' he remarked. 'Must 'ave unsot his reason.'

'Unnecessary!' I said.

'Reminded me o' the time 'at Tip Taylor got his tooth pulled,' said he. 'Shook 'im up so 'at he thought he'd had his neck put out o' ji'nt.'

Sol Rollin was one of my studies that winter. He was a carpenter by trade and his oddities were new and delightful. He whistled as he worked, he whistled as he read, he whistled right merrily as he walked up and down the streets—a short, slight figure with a round boyish face and a fringe of iron-grey hair under his chin. The little man had one big passion—that for getting and saving. The ancient thrift of his race had pinched him small and narrow as a foot is stunted by a tight shoe. His mind was a bit out of register as we say in the printing business. His vocabulary was rich and vivid and stimulating.

'Somebody broke into the arsenic today,' he announced, one evening, at the supper table.

'The arsenic,' said somebody, 'what arsenic?'

'Why the place where they keep the powder,' he answered.

'Oh! the arsenal.'

'Yes, the arsenal,' he said, cackling with laughter at his error. Then he grew serious.

'Stole all the ambition out of it,' he added.

'You mean ammunition, don't you, Solomon?' his wife enquired.

'Certainly,' said he, 'wasn't that what I said.'

When he had said a thing that met his own approval Sol Rollin would cackle most cheerfully and then crack a knuckle by twisting a finger. His laugh was mostly out of register also. It had a sad lack of relevancy. He laughed on principle rather than provocation. Some sort of secret comedy of which the world knew nothing, was passing in his mind; it seemed to have its exits and its entrances, its villain, its clown and its miser who got all the applause.

While working his joy was unconfined. Many a time I have sat and watched him in his little shop, its window dim with cobwebs. Sometimes he would stop whistling and cackle heartily as he worked his plane or drew his pencil to the square. I have even seen him drop his tools and give his undivided attention to laughter. He did not like to be interrupted—he loved his own company the best while he was 'doin' business'. I went one day when he was singing the two lines and their quaint chorus which was all he ever sang in my hearing; which gave him great relief, I have no doubt, when lip weary with whistling:

Sez I 'Dan'l Skinner, I thank yer mighty mean

To send me up the river, With a sev'n dollar team'

Lul-ly, ul—ly, diddie ul—ly, diddleul—lydee, Oh,

lul-ly, ul—ly, diddle ul—ly, diddle ul—ly dee.

'Mr Rollin!' I said.

Yes siree,' said he, pausing in the midst of his chorus to look up at me.

'Where can I get a piece of yellow pine?'

'See 'n a minute,' he said. Then he continued his sawing and his song, '"Says I Dan Skinner, I thank yer mighty mean"—what d' ye want it fer?' he asked stopping abruptly.

'Going to make a ruler,' I answered.

'"T' sen' me up the river with a seven dollar team,"' he went on, picking out a piece of smooth planed lumber, and handing it to me.

'How much is it worth?' I enquired.

He whistled a moment as he surveyed it carefully.

''Bout one cent,' he answered seriously.

I handed him the money and sat down awhile to watch him as he went on with his work. It was the cheapest amusement I have yet enjoyed. Indeed Sol Rollin became a dissipation, a subtle and seductive habit that grew upon me and on one pretext or another I went every Saturday to the shop if I had not gone home.

'What ye goin' t' be?'

He stopped his saw, and looked at me, waiting for my answer.

At last the time had come when I must declare myself and I did.

'A journalist,' I replied.

'What's that?' he enquired curiously.

'An editor,' I said.

'A printer man?'

'A printer man.'

'Huh!' said he. 'Mebbe I'll give ye a job. Sairey tol' me I'd orter t' 'ave some cards printed. I'll want good plain print: Solomon Rollin, Cappenter 'n J'iner, Hillsborough, NY—soun's putty good don't it.'

'Beautiful,' I answered.

'I'll git a big lot on 'em,' he said. 'I'll want one for Sister Susan 'at's out in Minnesoty—no, I guess I'll send 'er tew, so she can give one away—an' one fer my brother, Eliphalet, an' one apiece fer my three cousins over 'n Vermont, an' one fer my Aunt Mirandy. Le's see-tew an' one is three an' three is six an' one is seven. Then I'll git a few struck off fer the folks here—guess they'll thank I'm gittin' up 'n the world.'

He shook and snickered with anticipation of the glory of it. Pure vanity inspired him in the matter and it had in it no vulgar consideration of business policy. He whistled a lively tune as he bent to his work again.

'Yer sister says ye're a splendid scholar!' said he. 'Hear'n 'er braggin' 'bout ye t'other night; she thinks a good deal o' her brother, I can tell ye. Guess I know what she's gain' t' give ye Crissmus.'

'What's that?' I asked, with a curiosity more youthful than becoming.

'Don't ye never let on,' said he.

'Never,' said I.

'Hear'n 'em tell,' he said,' 'twas a gol' lockup, with 'er pictur' in it.'

'Oh, a locket!' I exclaimed.

'That's it,' he replied, 'an' pure gol', too.'

I turned to go.

'Hope she'll grow up a savin' woman,' he remarked. "Fraid she won't never be very good t' worlt.'

'Why not?' I enquired.

'Han's are too little an' white,' he answered.

'She won't have to,' I said.

He cackled uproariously for a moment, then grew serious.

'Her father's rich,' he said, 'the richest man o' Faraway, an I guess she won't never hev anything t' dew but set'n sing an' play the melodium.'

'She can do as she likes,' I said.

He stood a moment looking down as if meditating on the delights he had pictured.

'Gol!' he exclaimed suddenly.

My subject had begun to study me, and I came away to escape further examination.

Chapter 18

I ought to say that I have had and shall have to chronicle herein much that would seem to indicate a mighty conceit of myself. Unfortunately the little word 'I' throws a big shadow in this history. It looms up all too frequently in every page for the sign of a modest man. But, indeed, I cannot help it, for he was the only observer of all there is to tell. Now there is much, for example, in the very marrow of my history—things that never would have happened, things that never would have been said, but for my fame as a scholar. My learning was of small account, for, it must be remembered, I am writing of a time when any degree of scholarship was counted remarkable among the simple folk of Faraway.

Hope took singing lessons and sang in church every Sunday. David or Uncle Eb came down for us often of a Saturday and brought us back before service in the morning. One may find in that town today many who will love to tell him of the voice and beauty and sweetness of Hope Brower those days, and of what they expected regarding her and me. We went out a good deal evenings to concerts, lectures at the churches or the college, or to visit some of the many people who invited us to their homes.

We had a recess of two weeks at the winter holidays and David Brower came after us the day the term ended. O, the great happiness of that day before Christmas when we came flying home in the sleigh behind a new team of greys and felt the intoxication of the frosty air, and drove in at dusk after the lamps were lit and we could see mother and Uncle Eb and Grandma Bisnette looking out of the window, and a steaming dinner on the table! I declare! it is long since then, but I cannot ever think of that time without wiping my glasses and taking a moment off. Tip Taylor took the horses and we all came in where the kettle was singing on the stove and loving hands helped us out of our wraps. The supper was a merry feast, the like of which one may find only by returning to his boyhood. Mack! that is a long journey for some of us.

Supper over and the dishes out of the way we gathered about the stove with cider and butternuts.

'Well,' said Hope, 'I've got some news to tell you—this boy is the best scholar of his age in this county.'

'Thet so?' said David.

Uncle Eb stopped his hmnmer that was lifted to crack a butternut and pulled his chair close to Hope's. Elizabeth looked at her daughter and then at me, a smile and a protest in her face.

'True as you live,' said Hope. 'The master told me so. He's first in everything, and in the Town Hall the other night he spelt everybody down.'

'What! In Hillsborough?' Uncle Eb asked incredulously.

'Yes, in Hillsborough,' said Hope, 'and there were doctors and lawyers and college students and I don't know who all in the match.'

'Most reemarkable!' said David Brower.

'Treemenjious!' exclaimed Uncle Eb.

'I heard about it over at the mills t'day,' said Tip Taylor.

'Merd Dieu!' exclaimed Grandma Bisnette, crossing herself.

Elizabeth Brower was unable to stem this tide of enthusiasm. I had tried to stop it, but, instantly, it had gone beyond my control. If I could be hurt by praise the mischief had been done.

'It's very nice, indeed,' said she soberly. 'I do hope it won't make him conceited. He should remember that people do not always mean what they say.'

'He's too sensible for that, mother,' said David.

'Shucks!' said Uncle Eb, 'he ain' no fool if he is a good speller—not by a dum sight!'

'Tip,' said David, 'you'll find a box in the sleigh 'at come by express. I wish ye'd go'n git it.'

We all stood looking while Tip brought it in and pried off the top boards with a hatchet.

'Careful, now!' Uncle Eb cautioned him. 'Might spile sumthin'.'

The top off, Uncle Eb removed a layer of pasteboard. Then he pulled out a lot of coloured tissue paper, and under that was a package, wrapped and tied. Something was written on it. He held it up and tried to read the writing.

'Can't see without my spectacles,' he said, handing it to me.

'For Hope,' I read, as I passed it to her.

'Hooray!' said Uncle Eb, as he lifted another, and the last package, from the box.

'For Mrs Brower,' were the words I read upon that one.

The strings were cut, the wrappers torn away, and two big rolls of shiny silk loosened their coils on the table. Hope uttered a cry of delight. A murmur of surprise and admiration passed from one to another. Elizabeth lifted a rustling fold and held it to the lamplight We passed our hands over the smooth sheen of the silk.

'Wall, I swan!' said Uncle Eb. 'Jes' like a kitten's ear!'

'Eggzac'ly!' said David Brower.

Elizabeth lifted the silk and let it flow to her feet Then for a little she looked down, draping it to her skirt and moving her foot to make the silk rustle. For the moment she was young again.

'David,' she said, still looking at the glory of glossy black that covered her plain dress.

'Well, mother,' he answered.

'Was you fool enough t' go'n buy this stuff fer me?'

'No, mother—it come from New York City,' he said.

'From New York City?' was the exclamation of all.

Elizabeth Brower looked thoughtfully at her husband.

'Clear from New York City?' she repeated.

'From New York City,' said he.

'Wall, of all things!' said Uncle Eb, looking over his spectacles from one to another.

'It's from the Livingstone boy,' said Mrs Brower. 'I've heard he's the son of a rich man.'

''Fraid he took a great fancy t' Hope,' said David.

'Father,' said the girl, you've no right to say that. I'm sure he never cared a straw for me.'

'I don't think we ought to keep it,' said Mrs Brower, looking up thoughtfully.

'Shucks and shavin's!' said Uncle Eb. 'Ye don't know but what I had it sent myself.'

Hope went over and put her arms around his neck.

'Did you, Uncle Eb?' she asked. 'Now you tell me the truth, Uncle Eb.'

'Wouldn't say 't I did,' he answered, 'but I don' want 'a see ye go sendin' uv it back. Ye dunno who sent it.'

'What'll I do with it?' Mrs Brower asked, laughing in a way that showed a sense of absurdity. 'I'd a been tickled with it thirty years ago, but now-folks 'ud think I was crazy.'

'Never heard such fol de rol,' said Uncle Eb. 'If ye move t' the village it'll come handy t' go t' meetin' in.'

That seemed to be unanswerable and conclusive, at least for the time being, and the silk was laid away. We sat talking until late bedtime, Hope and I, telling of our studies and of the many people we had met in Hillsborough.

We hung up our stockings just as we had always done Christmas Eve, and were up betimes in the morning to find them filled with many simple but delightful things, and one which I treasure to this day—the locket and its picture of which I had been surreptitiously informed.

At two o'clock we had a fine dinner of roast turkey and chicken pie, with plenty of good cider, and the mince pie, of blessed memory, such as only a daughter of New England may dare try to make.

Uncle Eb went upstairs after dinner and presently we heard him descending with a slow and heavy foot. I opened the stair door and there he stood with the old bass viol that had long lain neglected in a dusty corner of the attic. Many a night I had heard it groan as the strings loosened, in the years it had lain on its back, helpless and forgotten. It was like a dreamer, snoring in his sleep, and murmuring of that he saw in his dreams. Uncle Eb had dusted and strung it and glued its weaker joints. He sat down with it, the severe look of old upon his face, and set the strings roaring as he tuned them. Then he brought the sacred treasure to me and leaned it against my shoulder.

'There that's a Crissmus present fer ye, Willie,' said he. 'It may help ye t' pass away the time once in a while.'

I thanked him warmly.

''S a reel firs'-class instrument,' he said. 'Been a rip snorter 'n its day.' He took from his bosom then the old heart pin of silver that he had always worn of a Sunday.

'Goin' t' give ye thet, too,' he said. 'Dunno's ye'll ever care to wear it, but I want ye should hev sumthin' ye can carry'n yer pocket t' remember me by.'

I did not dare trust myself to speak, and I sat helplessly turning that relic of a better day in my fingers.

'It's genuwine silver,' said he proudly.

I took his old hand in mine and raised it reverently to my lips.

'Hear'n 'em tell 'bout goin' t' the village, an' I says t' myself, "Uncle Eb," says I, "we'll hev t' be goin'. 'Tain' no place fer you in the village."'

'Holden,' said David Brower, 'don't ye never talk like that ag'in. Yer just the same as married t' this family, an' ye can't ever git away from us.'

And he never did until his help was needed in other and fairer fields, I am sure, than those of Faraway—God knows where.

Chapter 19

Tip Taylor was, in the main, a serious-minded man. A cross eye enhanced the natural solemnity of his countenance. He was little given to talk or laughter unless he were on a hunt, and then he only whispered his joy. He had seen a good bit of the world through the peek sight of his rifle, and there was something always in the feel of a gun that lifted him to higher moods. And yet one could reach a tender spot in him without the aid of a gun. That winter vacation I set myself to study things for declamation—specimens of the eloquence of Daniel Webster and Henry Clay and James Otis and Patrick Henry. I practiced them in the barn, often, in sight and hearing of the assembled herd and some of those fiery passages were rather too loud and threatening for the peace and comfort of my audience. The oxen seemed always to be expecting the sting of the bull whip; they stared at me timidly, tilting their ears every moment, as if to empty them of a heavy load; while the horses snorted with apprehension. This haranguing of the herd had been going on a week or more when Uncle Eb and I, returning from a distant part of the farm, heard a great uproar in the stable. Looking in at a window we saw Tip Taylor, his back toward us, extemporising a speech. He was pressing his argument with gestures and the tone of thunder. We listened a moment, while a worried look came over the face of Uncle Eb. Tip's words were meaningless save for the secret aspiration they served to advertise. My old companion thought Tip had gone crazy, and immediately swung the door and stepped in. The orator fell suddenly from his lofty altitude and became a very sober looking hired man.

'What's the matter?' Uncle Eb enquired.

'Practicin',' said Tip soberly, as he turned slowly, his face damp and red with exertion.

'Fer what?' Uncle Eb enquired.

'Fer the 'sylum, I guess,' he answered, with a faint smile.

'Ye don' need no more practice,' Uncle Eb answered. 'Looks t' me as though ye was purty well prepared.'

To me there was a touch of pathos in this show of the deeper things in Tip's nature that had been kindled to eruption by my spouting. He would not come in to dinner that day, probably from an unfounded fear that we would make fun of his flight—a thing we should have been far from doing once we understood him.

It was a bitter day of one of the coldest winters we had ever known. A shrieking wind came over the hills, driving a scud of snow before it The stock in the stables, we all came in, soon after dinner, and sat comfortably by the fire with cider, checkers and old sledge. The dismal roar of the trees and the wind-wail in the chimney served only to increase our pleasure. It was growing dusk when mother, peering through the sheath of frost on a window pane, uttered an exclamation of surprise.

'Why! who is this at the door?' said she. 'Why! It's a man in a cutter.' Father was near the door and he swung it open quickly. There stood a horse and cutter, a man sitting in it, heavily muffled. The horse was shivering and the man sat motionless.

'Hello!' said David Brower in a loud voice.

He got no answer and ran bareheaded to the sleigh.

'Come, quick, Holden,' he called, 'it's Doctor Bigsby.'

We all ran out then, while David lifted the still figure in his arms.

'In here, quick!' said Elizabeth, opening the door to the parlour. 'Musn't take 'im near the stove.'

We carried him into the cold room and laid him down, and David and I tore his wraps open while the others ran quickly after snow.

I rubbed it vigorously upon his face and ears, the others meantime applying it to his feet and arms, that had been quickly stripped. The doctor stared at us curiously and tried to speak.

'Get ap, Dobbin!' he called presently, and ducked as if urging his horse. 'Get ap, Dobbin! Man'll die 'fore ever we git there.'

We all worked upon him with might and main. The white went slowly out of his face. We lifted him to a sitting posture. Mother and Hope and Uncle Eb were rubbing his hands and feet.

'Where am I?' he enquired, his face now badly swollen.

'At David Brower's,' said I.

'Huh?' he asked, with that kindly and familiar grunt of interrogation.

'At David Brower's,' I repeated.

'Well, I'll have t' hurry,' said he, trying feebly to rise. 'Man's dyin' over—' he hesitated thoughtfully, 'on the Plains,' he added, looking around at us.

Grandma Bisnette brought a lamp and held it so the light fell on his face. He looked from one to another. He drew one of his hands away and stared at it.

'Somebody froze?' he asked.

'Yes,' said I.

'Hm! Too bad. How'd it happen?' he asked. 'I don't know.'

'How's the pulse?' he enquired, feeling for my wrist.

I let him hold it in his hand.

'Will you bring me some water in a glass?' he enquired, turning to Mrs Brower, just as I had seen him do many a time in Gerald's illness. Before she came with the water his head fell forward upon his breast, while he muttered feebly. I thought then he was dead, but presently he roused himself with a mighty effort.

'David Brower!' he called loudly, and trying hard to rise, 'bring the horse! bring the horse! Mus' be goin', I tell ye. Man's dyin' over—on the Plains.'

He went limp as a rag then. I could feel his heart leap and struggle feebly.

'There's a man dyin' here,' said David Brower, in a low tone. 'Ye needn't rub no more.

'He's dead,' Elizabeth whispered, holding his hand tenderly, and looking into his half-closed eyes. Then for a moment she covered her own with her handkerchief, while David, in a low, calm tone, that showed the depth of his feeling, told us what to do.

Uncle Eb and I watched that night, while Tip Taylor drove away to town. The body lay in the parlour and we sat by the stove in the room adjoining. In a half-whisper we talked of the sad event of the day.

'Never oughter gone out a day like this,' said Uncle Eb. 'Don' take much t' freeze an ol' man.'

'Got to thinking of what happened yesterday and forgot the cold,' I said.

'Bad day t' be absent-minded,' whispered Uncle Eb, as he rose and tiptoed to the window and peered through the frosty panes. 'May o' got faint er sumthin'. Ol' hoss brought 'im right here—been here s' often with 'in'.'

He took the lantern and went out a moment. The door creaked upon its frosty hinges when he opened it.

'Thirty below zero,' he whispered as he came in. 'Win's gone down a leetle bit, mebbe.'

Uncanny noises broke in upon the stillness of the old house. Its timbers, racked in the mighty grip of the cold, creaked and settled. Sometimes there came a sharp, breaking sound, like the crack of bones.

'If any man oughter go t' Heaven, he had,' said Uncle Eb, as he drew on his boots.

'Think he's in Heaven?' I asked.

'Hain't a doubt uv it,' said he, as he chewed a moment, preparing for expectoration.

'What kind of a place do you think it is?' I asked.

'Fer one thing,' he said, deliberately, 'nobody'll die there, 'less he'd ought to; don't believe there's goin' t' be any need o' swearin' er quarrellin'. To my way o' thinkin' it'll be a good deal like Dave Brower's farm—nice, smooth land and no stun on it, an' hills an' valleys an' white clover aplenty, an' wheat an' corn higher'n a man's head. No bull thistles, no hard winters, no narrer contracted fools; no long faces, an' plenty o' work. Folks sayin' "How d'y do" 'stid o' "goodbye", all the while—comin' 'stid o' gain'. There's goin' t' be some kind o' fun there. I ain' no idee what 'tis. Folks like it an' I kind o' believe 'at when God's gin a thing t' everybody he thinks purty middlin' well uv it.'

'Anyhow, it seems a hard thing to die,' I remarked.

'Seems so,' he said thoughtfully. 'Jes' like ever'thing else—them 'at knows much about it don' have a great deal t' say. Looks t' me like this: I cal'ate a man hes on the everidge ten things his heart is sot on—what is the word I want—?'

'Treasures?' I suggested.

'Thet's it,' said he. 'Ev'ry one hes about ten treasures. Some hev more—some less. Say one's his strength, one's his plan, the rest is them he loves, an' the more he loves the better 'tis fer him. Wall, they begin t' go one by one. Some die, some turn agin' him. Fin's it hard t' keep his allowance. When he's only nine he's lost eggzac'ly one-tenth uv his dread o' dyin'. Bime bye he counts up—one-two-three-four-five-an' thet's all ther is left. He figgers it up careful. His strength is gone, his plan's a fillure, mebbe, an' this one's dead an' thet one's dead, an' t'other one better be. Then 's 'bout half-ways with him. If he lives till the ten treasures is all gone, God gives him one more—thet's death. An' he can swop thet off an' git back all he's lost. Then he begins t' think it's a purty dum good thing, after all. Purty good thing, after all,' he repeated, gaping as he spoke.

He began nodding shortly, and soon he went asleep in his chair.

Chapter 20

We went back to our work again shortly, the sweetness and the bitterness of life fresh in our remembrance. When we came back, 'hook an' line', for another vacation, the fields were aglow with colour, and the roads where Dr Bigsby had felt the sting of death that winter day were now over drifted with meadow-music and the smell of clover. I had creditably taken examination for college, where I was to begin my course in the fall, with a scholarship. Hope had made remarkable progress in music and was soon going to Ogdensburg for instruction.

A year had gone, nearly, since Jed Feary had cautioned me about falling in love. I had kept enough of my heart about me 'to do business with', but I had continued to feel an uncomfortable absence in the region of it. Young men at Hillsborough—many of whom, I felt sure, had a smarter look than I—had bid stubbornly for her favour. I wondered, often, it did not turn her head—this tribute of rustic admiration. But she seemed to be all unconscious of its cause and went about her work with small conceit of herself. Many a time they had tried to take her from my arm at the church door—a good-natured phase of youthful rivalry there in those days—but she had always said, laughingly, 'No, thank you,' and clung all the closer to me. Now Jed Feary had no knowledge of the worry it gave me, or of the peril it suggested. I knew that, if I felt free to tell him all, he would give me other counsel. I was now seventeen and she a bit older, and had I not heard of many young men and women who had been engaged—aye, even married—at that age? Well, as it happened, a day before she left us, to go to her work in Ogdensburg, where she was to live with her uncle, I made an end of delay. I considered carefully what a man ought to say in the circumstances, and I thought I had near an accurate notion. We were in the garden—together—the playground of our childhood.

'Hope, I have a secret to tell you,' I said.

'A secret,' she exclaimed eagerly. 'I love secrets.'

'A great secret,' I repeated, as I felt my face burning.

'Why—it must be something awful!'

'Not very,' I stammered. Having missed my cue from the beginning, I was now utterly confused.

'William!' she exclaimed, 'what is the matter of you.'

'I—I am in love,' said I, very awkwardly.

'Is that all?' she answered, a trace of humour in her tone. 'I thought it was bad news.'

I stooped to pick a rose and handed it to her.

'Well,' she remarked soberly, but smiling a little, as she lifted the rose to her lips, 'is it anyone I know?'

I felt it was going badly with me, but caught a sudden inspiration.

'You have never seen her,' I said.

If she had suspected the truth I had turned the tables on her, and now she was guessing. A quick change came into her face, and, for a moment, it gave me confidence.

'Is she pretty?' she asked very seriously as she dropped the flower and looked down crushing it beneath her foot.

'She is very beautiful—it is you I love, Hope.'

A flood of colour came into her cheeks then, as she stood a moment looking down at the flower in silence.

'I shall keep your secret,' she said tenderly, and hesitating as she spoke, 'and when you are through college—and you are older—and I am older—and you love me as you do now—I hope—I shall love you, too—as—I do now.'

Her lips were trembling as she gave me that sweet assurance—dearer to me—far dearer than all else I remember of that golden time—and tears were coursing down her cheeks. For myself I was in a worse plight of emotion. I dare say she remembered also the look of my face in that moment.

'Do not speak of it again,' she said, as we walked away together on the shorn sod of the orchard meadow, now sown with apple blossoms, 'until we are older, and, if you never speak again, I shall know you—you do not love me any longer.'

The dinner horn sounded. We turned and walked slowly back

'Do I look all right?' she asked, turning her face to me and smiling sweetly.

'All right,' I said. 'Nobody would know that anyone loved you—except for your beauty and that one tear track on your cheek.'

She wiped it away as she laughed.

'Mother knows anyway,' she said, 'and she has given me good advice. Wait!' she added, stopping and turning to me. 'Your eyes are wet!'

I felt for my handkerchief.

'Take mine,' she said.

Elder Whitmarsh was at the house and they were all sitting down to dinner as we came in.

'Hello!' said Uncle Eb. 'Here's a good-lookin' couple. We've got a chicken pie an' a Baptis' minister fer dinner an' both good. Take yer pew nex' t' the minister,' he added as he held the chair for me.

Then we all bowed our heads and I felt a hearty amen for the elder's words:

'O Lord, may all our doing and saying and eating and drinking of this day be done, as in Thy sight, for our eternal happiness—and for Thy glory. Amen.'

Chapter 21

We have our secrets, but, guard them as we may, it is not long before others have them also. We do much talking without words. I once knew a man who did his drinking secretly and his reeling in public, and thought he was fooling everybody. That shows how much easier it is for one to fool himself than to fool another. What is in a man's heart is on his face, and is shortly written all over him. Therein is a mighty lesson.

Of all people I ever knew Elizabeth Brower had the surest eye for looking into one's soul, and I, myself, have some gift of penetration. I knew shortly that Mrs Brower—wise and prudent woman that she was—had suspected my love for Hope and her love for me, and had told her what she ought to say if I spoke of it.

The maturity of judgement in Hope's answer must have been the result of much thought and counsel, it seemed to me.

'If you do not speak again I shall know you do not love me any longer,' she had said. They were brave words that stood for something very deep in the character of those people—a self-repression that was sublime, often, in their women. As I said them to myself, those lonely summer days in Faraway, I saw in their sweet significance no hint of the bitterness they were to bring. But God knows I have had my share of pleasure and no more bitterness than I deserved.

It was a lonely summer for me. I had letters from Hope—ten of them—which I still keep and read, often with something of the old pleasure—girlish letters that told of her work and friends, and gave me some sweet counsel and much assurance between the lines.

I travelled in new roads that vacation time. Politics and religion, as well as love, began to interest me. Slavery was looming into the proportion of a great issue, and the stories of cruelty and outrage on the plantations of the South stirred my young blood and made it ready for the letting of battle, in God's time. The speeches in the Senate were read aloud in our sitting-room after supper—the day the Tribune came—and all lent a tongue to their discussion. Jed Feary was with us one evening, I remember, when our talk turned into long ways, the end of which I have never found to this day. Elizabeth had been reading of a slave, who, according to the paper, had been whipped to death.

'If God knows 'at such things are bein' done, why don't he stop 'em?' David asked.

'Can't very well,' said Jed Feary.

'Can, if he's omnipotent,' said David.

'That's a bad word—a dangerous one,' said the old poet, dropping his dialect as he spoke. 'It makes God responsible for evil as well as good. The word carries us beyond our depth. It's too big for our boots. I'd ruther think He can do what's doable an' know what's knowable. In the beginning he gave laws to the world an' these laws are unchangeable, or they are not wise an' perfect. If God were to change them He would thereby acknowledge their imperfection. By this law men and races suffer as they struggle upward. But if the law is unchangeable, can it be changed for a better cause even than the relief of a whipped slave? In good time the law shall punish and relieve. The groans of them that suffer shall hasten it, but there shall be no change in the law. There can be no change in the law.'

'Leetle hard t' tell jest how powerful God is,' said Uncle Eb. 'Good deal like tryin' t' weigh Lake Champlain with a quart pail and a pair o' steelyards.'

'If God's laws are unchangeable, what is the use of praying?' I asked.

'He can give us the strength to bear, the will to obey him an' light to guide us,' said the poet. 'I've written out a few lines t' read t' Bill here 'fore he goes off t' college. They have sumthin' t' say on this subject. The poem hints at things he'd ought 'o learn purty soon—if he don't know 'em now.'

The old poet felt in his pockets as he spoke, and withdrew a folded sheet of straw-coloured wrapping paper and opened it. I was 'Bill'-plain 'Bill'—to everybody in that country, where, as you increased your love of a man, you diminished his name. I had been called Willie, William and Billy, and finally, when I threw the strong man of the township in a wrestling match they gave me this full token of confidence. I bent over the shoulder of Jed Feary for a view of the manuscript, closely written with a lead pencil, and marked with many erasures.

'Le's hear it,' said David Brower.

Then I moved the lamp to his elbow and he began reading:

'A talk with William Brower on the occasion of his going away to college and writ out in rhyme for him by his friend Jedediah Feary to be a token of respect.

The man that loses faith in God, ye'll find out every time,

Has found a faith in his own self that's mighty nigh sublime.

He knows as much as all the saints an' calls religion flighty,

An' in his narrow world assumes the place o' God Almighty.

But don't expect too much o' God, it wouldn't be quite fair

If fer everything ye wanted ye could only swap a prayer;

I'd pray fer yours an' you fer mine an' Deacon Henry Hospur

He wouldn't hev a thing t' do but lay a-bed an' prosper.

If all things come so easy, Bill, they'd hev but little worth,

An' someone with a gift O' prayer 'ud mebbe own the earth.

It's the toil ye give t' git a thing—the sweat an' blood an' trouble

We reckon by—an' every tear'll make its value double.

There's a money O' the soul, my boy, ye'll find in after years,

Its pennies are the sweat drops an' its dollars are the tears;
An' love is the redeemin' gold that measures what they're worth,
An' ye'll git as much in Heaven as ye've given out on earth.
Fer the record o' yer doin'—I believe the soul is planned
With an automatic register t, tell jest how ye stand,
An' it won't take any cipherin' t' show that fearful day,
If ye've multiplied yer talents well, er thrown 'em all away.
When yer feet are on the summit, an' the wide horizon clears,
An' ye look back on yer pathway windin' thro' the vale o' tears;
When ye see how much ye've trespassed an' how fur ye've gone astray,
Ye'll know the way o' Providence ain't apt t' be your way.
God knows as much as can be known, but I don't think it's true
He knows of all the dangers in the path o' me an' you.
If I shet my eyes an' hurl a stone that kills the King o' Siam,
The chances are that God'll be as much surprised as I am.
If ye pray with faith believin', why, ye'll certnly receive,
But that God does what's impossible is more than I'll believe.
If it grieves Him when a sparrow falls, it's sure as anything,
He'd hev turned the arrow if He could, that broke the sparrow's wing.
Ye can read old Nature's history thet's writ in rocks an' stones,
Ye can see her throbbin' vitals an' her mighty rack o' hones.
But the soul o' her—the livin' God, a little child may know
No lens er rule o' cipherin' can ever hope t' show.
There's a part o' Cod's creation very handy t' yer view,
Al' the truth o' life is in it an' remember, Bill, it's you.
An' after all yer science ye must look up in yer mind,

An' learn its own astronomy the star o' peace t' find.

There's good old Aunt Samanthy Jane thet all her journey long

Has led her heart to labour with a reveille of song.

Her folks hev robbed an' left her but her faith in goodness grows,

She hasn't any larnin', but I tell ye Bill, she knows!

She's hed her share o' troubles; I remember well the day

We took her t' the poorhouse—she was singin' all the way;

Ye needn't be afraid t' come where stormy Jordan flows,

If all the larnin' ye can git has taught ye halfshe knows.'

I give this crude example of rustic philosophy, not because it has my endorsement—God knows I have ever felt it far beyond me—but because it is useful to those who may care to know the man who wrote it. I give it the poor fame of these pages with keen regret that my friend is now long passed the praise or blame of this world.

Chapter 22

The horse played a part of no small importance in that country. He was the coin of the realm, a medium of exchange, a standard of value, an exponent of moral character. The man that travelled without a horse was on his way to the poorhouse. Uncle Eb or David Brower could tell a good horse by the sound of his footsteps, and they brought into St Lawrence County the haughty Morgans from Vermont. There was more pride in their high heads than in any of the good people. A Northern Yankee who was not carried away with a fine horse had excellent self-control. Politics and the steed were the only things that ever woke him to enthusiasm, and there a man was known as he traded. Uncle Eb used to say that one ought always to underestimate his horse 'a leetle fer the sake of a reputation'.

We needed another horse to help with the haying, and Bob Dean, a tricky trader, who had heard of it, drove in after supper one evening, and offered a rangy brown animal at a low figure. We looked him over, tried him up and down the road, and then David, with some shrewd suspicion, as I divined later, said I could do as I pleased. I bought the horse and led him proudly to the stable. Next morning an Irishman, the extra man for the haying, came in with a worried look to breakfast.

'That new horse has a chittern' kind of a coff,' he said.

'A cough?' said I.

"Tain't jist a coff, nayther,' he said, 'but a kind of toom!'

With the last word he obligingly imitated the sound of the cough. It threw me into perspiration.

'Sounds bad,' said Uncle Eb, as he looked at me and snickered.

"Fraid Bill ain't much of a jockey,' said David, smiling.

'Got a grand appetite—that hoss has,' said Tip Taylor.

After breakfast Uncle Eb and I hitched him to the light buggy and touched him up for a short journey down the road. In five minutes he had begun to heave and whistle. I felt sure one could have heard him half a mile away. Uncle Eb stopped him and began to laugh.

'A whistler,' said he, 'sure's yer born. He ain't wuth a bag o' beans. But don't ye never let on. When ye git licked ye musn't never fin' fault. If anybody asks ye 'bout him tell 'em he's all ye expected.'

We stood waiting a moment for the horse to recover himself. A team was nearing us.

'There's Bob Dean,' Uncle Eb whispered. 'The durn scalawag! Don't ye say a word now.

'Good-mornin'!' said Dean, smiling as he pulled up beside us.

'Nice pleasant mornin'!' said Uncle Eb, as he cast a glance into the sky.

'What ye standin' here for?' Dean asked.

Uncle Eb expectorated thoughtfully.

'Jest a lookin' at the scenery,' said he. 'Purty country, right here! Alwus liked it.'

'Nice lookin' hoss ye got there,' said Dean.

'Grand hoss!' said Uncle Eb, surveying him proudly. 'Most reemarkable hoss.'

'Good stepper, too,' said Dean soberly.

'Splendid!' said Uncle Eb. 'Can go a mile without ketchin' his breath.'

'Thet so?' said Dean.

'Good deal like Lucy Purvis,' Uncle Eb added. 'She can say the hull mul'plication table an' only breathe once. Ye can learn sumthin' from a hoss like thet. He's good as a deestric' school—thet hoss is.'

Yes, sir, thet hoss is all right,' said Dean, as he drove away.

'Righter'n I expected,' Uncle Eb shouted, and then he covered his mouth, shaking with suppressed laughter.

'Skunk!' he said, as we turned the animal and started to walk him home. 'Don't min' bein' beat, but I don't like t' hev a man rub it in on me. I'll git even with him mebbe.'

And he did. It came about in this way. We turned our new purchase into the pasture, and Uncle Eb and I drove away to Potsdam for a better nag. We examined all the horses in that part of the country. At last we chanced upon one that looked like the whistler, save that he had a white stocking on one hind foot.

'Same age, too,' said Uncle Eb, as he looked into his mouth.

'Can pass anything on the road,' said his owner.

'Can he?' said Uncle Eb, who had no taste for slow going. 'Hitch him up an' le's see what he can do.'

He carried us faster than we had ever ridden before at a trot, and coming up behind another team the man pulled out, let the reins loose on his back, and whistled. If anyone had hit him with a log chain the horse could not have moved quicker. He took us by the other team like a flash, on the dead run and three in the buggy.

'He'll do all right,' said Uncle Eb, and paid for the horse.

It was long after dark when we started home, leading him behind, and near midnight when we arrived.

In the morning I found Uncle Eb in the stable showing him to the other help. To my surprise the white stocking had disappeared.

'Didn't jes' like that white stockin',' he said, as I came in. 'Wondered how he'd look without it.'

They all agreed this horse and the whistler were as much alike as two peas in appearance. Breakfast over Uncle Eb asked the Irishman to hitch him up.

'Come Bill,' said he, 'le's take a ride. Dean'll be comm' 'long bym bye on his way t' town with that trotter o' his'n. 'Druther like to meet him.'

I had only a faint idea of his purpose. He let the horse step along at top speed going up the road and when we turned about he was breathing heavily. We jogged him back down the road a mile or so, and when I saw the blazed face of Dean's mare, in the distance, we pulled up and shortly stopped him. Dean came along in a moment.

'Nice mornin'!' said he.

'Grand!' said Uncle Eb.

'Lookin' at the lan'scape ag'in?'

'Yes; I've jes' begun t' see what a putty country this is,' said Uncle Eb.

'How's the boss?'

'Splendid! Gives ye time t' think an' see what yer passin'. Like t' set 'n think once in a while. We don't do enough thinkin' here in this part o' the country.'

'Yd orter buy this mare an learn how t' ride fast,' said Dean.

'Thet one,' said Uncle Eb, squinting at the mare, 'why she can't go fast 'nough.'

'She can't, hey?' said Dean, bridling with injured pride. 'I don't think there's anything in this town can head her.'

'Thunder!' said Uncle Eb, 'I can go by her with this ol' plug easy 'twixt here an' our gate. Ye didn't know what ye was sellin'.'

'If ye pass her once I'll give her to ye,' said he.

'Mean it?' said Uncle Eb.

'Sartin,' said he, a little redder in the face.

'An' if I don't I'll give ye the whistler,' said Uncle Eb as he turned about.

The mare went away, under the whip, before we had fairly started. She was going a fifty shot but in a moment we were lapping upon her hind wheel. Dean threw a startled glance over his shoulder. Then he shouted to the mare. She quickened her pace a little but we kept our position. Uncle Eb was leaning over the dasher his white locks flying. He had something up his sleeve, as they say, and was not yet ready to use it. Then Dean began to shear over to cut us off—a nasty trick of the low horseman. I saw Uncle Eb glance at the ditch ahead. I knew what was coming and took a firm hold of the seat. The ditch was a bit rough, but Uncle Eb had no lack of courage. He turned the horse's head, let up on the reins and whistled. I have never felt such a thrill as then. Our horse leaped into the deep grass running like a wild deer.

'Hi there! hi there!' Uncle Eb shouted, bouncing in his seat, as we went over stones and hummocks going like the wind.

'Go, ye brown devil!' he yelled, his hat flying off as he shook the reins.

The mare lost her stride; we flashed by and came up into the road. Looking back I saw her jumping up and down a long way behind us and Dean whipping her. Uncle Eb, his hands over the dasher, had pulled down to a trot Ahead of us we could see our folks—men and women—at the gate looking down the road at us waving hats and handkerchiefs. They had heard the noise of the battle. Uncle Eb let up on the reins and looked back snorting with amusement. In a moment we pulled up at our gate. Dean came along slowly.

'Thet's a putty good mare,' said Uncle Eb.

'Yer welcome to her,' said Dean sullenly.

'Wouldn't hev her,' said Uncle Eb.

'Why not?' said the trader a look of relief coming over his face.

'Can't go fast enough for my use,' Uncle Eb answered. 'Ye can jest hitch her in here awhile an' the first day ye come over with a hundred dollars ye can hev her 'n the whistler, both on 'em. Thet whistler's a grand hoss! Can hold his breath longer'n any hoss I ever knew!'

The sum named was that we had paid him for the highly accomplished animal. Dean had the manhood to pay up then and there and said he would send for the other horse, which he never did.

'Guess he won't bother us any more when we stop t' look at the scenery,' said Uncle Eb, laughing as Dean drove away. 'Kind o' resky business buyin' hosses,' he added. 'Got t' jedge the owner as well as the hoss. If there's anything the matter with his conscience it'll come out in the hoss somewhere every time. Never knew a mean man t' own a good hoss. Remember, boy, 's a lame soul thet drives a limpin' hoss.'

'No use talkin'; Bill ain' no jedge uv a hoss' said David Brower. 'He'll hev t' hev an education er he'll git t' the poorhouse someday sartin.'

'Wall he's a good jedge o' gals anyway,' said Uncle Eb.

As for myself I was now hopelessly confirmed in my dislike of farming and I never traded horses again.

Chapter 23

Late in August Uncle Eb and I took our Black Hawk stallion to the fair in Hillsborough and showed him for a prize. He was fit for the eye of a king when we had finished grooming him, that morning, and led him out, rearing in play, his eyes flashing from under his broad plume, so that all might have a last look at him. His arched neck and slim barrel glowed like satin as the sunlight fell upon him. His black mane flew, he shook the ground with his hoofs playing at the halter's end. He hated a harness and once in it lost half his conceit. But he was vainest of all things in Faraway when we drove off with him that morning.

All roads led to Hillsborough fair time. Up and down the long hills we went on a stiff jog passing lumber wagons with generations enough in them to make a respectable genealogy, the old people in chairs; light wagons that carried young men and their sweethearts, backswoodsmen coming out in ancient vehicles upon reeling, creaking wheels to get food for a year's reflection—all thickening the haze of the late summer with the dust of the roads. And Hillsborough itself was black with people. The shouts of excited men, the neighing of horses, the bellowing of cattle, the wailing of infants, the howling of vendors, the pressing crowd, had begun to sow the seed of misery in the minds of those accustomed only to the peaceful quietude of the farm. The staring eye, the palpitating heart, the aching head, were successive stages in the doom of many. The fair had its floral hall carpeted with sawdust and redolent of cedar, its dairy house, its mechanics' hall sacred to farming implements, its long sheds full of sheep and cattle, its dining-hall, its temporary booths of rough lumber, its half-mile track and grandstand. Here voices of beast and vendor mingled in a chorus of cupidity and distress. In Floral Hall Sol Rollin was on exhibition. He gave me a cold nod, his lips set for a tune as yet inaudible. He was surveying sundry examples of rustic art that hung on the circular railing of the gallery and trying to preserve a calm breast. He was looking at Susan Baker's painted cow that hung near us.

'Very descriptive,' he said when I pressed him for his notion of it. 'Rod Baker's sister Susan made thet cow. Gits tew dollars an' fifty cents every fair time—wish I was dewin 's well.'

'That's one of the most profitable cows in this country,' I said.

'Looks a good deal like a new breed.'

'Yes,' he answered soberly, then he set his lips, threw a sweeping glance into the gallery, and passed on.

Susan Baker's cow was one of the permanent features of the county fair, and was indeed a curiosity not less remarkable than the sacred ox of Mr Barnum.

Here also I met a group of the pretty girls who had been my schoolmates. They surrounded me, chattering like magpies.

'There's going to be a dance at our house tonight,' said one of them, 'and you must come.'

'I cannot, I must go home,' I said.

'Of course!' said a red-cheeked saucy miss. 'The stuck-up thing! He wouldn't go anywhere unless he could have his sister with him.'

Then they went away laughing.

I found Ab Thomas at the rifle range. He was whittling as he considered a challenge from Tip Taylor to shoot a match. He turned and 'hefted' the rifle, silently, and then he squinted over the barrel two or three times.

'Dunno but what I'll try ye once,' he said presently, 'jes t' see.'

Once started they grew red in their faces and shot themselves weary in a reckless contest of skill and endurance. A great hulking fellow, half drunk and a bit quarrelsome, came up, presently, and endeavoured to help Ab hold his rifle. The latter brushed him away and said nothing for a moment. But every time he tried to take aim the man jostled him.

An looked up slowly and calmly, his eyebrows tilted for his aim, and said, 'Go off I tell ye.' Then he set himself and took aim again.

'Le'me hold it,' said the man, reaching for the barrel. 'Shoot better if I do the aimin'.' A laugh greeted this remark. Ab looked up again. There was a quick start in his great slouching figure.

'Take yer hand off o' thet,' he said a little louder than before.

The man, aching for more applause, grew more impertinent. Ab quietly handed the rifle to its owner. Then something happened suddenly. It was so quickly over I am not quite sure of the order of business, but anyhow he seized the intruder by the shoulders flinging him down so heavily it knocked the dust out of the grass.

'A fight!' somebody shouted and men and boys came runing from all sides. We were locked in a pushing crowd before I could turn. The intruder lay stunned a moment. Then he rose, bare headed, his back covered with dust, pushed his way out and ran.

Ab turned quietly to the range.

'Hedn't orter t' come an' try t' dew my aimin',' he said mildly, by way of protest, 'I won't hev it.'

Then he enquired about the score and calmly took aim again. The stallion show came on that afternoon.

'They can't never beat thet hoss,' Uncle Eb had said to me.

''Fraid they will,' I answered. 'They're better hitched for one thing.'

'But they hain't got the ginger in 'em,' said he, 'er the git up 'n git. If we can show what's in him the Hawk'll beat 'em easy.'

If we won I was to get the prize but I had small hope of winning. When I saw one after another prance out, in sparkling silver harness adorned with rosettes of ribbon—light stepping, beautiful creatures all of them—I could see nothing but defeat for us. Indeed I could see we had been too confident. I dreaded the moment when Uncle Eb should drive down with Black Hawk in a plain leather harness, drawing a plainer buggy. I had planned to spend the prize money taking Hope to the harvest ball at Rickard's, and I had worked hard to put the Hawk in good fettle. I began to feel the bitterness of failure.

'Black Hawk! Where is Black Hawk?' said one of the judges loudly.

'Owned by David Brower o' Faraway,' said another looking at his card.

Where indeed was Uncle Eb? I got up on the fence and looked all about me anxiously. Then I heard a great cheering up the track. Somebody was coming down, at a rapid pace, riding a splendid moving animal, a knee rising to the nose at each powerful stride. His head and flying mane obscured the rider but I could see the end of a rope swinging in his hand. There was something familiar in the easy high stride of the horse. The cheers came on ahead of him like foam before a breaker. Upon my eyes! it was Black Hawk, with nothing but a plain rope halter on his head, and Uncle Eb riding him.

'G'lang there!' he shouted, swinging the halter stale to the shining flank. 'G'lang there!' and he went by, like a flash, the tail of Black Hawk straight out behind him, its end feathering in the wind. It was a splendid thing to see—that white-haired man, sitting erect on the flying animal, with only a rope halter in his hand. Every man about me was yelling. I swung my hat, shouting myself hoarse. When Uncle Eb came back the Hawk was walking quietly in a crowd of men and boys eager to feel his silken sides. I crowded through and held the horse's nose while Uncle Eb got down.

'Thought I wouldn't put no luther on him,' said Uncle Eb, 'God's gin' 'im a good 'nuff harness.'

The judges came and looked him over.

'Guess he'll win the prize all right,' said one of them.

And he did. When we came home that evening every horse on the road thought himself a trotter and went speeding to try his pace with everything that came up beside him. And many a man of Faraway, that we passed, sent up a shout of praise for the Black Hawk.

But I was thinking of Hope and the dance at Rickard's. I had plenty of money now and my next letter urged her to come home at once.

Chapter 24

Hope returned for a few days late in August. Invitations were just issued for the harvest dance at Rickard's.

'You mus' take 'er,' said Uncle Eb, the day she came. 'She's a purty dancer as a man ever see. Prance right up an' tell 'er she mus' go. Don' want 'O let anyone git ahead O' ye.'

'Of course I will go,' she said in answer to my invitation, 'I shouldn't think you were a beau worth having if you did not ask me.'

The yellow moon was peering over Woody Ledge when we went away that evening. I knew it was our last pleasure seeking in Faraway, and the crickets in the stubble filled the silence with a kind of mourning.

She looked so fine in her big hat and new gown with its many dainty accessories of lace and ribbon, adjusted with so much patting and pulling, that as she sat beside me, I hardly dared touch her for fear of spoiling something. When she shivered a little and said it was growing cool I put my arm about her, and, as I drew her closer to my side, she turned her hat, obligingly, and said it was a great nuisance.

I tried to kiss her then, but she put her hand over my mouth and said, sweetly, that I would spoil everything if I did that.

'I must not let you kiss me, William,' she said, 'not—not for all in the world. I'm sure you wouldn't have me do what I think is wrong—would you?'

There was but one answer to such an appeal, and I made myself as happy as possible feeling her head upon my shoulder and her soft hair touching my cheek. As I think of it now the trust she put in me was something sublime and holy.

'Then I shall talk about—about our love,' I said, 'I must do something.'

'Promised I wouldn't let you,' she said. Then she added after a moment of silence, 'I'll tell you what you may do—tell me what is your ideal in a woman—the one you would love best of all. I don't think that would be wicked—do you?'

'I think God would forgive that,' I said. 'She must be tall and slim, with dainty feet and hands, and a pair of big eyes, blue as a violet, shaded with long dark lashes. And her hair must be wavy and light with a little tinge of gold in it. And her cheek must have the pink of the rose and dimples that show in laughter. And her voice—that must have music in it and the ring of kindness and good-nature. And her lips—let them show the crimson of her blood and be ready to give and receive a kiss when I meet her.'

She sighed and nestled closer to me.

'If I let you kiss me just once,' she whispered, 'you will not ask me again—will you?'

'No, sweetheart, I will not,' I answered. Then we gave each other such a kiss as may be known once and only once in a lifetime.

'What would you do for the love of a girl like that?' she whispered.

I thought a moment, sounding depths of undiscovered woe to see if there were anything I should hesitate to suffer and there was nothing.

'I'd lay me doun an' dee,' I said.

And I well remember how, when I lay dying, as I believed, in rain and darkness on the bloody field of Bull Run, I thought of that moment and of those words.

'I cannot say such beautiful things as you,' she answered, when I asked her to describe her ideal. 'He must be good and he must be tall and handsome and strong and brave.'

Then she sang a tender love ballad. I have often shared the pleasure of thousands under the spell of her voice, but I have never heard her sing as to that small audience on Faraway turnpike.

As we came near Rickard's Hall we could hear the fiddles and the calling off.

The windows on the long sides of the big house were open. Long shafts of light shot out upon the gloom. It had always reminded me of a picture of Noah's ark that hung in my bedroom and now it seemed to be floating, with resting oars of gold, in a deluge of darkness. We were greeted with a noisy welcome, at the door. Many of the boys and girls came, from all sides of the big hall, and shook hands with us. Enos Brown, whose long forelocks had been oiled for the occasion and combed down so they touched his right eyebrow, was panting in a jig that jarred the house. His trouser legs were caught on the tops of his fine boots. He nodded to me as I came in, snapped his fingers and doubled his energy. It was an exhibition both of power and endurance. He was damp and apologetic when, at length, he stopped with a mighty bang of his foot and sat down beside me. He said he was badly out of practice when I offered congratulations. The first fiddler was a small man, with a short leg, and a character that was minus one dimension. It had length and breadth but no thickness. He sat with his fellow player on a little platform at one end of the room. He was an odd man who wandered all over the township with his fiddle. He played by ear, and I have seen babies smile and old men dance when his bow was swaying. I remember that when I heard it for the first time, I determined that I should be a fiddler if I ever grew to be a man. But David told me that fiddlers were a worthless lot, and that no wise man should ever fool with a fiddle. One is lucky, I have since learned, if any dream of yesterday shall stand the better light of today or the more searching rays of tomorrow.

'Choose yer partners fer Money Musk!' the caller shouted.

Hope and I got into line, the music started, the circles began to sway. Darwin Powers, an old but frisky man, stood up beside the fiddlers, whistling, with sobriety and vigour, as they played. It was a pleasure to see some of the older men of the neighbourhood join the dizzy riot by skipping playfully in the corners. They tried to rally their unwilling wives, and generally a number of them were dancing before the night was over. The life and colour of the scene, the fresh, young faces of the girls some of them models of rustic beauty—the playful antics of the young men, the merrymaking of their fathers, the laughter, the airs of gallantry, the glances of affection—there is a magic in the thought of it all that makes me young again.

There were teams before and behind us when we came home, late at night, so sleepy that the stars went reeling as we looked at them.

'This night is the end of many things,' I remarked.

'And the beginning of better ones, I hope,' was her answer.

'Yes, but they are so far away,' I said, 'you leave home to study and I am to be four years in college-possibly I can finish in three.'

'Perfectly terrible!' she said, and then she added the favourite phrase and tone of her mother: 'We must be patient.'

'I am very sorry of one thing,' I said. 'What's that?'

'I promised not to ask you for one more kiss.'

'Well then,' said she, 'you—you—needn't ask me.' And in a moment I helped her out at the door.

Chapter 25

David Brower had prospered, as I have said before, and now he was chiefly concerned in the welfare of his children. So, that he might give us the advantages of the town, he decided either to lease or sell his farm—by far the handsomest property in the township. I was there when a buyer came, in the last days of that summer. We took him over the smooth acres from Lone Pine to Woody Ledge, from the top of Bowman's Hill to Tinkie Brook in the far valley. He went with us through every tidy room of the house. He looked over the stock and the stables.

'Wall! what's it wuth?' he said, at last, as we stood looking down the fair green acres sloping to the sugar bush.

David picked up a stick, opened his knife, and began to whittle thoughtfully, a familiar squint of reflection in his face. I suppose he thought of all it had cost him—the toil of many years, the strength of his young manhood, the youth and beauty of his wife, a hundred things that were far better than money.

'Fifteen thousan' dollars,' he said slowly—'not a cent less.' The man parleyed a little over the price.

'Don' care t' take any less t'day,' said David calmly. 'No harm done.'

'How much down?'

David named the sum.

'An' possession?'

'Next week'

'Everything as it stan's?'

'Everything as it stan's 'cept the beds an' bedding.'

'Here's some money on account,' he said. 'We'll close t'morrer?'

'Close t'morrer,' said David, a little sadness in his tone, as he took the money.

It was growing dusk as the man went away. The crickets sang with a loud, accusing, clamour. Slowly we turned and went into the dark house, David whistling under his breath. Elizabeth was resting in her chair. She was humming an old hymn as she rocked.

'Sold the farm, mother,' said David.

She stopped singing but made no answer. In the dusk, as we sat down, I saw her face leaning upon her hand. Over the hills and out of the fields around us came many voices—the low chant in the stubble, the baying of a hound in the far timber, the cry of the tree toad—a tiny drift of odd things (like that one sees at sea) on the deep eternal silence of the heavens. There was no sound in the room save the low creaking of the rocker in which Elizabeth sat. After all the going, and coming, and doing, and saying of many years here was a little spell of silence and beyond lay the untried things of the future. For me it was a time of reckoning.

'Been hard at work here all these years, mother,' said David. 'Oughter be glad t' git away.'

'Yes,' said she sadly, 'it's been hard work. Years ago I thought I never could stan' it. But now I've got kind o' used t' it.'

'Time ye got used t' pleasure 'n comfort,' he said. 'Come kind o' hard, at fast, but ye mus' try t' stan' it. If we're goin' t' hev sech flin in Heaven as Deacon Hospur tells on we oughter begin t' practice er we'll be 'shamed uv ourselves.'

The worst was over. Elizabeth began to laugh.

At length a strain of song came out of the distance.

'Maxwelton's braes are bonnie where early falls the dew.'

'It's Hope and Uncle Eb,' said David while I went for the lantern. 'Wonder what's kep' 'em s' late.'

When the lamps were lit the old house seemed suddenly to have got a sense of what had been done. The familiar creak of the stairway as I went to bed had an appeal and a protest. The rude chromo of the voluptuous lady, with red lips and the name of Spring, that had always hung in my chamber had a mournful, accusing look. The stain upon her cheek that had come one day from a little leak in the roof looked now like the path of a tear drop. And when the wind came up in the night and I heard the creaking of Lone Pine it spoke of the doom of that house and its own that was not far distant.

We rented a new home in town, that week, and were soon settled in it. Hope went away to resume her studies the same day I began work in college.

Chapter 26

Not much in my life at college is essential to this history—save the training. The students came mostly from other and remote parts of the north country—some even from other states. Coming largely from towns and cities they were shorn of those simple and rugged traits, that distinguished the men o' Faraway, and made them worthy of what poor fame this book may afford. In the main they were like other students the world over, I take it' and mostly, as they have shown, capable of wiling their own fame. It all seemed very high and mighty and grand to me especially the names of the courses. I had my baptism of Sophomoric scorn and many a heated argument over my title to life, liberty and the pursuit of learning. It became necessary to establish it by force of arms, which I did decisively and with as little delay as possible. I took much interest in athletic sports and was soon a good ball player, a boxer of some skill, and the best wrestler in college. Things were going on comfortably when an upper classman met me and suggested that on a coming holiday, the Freshmen ought to wear stove-pipe hats. Those hats were the seed of great trouble.

'Stove-pipe hats!' I said thoughtfully.

'They're a good protection,' he assured me.

It seemed a very reasonable, not to say a necessary precaution. A man has to be young and innocent sometime or what would become of the Devil. I did not see that the stove-pipe hat was the red rag of insurrection and, when I did see it' I was up to my neck in the matter.

You see the Sophs are apt to be very nasty that day,' he continued.

I acknowledged they were quite capable of it.

'And they don't care where they hit,' he went on.

I felt of my head that was still sore, from a forceful argument of the preceding day, and admitted there was good ground for the assertion.

When I met my classmen, that afternoon, I was an advocate of the 'stove-pipe' as a means of protection. There were a number of husky fellows, in my class, who saw its resisting power and seconded my suggestion. We decided to leave it to the ladies of the class and they greeted our plan with applause. So, that morning, we arrayed ourselves in high hats, heavy canes and fine linen, marching together up College Hill. We had hardly entered the gate before we saw the Sophs forming in a thick rank outside the door prepared, as we took it, to resist our entrance. They outnumbered us and were, in the main, heavier but we had a foot or more of good stiff material between each head and harm. Of just what befell us, when we got to the enemy, I have never felt sure. Of the total inefficiency of the stove-pipe hat as an article of armour, I have never had the slightest doubt since then. There was a great flash and rattle of canes. Then the air was full of us. In the heat of it all prudence went to the winds. We hit out right and left, on both sides, smashing hats and bruising heads and hands. The canes went down in a jiffy and then we closed with each other hip and thigh. Collars were ripped off, coats were torn, shirts were gory from the blood of noses, and in this condition the most of us were rolling and tumbling on the ground. I had flung a man, heavily, and broke away and was tackling another when I heard a hush in the tumult and then the voice of the president. He stood on the high steps, his grey head bare, his right hand lifted. It must have looked like carnage from where he stood.

'Young gentlemen!' he called. 'Cease, I command you. If we cannot get along without this thing we will shut up shop.'

Well, that was the end of it and came near being the end of our careers in college. We looked at each other, torn and panting and bloody, and at the girls, who stood by, pale with alarm. Then we picked up the shapeless hats and went away for repairs. I had heard that the path of learning was long and beset with peril but I hoped, not without reason, the worst was over. As I went off the campus the top of my hat was hanging over my left ear, my collar and cravat were turned awry, my trousers gaped over one knee. I was talking with a fellow sufferer and patching the skin on my knuckles, when suddenly I met Uncle Eb.

'By the Lord Harry!' he said, looking me over from top to toe, 'teacher up there mus' be purty ha'sh.'

'It wa'n't the teacher,' I said.

'Must have fit then.'

'Fit hard,' I answered, laughing.

'Try t' walk on ye?'

'Tried t' walk on me. Took several steps too,' I said stooping to brush my trousers.

'Hm! guess he found it ruther bad walkin' didn't he?' my old friend enquired. 'Leetle bit rough in spots?'

'Little bit rough, Uncle Eb—that's certain.'

'Better not go hum,' he said, a great relief in his face. 'Look 's if ye'd been chopped down an' sawed—an' split—an' throwed in a pile. I'll go an' bring over some things fer ye.'

I went with my friend, who had suffered less damage, and Uncle Eb brought me what I needed to look more respectable than I felt.

The president, great and good man that he was, forgave us, finally, after many interviews and such wholesome reproof as made us all ashamed of our folly.

In my second year, at college, Hope went away to continue her studies in New York She was to live in the family of John Fuller, a friend of David, who had left Faraway years before and made his fortune there in the big city. Her going filled my days with a lingering and pervasive sadness. I saw in it sometimes the shadow of a heavier loss than I dared to contemplate. She had come home once a week from Ogdensburg and I had always had a letter between times. She was ambitious and, I fancy, they let her go, so that there should be no danger of any turning aside from the plan of my life, or of hers; for they knew our hearts as well as we knew them and possibly better.

We had the parlour to ourselves the evening before she went away, and I read her a little love tale I had written especially for that occasion. It gave us some chance to discuss the absorbing and forbidden topic of our lives.

'He's too much afraid of her,' she said, 'he ought to put his arm about her waist in that love scene.'

'Like that,' I said, suiting the action to the word.

'About like that,' she answered, laughing, 'and then he ought to say something very, very, nice to her before he proposes—something about his having loved her for so long—you know.'

'And how about her?' I asked, my arm still about her waist.

'If she really loves him,' Hope answered, 'she would put her arms about his neck and lay her head upon his shoulder, so; and then he might say what is in the story.' She was smiling now as she looked up at me.

'And kiss her?'

'And kiss her,' she whispered; and, let me add, that part of the scene was in nowise neglected.

'And when he says: "will you wait for me and keep me always in your heart?" what should be her answer,' I continued.

'Always!' she said.

'Hope, this is our own story,' I whispered. 'Does it need any further correction?'

'It's too short—that's all,' she answered, as our lips met again.

Just then Uncle Eb opened the door, suddenly.

'Tut tut!' he said tuning quickly about

'Come in, Uncle Eb,' said Hope, 'come right in, we want to see you.

In a moment she had caught him by the arm.

'Don' want 'o break up the meetin',' said he laughing.

'We don't care if you do know,' said Hope, 'we're not ashamed of it.'

'Hain't got no cause t' be,' he said. 'Go it while ye're young 'n full 'o vinegar! That's what I say every time. It's the best fun there is. I thought I'd like t' hev ye both come up t' my room, fer a minute, 'fore yer mother 'n father come back,' he said in a low tone that was almost a whisper.

Then he shut one eye, suggestively, and beckoned with his head, as we followed him up the stairway to the little room in which he slept. He knelt by the bed and pulled out the old skin-covered trunk that David Brower had given him soon after we came. He felt a moment for the keyhole, his hand trembling, and then I helped him open the trunk. From under that sacred suit of broadcloth, worn only on the grandest occasions, he fetched a bundle about the size of a man's head. It was tied in a big red handkerchief. We were both sitting on the floor beside him.

'Heft it,' he whispered.

I did so and found it heavier than I expected.

'What is it?' I asked.

'Spondoolix,' he whispered.

Then he untied the bundle—a close packed hoard of bankbills with some pieces of gold and silver at the bottom.

'Hain't never hed no use fer it,' he said as he drew out a layer of greenbacks and spread them with trembling fingers. Then he began counting them slowly and carefully.

'There!' he whispered, when at length he had counted a hundred dollars. 'There Hope! take thet an' put it away in yer wallet. Might come handy when ye're 'way fr'm hum.'

She kissed him tenderly.

'Put it 'n yer wallet an' say nothin'—not a word t' nobody,' he said.

Then he counted over a like amount for me.

'Say nothin',' he said, looking up at me over his spectacles. 'Ye'll hev t' spile a suit o' clothes purty often if them fellers keep a fightin' uv ye all the time.'

Father and mother were coming in below stairs and, hearing them, we helped Uncle Eb tie up his bundle and stow it away. Then we went down to meet them.

Next morning we bade Hope goodbye at the cars and returned to our home with a sense of loss that, for long, lay heavy upon us all.

Chapter 27

Uncle Eb and David were away buying cattle, half the week, but Elizabeth Brower was always at home to look after my comfort. She was up betimes in the morning and singing at her work long before I was out of bed. When the breakfast was near ready she came to my door with a call so fall of cheerfulness and good-nature it was the best thing in the day. And often, at night, I have known her to come into my room when I was lying awake with some hard problem, to see that I was properly covered or that my window was not open too far. As we sat alone together, of an evening, I have seen her listen for hours while I was committing the Odes of Horace with a curiosity that finally gave way to resignation. Sometimes she would look over my shoulder at the printed page and try to discern some meaning in it. When Uncle Eb was with us he would often sit a long time his head turned attentively as the lines came rattling off my tongue.

'Cur'us talk!' he said, one evening, as I paused a moment, while he crossed the room for a drink of water. 'Don' seem t' make no kind O' sense. I can make out a word here 'n there but fer good, sound, common sense I call it a purty thin crop.'

Hope wrote me every week for a time. A church choir had offered her a place soon after she went to the big city. She came home intending to surprise us all, the first summer but unfortunately, I had gone away in the woods with a party of surveyors and missed her. We were a month in the wilderness and came out a little west of Albany where I took a boat for New York to see Hope. I came down the North River between the great smoky cities, on either side of it, one damp and chilly morning. The noise, the crowds, the immensity of the town appalled me. At John Fuller's I found that Hope had gone home and while they tried to detain me longer I came back on the night boat of the same day. Hope and I passed each other in that journey and I did not see her until the summer preceding my third and last year in college—the faculty having allowed me to take two years in one. Her letters had come less frequently and when she came I saw a grand young lady of fine manners, her beauty shaping to an ampler mould, her form straightening to the dignity of womanhood.

At the depot our hands were cold and trembling with excitement—neither of us, I fancy, knowing quite how far to go in our greeting. Our correspondence had been true to the promise made her mother—there had not been a word of love in it—only now and then a suggestion of our tender feeling. We hesitated only for the briefest moment. Then I put my arm about her neck and kissed her.

'I am so glad to see you,' she said.

Well, she was charming and beautiful, but different, and probably not more different than was I. She was no longer the laughing, simple-mannered child of Faraway, whose heart was as one's hand before him in the daylight. She had now a bit of the woman's reserve—her prudence, her skill in hiding the things of the heart. I loved her more than ever, but somehow I felt it hopeless—that she had grown out of my life. She was much in request among the people of Hillsborough, and we went about a good deal and had many callers. But we had little time to ourselves. She seemed to avoid that, and had much to say of the grand young men who came to call on her in the great city. Anyhow it all hurt me to the soul and even robbed me of my sleep. A better lover than I would have made an end of dallying and got at the truth, come what might. But I was of the Puritans, and not of the Cavaliers, and my way was that which God had marked for me, albeit I must own no man had ever a keener eye for a lovely woman or more heart to please her. A mighty pride had come to me and I had rather have thrown my heart to vultures than see it an unwelcome offering. And I was quite out of courage with Hope; she, I dare say, was as much out of patience with me.

She returned in the late summer and I went back to my work at college in a hopeless fashion that gave way under the whip of a strong will.

I made myself as contented as possible. I knew all the pretty girls and went about with some of them to the entertainments of the college season. At last came the long looked for day of my graduation—the end of my student life.

The streets of the town were thronged, every student having the college colours in his coat lapel. The little company of graduates trembled with fright as the people crowded in to the church, whispering and faring themselves, in eager anticipation. As the former looked from the two side pews where they sat, many familiar faces greeted them—the faces of fathers and mothers aglow with the inner light of pride and pleasure; the faces of many they loved come to claim a share in the glory of that day. I found my own, I remember, but none of them gave me such help as that of Uncle Eb. However I might fare, none would feel the pride or disgrace of it more keenly than he. I shall never forget how he turned his head to catch every word when I ascended the platform. As I warmed to my argument I could see him nudging the arm of David, who sat beside him, as if to say, 'There's the boy that came over the hills with me in a pack basket.' When I stopped a moment, groping for the next word, he leaned forward, embracing his knee, firmly, as if intending to draw off a boot. It was all the assistance he could give me. When the exercises were over I found Uncle Eb by the front door of the church, waiting for me.

'Willie, ye done noble!' said he.

'Did my very best, Uncle Eb,' I replied.

'Liked it grand—I did, sartin.' 'Glad you liked it, Uncle Eb.'

'Showed great larnin'. Eho was the man 'at give out the pictur's?'

He meant the president who had conferred the degrees. I spoke the name.

'Deceivin' lookin' man, ain't he? Seen him often, but never took no pertick'lar notice of him before.'

'How deceiving?' I enquired.

'Talked so kind of plain,' he replied. 'I could understan' him as easy as though he'd been swappin' hosses. But when you got up, Bill'. Why, you jes' riz right up in the air an' there couldn't no dum fool tell what you was talkin' 'bout.'

Whereat I concluded that Uncle Eb's humour was as deep as it was kindly, but I have never been quite sure whether the remark was a compliment or a bit of satire.

Chapter 28

The folks of Faraway have been carefully if rudely pictured, but the look of my own person, since I grew to the stature of manhood, I have left wholly to the imagination of the reader. I will wager he knew long since what manner of man I was and has measured me to the fraction of an inch, and knows even the colour of my hair and eyes from having been so long in my company. If not—well, I shall have to write him a letter.

When Uncle Eb and I took the train for New York that summer day in 1860, some fifteen years after we came down Paradise Road with the dog and wagon and pack basket, my head, which, in that far day, came only to the latitude of his trouser pocket, had now mounted six inches above his own. That is all I can say here on that branch of my subject. I was leaving to seek my fortune in the big city; Uncle Eb was off for a holiday and to see Hope and bring her home for a short visit. I remember with what sadness I looked back that morning at mother and father as they stood by the gate slowly waving their handkerchiefs. Our home at last was emptied of its young, and even as they looked the shadow of old age must have fallen suddenly before them. I knew how they would go back into that lonely room and how, while the clock went on with its ticking, Elizabeth would sit down and cover her face a moment, while David would make haste to take up his chores.

We sat in silence a long time after the train was off, a mighty sadness holding our tongues. Uncle Eb, who had never ridden a long journey on the cars before, had put on his grand suit of broadcloth. The day was hot and dusty, and before we had gone far he was sadly soiled. But a suit never gave him any worry, once it was on. He sat calmly, holding his knee in his hands and looking out of the open window, a squint in his eyes that stood for some high degree of interest in the scenery.

'What do you think of this country?' I enquired.

'Looks purty fair,' said he, as he brushed his face with his handkerchief and coughed to clear his throat of the dust, 'but 'tain't quite so pleasant to the taste as some other parts o' the country. I ruther liked the flavour of Saint Lawrence all through, but Jefferson is a leetle gritty.'

He put down the window as he spoke.

'A leetle tobaccer'll improve it some,' he added, as his hand went down for the old silver box. 'The way these cars dew rip along! Consarned if it ain't like flyin'! Kind o' makes me feel like a bird.'

The railroad was then not the familiar thing it is now in the north country. The bull in the fields had not yet come to an understanding of its rights, and was frequently tempted into argument with a locomotive. Bill Fountain, who came out of a back township, one day had even tied his faithful hound to the rear platform.

Our train came to a long stop for wood and water near midday, and then we opened the lunch basket that mother had given us.

'Neighbour,' said a solemn-faced man, who sat in front of us, 'do you think the cars are ag'in the Bible? D'you think a Christian orter ride on 'em?'

'Sartin,' said Uncle Eb. 'Less the constable's after him—then I think he orter be on a balky hoss.'

'Wife'n I hes talked it over a good deal,' said the man. 'Some says it's ag'in the Bible. The minister 'at preaches over 'n our neighbourhood says if God hed wanted men t' fly he'd g'in 'em wings.'

'S'pose if he'd ever wanted 'm t' skate he'd hed 'em born with skates on?' said Uncle Eb.

'Danno,' said the man. 'It behooves us all to be careful. The Bible says "Go not after new things."'

'My friend,' said Uncle Eb, between bites of a doughnut, 'I don' care what I ride in so long as 'tain't a hearse. I want sumthin' at's comfortable an' purty middlin' spry. It'll do us good up here t' git jerked a few hunderd miles an' back ev'ry leetle while. Keep our j'ints limber. We'll live longer fer it, an' thet'll please God sure—cuz I don't think he's hankerin' fer our society—not a bit. Don' make no difference t' him whuther we ride 'n a spring wagon er on the cars so long's we're right side up 'n movin'. We need more steam; we're too dum slow. Kind o' think a leetle more steam in our religion wouldn't hurt us a bit. It's purty fur behind.'

We got to Albany in the evening, just in time for the night boat. Uncle Eb was a sight in his dusty broadcloth, when we got off the cars, and I know my appearance could not have been prepossessing. Once we were aboard the boat and had dusted our clothes and bathed our hands and faces we were in better spirits.

'Consarn it!' said Uncle Eb, as we left the washroom, 'le's have a durn good supper. I'll stan' treat.'

'Comes a leetle bit high,' he said, as he paid the bill, 'but I don' care if it does. 'Fore we left I says t' myself, "Uncle Eb," says I, "you go right in fer a good time an' don' ye count the pennies. Everybody's a right t' be reckless once in seventy-five year."'

We went to our stateroom a little after nine. I remember the berths had not been made up, and removing our boots and coats we lay down upon the bare mattresses. Even then I had a lurking fear that we might be violating some rule of steamboat etiquette. When I went to New York before I had dozed all night in the big cabin.

A dim light came through the shuttered door that opened upon the dinning-saloon where the rattle of dishes for a time put away the possibility of sleep.

'I'll be awful glad t' see Hope,' said Uncle Eb, as he lay gaping.

'Guess I'll be happier to see her than she will to see me,' I said.

'What put that in yer head?' Uncle Eb enquired.

''Fraid we've got pretty far apart,' said I.

'Shame on ye, Bill,' said the old gentleman. 'If thet's so ye ain't done right. Hedn't orter let a girl like thet git away from ye—th' ain't another like her in this world.'

'I know it' I said' 'but I can't help it. Somebody's cut me out Uncle Eb.'

''Tain't so,' said he emphatically. 'Ye want t' prance right up t' her.'

'I'm not afraid of any woman,' I said, with a great air of bravery, 'but if she don't care for me I ought not to throw myself at her.'

'Jerusalem!' said Uncle Eb, rising up suddenly, 'what hev I gone an' done?'

He jumped out of his berth quickly and in the dim light I could see him reaching for several big sheets of paper adhering to the back of his shirt and trousers. I went quickly to his assistance and began stripping off the broadsheets which, covered with some strongly adhesive substance, had laid a firm hold upon him. I rang the bell and ordered a light.

'Consam it all! what be they—plasters?' said Uncle Eb, quite out of patience.

'Pieces of brown paper, covered with—West India molasses, I should think,' said I.

'West Injy molasses!' he exclaimed. 'By mighty! That makes me hotter'n a pancake. What's it on the bed fer?'

'To catch flies,' I answered.

'An' ketched me,' said Uncle Eb, as he flung the sheet he was examining into a corner. 'My extry good suit' too!'

He took off his trousers, then, holding them up to the light.

'They're sp'ilt,' said he mournfully. 'Hed 'em fer more'n ten year, too.'

'That's long enough,' I suggested.

'Got kind o' 'tached to 'em,' he said, looking down at them and rubbing his chin thoughtfully. Then we had a good laugh.

'You can put on the other suit,' I suggested, 'and when we get to the city we'll have these fixed.'

'Leetle sorry, though,' said he, 'cuz that other suit don' look reel grand. This here one has been purty—purty scrumptious in its day—if I do say it.'

'You look good enough in anything that's respectable,' I said.

'Kind o' wanted to look a leetle extry good, as ye might say,' said Uncle Eb, groping in his big carpet-bag. 'Hope, she's terrible proud, an' if they should hev a leetle fiddlin' an' dancin' some night we'd want t' be as stylish as any on em. B'lieve I'll go'n git me a spang, bran' new suit, anyway, 'fore we go up t' Fuller's.'

As we neared the city we both began feeling a bit doubtful as to whether we were quite ready for the ordeal.

'I ought to,' I said. 'Those I'm wearing aren't quite stylish enough, I'm afraid.'

'They're han'some,' said Uncle Eb, looking up over his spectacles, 'but mebbe they ain't just as splendid as they'd orter be. How much money did David give ye?'

'One hundred and fifty dollars,' I said, thinking it a very grand sum indeed.

''Tain't enough,' said Uncle Eb, bolting up at me again. 'Leastways not if ye're goin' t' hev a new suit. I want ye t' be spick an' span.'

He picked up his trousers then, and took out his fat leather wallet.

'Lock the door,' he whispered.

'Pop goes the weasel!' he exclaimed, good-naturedly, and then he began counting the bills.

'I'm not going to take any more of your money, Uncle Eb,' I said.

'Tut, tut!' said he, 'don't ye try t' interfere. What d' ye think they'll charge in the city fer a reel, splendid suit?'

He stopped and looked up at me.

'Probably as much as fifty dollars,' I answered.

'Whew-w-w!' he whistled. 'Patty steep! It is sartin.'

'Let me go as I am,' said I. 'Time enough to have a new suit when I've earned it.'

'Wall,' he said, as he continued counting, 'I guess you've earnt it already. Ye've studied hard an' tuk first honours an' yer goin' where folks are purty middlin' proud'n haughty. I want ye t' be a reg'lar high stepper, with a nice, slick coat. There,' he whispered, as he handed me the money, 'take thet! An' don't ye never tell 'at I g'in it t' ye.'

I could not speak for a little while, as I took the money, for thinking of the many, many things this grand old man had done for me.

'Do ye think these boots'll do?' he asked, as he held up to the light the pair he had taken off in the evening.

'They look all right,' I said.

'Ain't got no decent squeak to 'em now, an' they seem t' look kind o' clumsy. How're your'n?' he asked.

I got them out from under the berth and we inspected them carefully deciding in the end they would pass muster.

The steward had made up our berths, when he came, and lit our room for us. Our feverish discussion of attire had carried us far past midnight, when we decided to go to bed.

'S'pose we musn't talk t' no strangers there 'n New York,' said Uncle Eb, as he lay down. 'I've read 'n the Tribune how they'll purtend t' be friends an' then grab yer money an' run like Sam Hill. If I meet any o' them fellers they're goin' t' find me purty middlin' poor comp'ny.'

We were up and on deck at daylight, viewing the Palisades. The lonely feeling of an alien hushed us into silence as we came to the noisy and thickening river craft at the upper end of the city. Countless window panes were shining in the morning sunlight. This thought was in my mind that somewhere in the innumerable host on either side was the one dearer to me than any other. We enquired our way at the dock and walked to French's Hotel, on Printing House Square. After breakfast we went and ordered all the grand new things we had planned to get. They would not be ready for two days, and after talking it over we decided to go and make a short call. Hope, who had been up and looking for us a long time, gave us a greeting so hearty we began to get the first feeling of comfort since landing. She was put out about our having had breakfast, I remember, and said we must have our things brought there at once.

'I shall have to stay at the hotel awhile,' I said, thinking of the new clothes.

'Why,' said Mrs Fuller, 'this girl has been busy a week fixing your rooms and planning for you. We could not hear of your going elsewhere. It would be downright ingratitude to her.'

A glow of red came into the cheeks of Hope that made me ashamed of my remark. I thought she looked lovelier in her pretty blue morning gown, covering a broad expanse of crinoline, than ever before.

'And you've both got to come and hear me sing tonight at the church,' said she. 'I wouldn't have agreed to sing if I had not thought you were to be here.'

We made ourselves at home, as we were most happy to do, and that afternoon I went down town to present to Mr Greeley the letter that David Brower had given me.

Chapter 29

I came down Broadway that afternoon aboard a big white omnibus, that drifted slowly in a tide of many vehicles. Those days there were a goodly show of trees on either side of that thoroughfare—elms, with here and there a willow, a sumach or a mountain ash. The walks were thronged with handsome people—dandies with high hats and flaunting neckties and swinging canes—beautiful women, each covering a broad circumference of the pavement, with a cone of crinoline that swayed over dainty feet. From Grace Church down it was much of the same thing we see now, with a more ragged sky line. Many of the great buildings, of white and red sandstone, had then appeared, but the street was largely in the possession of small shops—oyster houses, bookstores and the like. Not until I neared the sacred temple of the Tribune did I feel a proper sense of my own littleness. There was the fountain of all that wisdom which had been read aloud and heard with reverence in our household since a time I could but dimly remember. There sat the prophet who had given us so much—his genial views of life and government, his hopes, his fears, his mighty wrath at the prospering of cruelty and injustice.

'I would like to see Mr Horace Greeley,' I said, rather timidly, at the counter.

'Walk right up those stairs and turn to the left,' said a clerk, as he opened a gate for me.

Ascending, I met a big man coming down, hurriedly, and with heavy steps. We stood dodging each other a moment with that unfortunate co-ordination of purpose men sometimes encounter when passing each other. Suddenly the big man stopped in the middle of the stairway and held both of his hands above his head.

'In God's name! young man,' said he, 'take your choice.'

He spoke in a high, squeaky voice that cut me with the sharpness of its irritation. I went on past him and entered an open door near the top of the stairway.

'Is Mr Horace Greeley in?' I enquired of a young man who sat reading papers.

'Back soon,' said he, without looking up. 'Take a chair.'

In a little while I heard the same heavy feet ascending the stairway two steps at a time. Then the man I had met came hurriedly into the room.

'This is Mr Greeley,' said the young man who was reading.

The great editor turned and looked at me through gold-rimmed spectacles. I gave him my letter out of a trembling hand. He removed it from the envelope and held it close to his big, kindly, smooth-shaven face. There was a fringe of silky, silver hair, streaked with yellow, about the lower part of his head from temple to temple. It also encircled his throat from under his collar. His cheeks were fall and fair as a lady's, with rosy spots in them and a few freckles about his nose. He laughed as he finished reading the letter.

'Are you Dave Brower's boy?' he asked in a drawling falsetto, looking at me out of grey eyes and smiling with good humour.

'By adoption,' I answered.'

'He was an almighty good rassler,' he said, deliberately, as he looked again at the letter.'

'What do you want to do?' he asked abruptly.'

'Want to work on the Tribune,' I answered.'

'Good Lord! he said. 'I can't hire everybody.'

I tried to think of some argument, but what with looking at the great man before me, and answering his questions and maintaining a decent show of dignity, I had enough to do.

'Do you read the Tribune? he asked.'

'Read it ever since I can remember.'

'What do you think of the administration?

'Lot of dough faces! I answered, smiling, as I saw he recognised his own phrase. He sat a moment tapping the desk with his penholder.'

'There's so many liars here in New York,' he said, 'there ought to be room for an honest man. How are the crops?'

'Fair, I answered. 'Big crop of boys every year.'

'And now you're trying to find a market, he remarked.'

'Want to have you try them,' I answered.

'Well,' said he, very seriously, turning to his desk that came up to his chin as he sat beside it, 'go and write me an article about rats.'

'Would you advise-,' I started to say, when he interrupted me.

'The man that gives advice is a bigger fool than the man that takes it,' he fleered impatiently. 'Go and do your best!'

Before he had given me this injunction he had dipped his pen and begun to write hurriedly. If I had known him longer I should have known that, while he had been talking to me, that tireless mind of his had summoned him to its service. I went out, in high spirits, and sat down a moment on one of the benches in the little park near by, to think it all over. He was going to measure my judgement, my skill as a writer—my resources. 'Rats,' I said to myself thoughtfully. I had read much about them. They infested the ships, they overran the wharves, they traversed the sewers. An inspiration came to me. I started for the waterfront, asking my way every block or two. Near the East River I met a policeman—a big, husky, good-hearted Irishman.

'Can you tell me,' I said, 'who can give me information about rats?'

'Rats?' he repeated. 'What d' ye wan't' know about thim?'

'Everything,' I said. 'They've just given me a job on the New York Tribune,' I added proudly.

He smiled good-naturedly. He had looked through me at a glance.

'Just say "Tribune",' he said. 'Ye don't have t' say "New York Tribune" here. Come along wi' me.'

He took me to a dozen or more of the dock masters.

'Give 'im a lift, my hearty,' he said to the first of them. 'He's a green.'

I have never forgotten the kindness of that Irishman, whom I came to know well in good time. Remembering that day and others I always greeted him with a hearty 'God bless the Irish!' every time I passed him, and he would answer, 'Amen, an' save yer riverince.'

He did not leave me until I was on my way home loaded with fact and fable and good dialect with a savour of the sea in it.

Hope and Uncle Eb were sitting together in his room when I returned.

'Guess I've got a job,' I said, trying to be very cool about it..

'A job! said Hope eagerly, as she rose. 'Where?

'With Mr Horace Greeley,' I answered, my voice betraying my excitement.

'Jerusalem! said Uncle Eb. 'Is it possible?'

'That's grand! said Hope. 'Tell us about it.'

Then I told them of my interview with the great editor and of what I had done since.

'Ye done wonderful!' said Uncle Eb and Hope showed quite as much pleasure in her own sweet way.

I was for going to my room and beginning to write at once, but Hope said it was time to be getting ready for dinner.

When we came down at half-past six we were presented to our host and the guests of the evening—handsome men and women in full dress—and young Mr Livingstone was among them. I felt rather cheap in my frock coat, although I had thought it grand enough for anybody on the day of my graduation. Dinner announced, the gentlemen rose and offered escort to the ladies, and Hope and Mrs Fuller relieved our embarrassment by conducting us to our seats—women are so deft in those little difficulties. The dinner was not more formal than that of every evening in the Fuller home—for its master was a rich man of some refinement of taste—and not at all comparable to the splendid hospitality one may see every day at the table of a modern millionaire. But it did seem very wonderful to us, then, with its fine-mannered servants, its flowers, its abundant silver. Hope had written much to her mother of the details of deportment at John Fuller's table, and Elizabeth had delicately imparted to us the things we ought to know. We behaved well, I have since been told, although we got credit for poorer appetites than we possessed. Uncle Eb took no chances and refused everything that had a look of mystery and a suggestion of peril, dropping a droll remark, betimes, that sent a ripple of amusement around the table.

John Trumbull sat opposite me, and even then I felt a curious interest in him—a big, full bearded man, quite six feet tall, his skin and eyes dark, his hair iron-grey, his voice deep like David s. I could not get over the impression that I had seen him before—a feeling I have had often, facing men I could never possibly have met. No word came out of his firm mouth unless he were addressed, and then all in hearing listened to the little he had to say: it was never more than some very simple remark. In his face and form and voice there was abundant heraldry of rugged power and ox-like vitality. I have seen a bronze head of Daniel Webster which, with a full blonde beard and an ample covering of grey hair would have given one a fairly perfect idea of the look of John Trumbull. Imagine it on a tall, and powerful body and let it speak with a voice that has in it the deep and musical vibration one may hear in the looing of an ox and you shall see, as perfectly as my feeble words can help you to do, this remarkable man who, must, hereafter, play before you his part—compared to which mine is as the prattle of a child—in this drama of God's truth.

'You have not heard,' said Mrs Fuller addressing me, 'how Mr Trumbull saved Hope's life.'

'Saved Hope's life!' I exclaimed.

'Saved her life,' she repeated, 'there isn't a doubt of it. We never sent word of it for fear it would give you all needless worry. It was a day of last winter—fell crossing Broadway, a dangerous place' he pulled her aside just in time—the horse's feet were raised above her—she would have been crushed in a moment He lifted her in his arms and carried her to the sidewalk not a bit the worse for it.

'Seems as if it were fate,' said Hope. 'I had seen him so often and wondered who he was. I recall a night when I had to come home alone from rehearsal. I was horribly afraid. I remember passing him under a street lamp. If he had spoken to me, then, I should have dropped with fear and he would have had to carry me home that time.

'It's an odd thing a girl like you should ever have to walk home alone,' said Mr Fuller. 'Doesn't speak well for our friend Livingstone or Burnham there or Dobbs.

'Mrs Fuller doesn't give us half a chance,' said Livingstone, 'she guards her day and night. It's like the monks and the Holy Grail.

'Hope is independent of the young men,' said Mrs Fuller as we rose from the table. 'If I cannot go with her myself, in the carriage, I always send a maid or a manservant to walk home with her. But Mr Fuller and I were out of town that night and the young men missed their great opportunity.

'Had a differ'nt way o' sparkin' years ago,' said Uncle Eb. 'Didn't never hev it please anybody but the girl then. If ye liked a girl ye went an' sot up with her an' gin her a smack an' tol' her right out plain an' square what ye wanted. An' thet settled it one way er t' other. An' her mother she step' in the next room with the door half-open an' never paid no 'tention. Recollec' one col'night when I was sparkin' the mother hollered out o' bed, "Lucy, hev ye got anythin 'round ye?" an' she hollered back, "Yis, mother," an' she hed too but 'twan't nothin' but my arm.'

They laughed merrily, over the quaint reminiscence of my old friend and the quainter way he had of telling it. The rude dialect of the backwoodsman might have seemed oddly out of place, there, but for the quiet, unassuming manner and the fine old face of Uncle Eb in which the dullest eye might see the soul of a gentleman.

'What became of Lucy?' Mr Fuller enquired, laughingly. 'You never married her.'

'Lucy died,' he answered soberly; 'thet was long, long ago.'

Then he went away with John Trumbull to the smoking-room where I found them, talking earnestly in a corner, when it was time to go to the church with Hope.

Chapter 30

Hope and Uncle Eb and I went away in a coach with Mrs Fuller. There was a great crowd in the church that covered, with sweeping arches, an interior more vast than any I had ever entered. Hope was gowned in white silk, a crescent of diamonds in her hair—a birthday gift from Mrs Fuller; her neck and a part of her full breast unadorned by anything save the gifts of God—their snowy whiteness, their lovely curves.

First Henry Cooper came on with his violin—a great master as I now remember him. Then Hope ascended to the platform, her dainty kid slippers showing under her gown, and the odious Livingstone escorting her. I was never so madly in love or so insanely jealous. I must confess it for I am trying to tell the whole truth of myself—I was a fool. And it is the greater folly that one says ever 'I was,' and never 'I am' in that plea. I could even see it myself then and there, but I was so great a fool I smiled and spoke fairly to the young man although I could have wrung his neck with rage. There was a little stir and a passing whisper in the crowd as she stood waiting for the prelude. Then she sang the ballad of Auld Robin Grey—not better than I had heard her sing it before, but so charmingly there were murmurs of delight going far and wide in the audience when she had finished. Then she sang the fine melody of 'Angels ever Bright and Fair', and again the old ballad she and I had heard first from the violin of poor Nick Goodall.

By yon bonnie bank an' by yon bonnie bonnie brae

The sun shines bright on Loch Lomond

Where me an' me true love were ever won't if gae

On the bonnie, bonnie bank o' Loch Lomond.

Great baskets of roses were handed to her as she came down from the platform and my confusion was multiplied by their number for I had not thought to bring any myself.

I turned to Uncle Eb who, now and then, had furtively wiped his eyes. 'My stars!' he whispered, 'ain't it reemarkable grand! Never heard ner seen nothin' like thet in all my born days. An' t' think it's my little Hope.'

He could go no further. His handkerchief was in his hand while he took refuge in silence.

Going home the flowers were heaped upon our laps and I, with Hope beside me, felt some restoration of comfort.

'Did you see Trumbull?' Mrs Fuller asked. 'He sat back of us and did seem to enjoy it so much—your singing. He was almost cheerful.

'Tell me about Mr Trumbull,' I said. 'He is interesting.

'Speculator,' said Mrs Fuller. 'A strange man, successful, silent, unmarried and, I think, in love. Has beautiful rooms they say on Gramercy Park. Lives alone with an old servant. We got to know him through the accident. Mr Fuller and he have done business together—a great deal of it since then. Operates in the stock market.

A supper was waiting for us at home and we sat a long time at the table. I was burning for a talk with Hope but how was I to manage it? We rose with the others and went and sat down together in a corner of the great parlour. We talked of that night at the White Church in Faraway when we heard Nick Goodall play and she had felt the beginning of a new life.

'I've heard how well you did last year,' she said, 'and how nice you were to the girls. A friend wrote me all about it. How attentive you were to that little Miss Brown!

'But decently polite,' I answered. 'One has to have somebody or—or be a monk.

'One has to have somebody!' she said, quickly, as she picked at the flower on her bosom and looked down at it soberly. 'That is true one has to have somebody and, you know, I haven't had any lack of company myself. By the way, I have news to tell you.

She spoke slowly and in a low voice with a touch of sadness in it. I felt the colour mounting to my face.

'News!' I repeated. 'What news, I-lope?

'I am going away to England,' she said, 'with Mrs Fuller if—if mother will let me. I wish you would write and ask her to let me go.

I was unhorsed. What to say I knew not, what it meant I could vaguely imagine. There was a moment of awkward silence.

'Of course I will ask her if you wish to go,' I said. 'When do you sail?

'They haven't fixed the day yet.

She sat looking down at her fan, a beautiful, filmy thing between braces of ivory. Her knees were crossed, one dainty foot showing under ruffles of lace. I looked at her a moment dumb with admiration.

'What a big man you have grown to be Will,' she said presently. 'I am almost afraid of you now.

She was still looking down at the fan and that little foot was moving nervously. Now was my time. I began framing an avowal. I felt a wild impulse to throw my strong arms about her and draw her close to me and feel the pink velvet of her fair face upon mine. If I had only done it! But what with the strangeness and grandeur of that big room, the voices of the others who were sitting in the library, near by, the mystery of the spreading crinoline that was pressing upon my knees, I had not half the courage of a lover.

'My friend writes me that you are in love,' she said, opening her fan and moving it slowly, as she looked up at me.

'She is right I must confess it,' I said, 'I am madly, hopelessly in love. It is time you knew it Hope and I want your counsel.

She rose quickly and turned her face away.

'Do not tell me—do not speak of it again—I forbid you,' she answered coldly.

Then she stood silent. I rose to take her hand and ask her to tell me why, a pretty rankling in my heart, Soft footsteps and the swish of a gown were approaching. Before I could speak Mrs Fuller had come through the doorway.

'Come Hope,' she said, 'I cannot let you sit up late—you are worn out, my dear.

Then Hope bade us both good-night and went away to her room. If I had known as much about women then, as now, I should have had it out, with short delay, to some understanding between us. But in that subject one loves and learns. And one thing I have learned is this, that jealousy throws its illusions on every word and look and act. I went to my room and sat down for a bit of reckoning. Hope had ceased to love me, I felt sure, and how was I to win her back?

After all my castle building what was I come to?

I heard my door open presently, and then I lifted my head. Uncle Eb stood near me in his stocking feet and shirt-sleeves.

'In trouble,' he whispered.

'In trouble,' I said.

''Bout Hope?'

'It's about Hope.'

'Don't be hasty. Hope'll never go back on you,' he whispered. 'She doesn't love me,' I said impulsively. 'She doesn't care the snap of her finger for me.

'Don't believe it,' he answered calmly. 'Not a single word of it. Thet woman—she's tryin' t' keep her away from ye—but 'twon't make no differ'nce. Not a bit.

'I must try to win her back—someway—somehow,' I whispered.

'Gi n ye the mitten?' he asked.

'That's about it,' I answered, going possibly too far in the depth of my feeling.

'Whew w!' he softly whistled. 'Wall, it takes two mittens t'make a pair—ye'll hev t'ask her ag in.

'Yes I cannot give her up,' I said decisively, 'I must try to win her back. It isn't fair. I have no claim upon her. But I must do it.

'Consarn it! women like t'be chased,' he said. 'It's their natur'. What do they fix up so fer—di'mon's an' silks an' satins—if 'tain't t'set men a chasm 'uv 'em? You'd otter enjoy it. Stick to her—jes' like a puppy to a root. Thet's my advice.'

'Hope has got too far ahead of me,' I said. 'She can marry a rich man if she wishes to, and I don't see why she shouldn't. What am I, anyhow, but a poor devil just out of college and everything to win? It makes me miserable to think here in this great house how small I am.'

'There's things goin' to happen,' Uncle Eb whispered. 'I can't tell ye what er when, but they're goin' to happen an' they're goin' to change everything.

We sat thinking a while then. I knew what he meant—that I was to conquer the world, somehow, and the idea seemed to me so absurd I could hardly help laughing as melancholy as I felt.

'Now you go to bed,' he said, rising and gently touching my head with his hand. 'There's things goin' t'happen, boy—take my word fer it.

I got in bed late at night but there was no sleep for me. In the still hours I lay quietly, planning my future, for now I must make myself worth having and as soon as possible.

Some will say my determination was worthy of a better lover but, bless you! I have my own way of doing things and it has not been always so unsuccessful.

Chapter 31

Hope was not at breakfast with us.

'The child is worn out,' said Mrs Fuller. 'I shall keep her in bed a day or two.

'Couldn't I see her a moment?' I enquired.

'Dear! no!' said she. 'The poor thing is in bed with a headache.' If Hope had been ill at home I should have felt free to go and sit by her as I had done more than once. It seemed a little severe to be shut away from her now but Mrs Fuller's manner had fore-answered any appeal and I held my peace. Having no children of her own she had assumed a sort of proprietorship over Hope that was evident—that probably was why the girl had ceased to love me and to write to me as of old. A troop of mysteries came clear to me that morning. Through many gifts and favours she had got my sweetheart in a sort of bondage and would make a marriage of her own choosing if possible.

'Is there anything you would like particularly for your breakfast? Mrs Fuller enquired.

'Hain't no way pertic'lar,' said Uncle Eb. 'I gen rally eat buckwheat pancakes an' maple sugar with a good strong cup o'tea.

Mrs Fuller left the room a moment.

'Dunno but I'll go out to the barn a minnit 'n take a look at the hosses,' he said when she came back.

'The stable is a mile away,' she replied smiling.

'Gran' good team ye druv us out with las' night,' he said. 'Hed a chance t'look 'em over a leetle there at the door. The off hoss is puffed some for'ard but if yer husband'll put on a cold bandage ev'ry night it'll make them legs smoother n a hound's tooth.

She thanked him and invited us to look in at the conservatory.

'Where's yer husband?' Uncle Eb enquired.

'He's not up yet,' said she, 'I fear he did not sleep well.

'Now Mis Fuller,' said Uncle Eb, as we sat waiting, 'if there s anything I can do t'help jes'le'me know what 'tis.

She said there was nothing. Presently Uncle Eb sneezed so powerfully that it rattled the crystals on the chandelier and rang in the brass medallions.

The first and second butlers came running in with a frightened look. There was also a startled movement from somebody above stairs.

'I do sneeze powerful, sometimes,' said Uncle Eb from under his red bandanna. "S enough if scare anybody.'

They brought in our breakfast then—a great array of tempting dishes. 'Jest hev four pancakes 'n a biled egg,' said Uncle Eb as he sipped his tea. 'Grand tea!' he added, 'strong enough if float a silver dollar too.

'Mrs Fuller,' I said rising, when we had finished, 'I thank you for your hospitality, but as I shall have to work nights, probably, I must find lodgings near the office.

'You must come and see us again,' she answered cordially. 'On Saturday I shall take Hope away for a bit of rest to Saratoga probably—and from there I shall take her to Hillsborough myself for a day or two.

'Thought she was goin' home with me,' said Uncle Eb.

'O dear no!' said Mrs Fuller, 'she cannot go now. The girl is ill and it's such a long journey.'

The postman came then with a letter for Uncle Eb.

It was from David Brower. He would have to be gone a week or so buying cattle and thought Uncle Eb had better come home as soon as convenient.

'They're lonesome,' he said, thoughtfully, after going over the letter again. "Tain't no wonder—they're gittin' old.'

Uncle Eb was older than either of them but he had not thought of that.

'Le's see; 's about eight o clock,' said he, presently. 'I've got t'go an' ten' to some business o' my own. I'll be back here sometime if day Mis Fuller an' I'll hev if see thet girl. Ye musn't never try if keep me 'way from her. She's sot on my knee too many year fer that—altogether too many.

We arranged to meet there at four. Then a servant brought us our hats. I heard Hope calling as we passed the stairway:

'Won't you come up a minute, Uncle Eb? I want to see you very much.'

Then Uncle Eb hurried upstairs and I came away.

I read the advertisements of board and lodging—a perplexing task for one so ignorant of the town. After many calls I found a place to my liking on Monkey Hill, near Printing House Square. Monkey Hill was the east end of William Street, and not in the least fashionable. There were some neat and cleanly looking houses on it of wood, and brick, and brown stone inhabited by small tradesmen; a few shops, a big stable and the chalet sitting on a broad, flat roof that covered a portion of the stableyard. The yard itself was the summit of Monkey Hill. It lay between two brick buildings and up the hill, from the walk, one looked into the gloomy cavern of the stable and under the low roof, on one side there were dump carts and old coaches in varying stages of infirmity. There was an old iron shop, that stood flush with the sidewalk, flanking the stableyard. A lantern and a mammoth key were suspended above the door and hanging upon the side of the shop was a wooden stair ascending to the chalet The latter had a sheathing of weather-worn clapboards. It stood on the rear end of the brick building, communicating with the front rooms above the shop. A little stair of five steps ascended from the landing to its red door that overlooked an ample yard of roofing, adorned with potted plants. The main room of the chalet where we ate our meals and sat and talked, of an evening, had the look of a ship's cabin. There were stationary seats along the wall covered with leathern cushions. There were port and starboard lanterns and a big one of polished brass that overhung the table. A ship's clock that had a noisy and cheerful tick, was set in the wall. A narrow passage led to the room in front and the latter had slanting sides. A big window of little panes, in its further end, let in the light of William Street. Here I found a home for myself, humble but quaint and cleanly. A thrifty German who, having long followed the sea, had married and thrown out his anchor for good and all, now dwelt in the chalet with his wife and two boarders—both newspaper men. The old shopkeeper in front, once a sailor himself, had put the place in shipshape and leased it to them.

Mine host bore the name of Opper and was widely known as 'All Right' Opper, from his habit of cheery approval. Everything and everybody were 'all right' to him so far as I could observe. If he were blessed or damned he said 'all right. To be sure he took exceptions, on occasions, but even then the affair ended with his inevitable verdict of 'all right'. Every suggestion I made as to terms of payment and arrangement of furniture was promptly stamped with this seal of approval.

I was comfortably settled and hard at work on my article by noon. At four I went to meet Uncle Eb. Hope was still sick in bed and we came away in a frame of mind that could hardly have been more miserable. I tried to induce him to stay a night with me in my new quarters.

'I mus'n't,' he said cheerfully.' 'Fore long I'm comin' down ag'in but I can't fool 'round no longer now. I'll jes'go n git my new clothes and put fer the steamboat. Want ye t'go 'n see Hope tomorrow. She's comm up with Mis Fuller next week. I'm goin' t' find out what's the matter uv her then. Somethin's wrong somewhere. Dunno what 'tis. She's all upsot.

Poor girl! it had been almost as heavy a trial to her as to me' cutting me off as she had done. Remembrances of my tender devotion to her, in all the years between then and childhood, must have made her sore with pity. I had already determined what I should do, and after Uncle Eb had gone that evening I wrote her a long letter and asked her if I might not still have some hope of her loving me. I begged her to let me know when I might come and talk with her alone. With what eloquence I could bring to bear I told her how my love had grown and laid hold of my life.

I finished my article that night and, in the morning, took it to Mr Greeley. He was at his desk writing and at the same time giving orders in a querulous tone to some workman who sat beside him. He did not look up as he spoke. He wrote rapidly, his nose down so close to the straggling, wet lines that I felt a fear of its touching them. I stood by, waiting my opportunity. A full-bearded man in his shirt-sleeves came hurriedly out of another room.

'Mr Greeley,' he said, halting at the elbow of the great editor.

'Yes, what is it?' the editor demanded nervously, his hand wobbling over the white page, as rapidly as before, his eyes upon his work.

'Another man garrotted this morning on South Street.

'Better write a paragraph,' he said, his voice snapping with impatience as he brushed the full page aside and began sowing his thoughts on another. 'Warn our readers. Tell 'em to wear brass collars with spikes in 'em till we get a new mayor.

The man went away laughing.

Mr Greeley threw down his pen, gathered his copy and handed it to the workman who sat beside him.

'Proof ready at five!' he shouted as the man was going out of the room.

'Hello! Brower,' he said bending to his work again. 'Thought you'd blown out the gas somewhere.

'Waiting until you reject this article,' I said.

He sent a boy for Mr Ottarson, the city editor. Meanwhile he had begun to drive his pen across the broadsheets with tremendous energy.

Somehow it reminded me of a man ploughing black furrows behind a fast walking team in a snow flurry. His mind was 'straddle the furrow' when Mr Ottarson came in. There was a moment of silence in which the latter stood scanning a page of the Herald he had brought with him.

'Ottarson!' said Mr Greeley, never slacking the pace of his busy hand, as he held my manuscript in the other, 'read this. Tell me what you think of it. If good, give him a show.

'The staff is full, Mr Greeley,' said the man of the city desk. His words cut me with disappointment.

The editor of the Tribune halted his hand an instant, read the last lines, scratching a word and underscoring another.

'Don't care!' he shrilled, as he went on writing. 'Used to slide downhill with his father. If he's got brains we'll pay him eight dollars a-week.

The city editor beckoned to me and I followed him into another room.

'If you will leave your address,' he said, 'I will let you hear from me when we have read the article.

With the hasty confidence of youth I began to discount my future that very day, ordering a full dress suit, of the best tailor, hat and shoes to match and a complement of neck wear that would have done credit to Beau Brummel. It gave me a start when I saw the bill would empty my pocket of more than half its cash. But I had a stiff pace to follow, and every reason to look my best.

Chapter 32

I took a walk in the long twilight of that evening. As it began to grow dark I passed the Fuller house and looked up at its windows. Standing under a tree on the opposite side of the avenue I saw a man come out of the door and walk away hurriedly with long strides. I met him at the next corner.

'Good-evening!' he said.

I recognised then the voice and figure of John Trumbull. 'Been to Fuller's,' said he.

'How is Hope?' I asked.

'Better,' said he. 'Walk with me?

'With pleasure,' said I, and then he quickened his pace.

We walked awhile in silence, going so fast! had hardly time to speak, and the darkness deepened into night. We hurried along through streets and alleys that were but dimly lighted, coming out at length on a wide avenue passing through open fields in the upper part of the city. Lights in cabin windows glowed on the hills around us. I made some remark about them but he did not hear me. He slackened pace in a moment and began whispering to himself' I could not hear what he said. I thought of bidding him good-night and returning but where were we and how could I find my way? We heard a horse coming presently at a gallop. At the first loud whack of the hoofs he turned suddenly and laying hold of my arm began to run. I followed him into the darkness of the open field. It gave me a spell of rare excitement for I thought at once of highwaymen—having read so much of them in the Tribune. He stopped suddenly and stooped low his hands touching the grass and neither spoke until the horse had gone well beyond us. Then he rose, stealthily, and looked about him in silence, even turning his face to the dark sky where only a few stars were visible.

'Well!' said he with a sort of grunt. 'Beats the devil! I thought it was. A wonderful thing was happening in the sky. A great double moon seemed to be flying over the city hooded in purple haze. A little spray of silver light broke out of it, as we looked, and shot backward and then floated after the two shining disks that were falling eastward in a long curve. They seemed to be so near I thought they were coming down upon the city. It occurred to me they must have some connection with the odd experience I had gone through. In a moment they had passed out of sight. We were not aware that we had witnessed a spectacle the like of which had not been seen in centuries, if ever, since God made the heavens. The great meteor of 1860.

'Let's go back,' said Trumbull. 'We came too far. I forgot myself.'

'Dangerous here?' I enquired.

'Not at all,' said he, 'but a long way out of town—tired?

'Rather,' I said, grateful for his evident desire to quiet my alarm.

'Come!' said he as we came back to the pavement, his hand upon my shoulder. 'Talk to me. Tell me—what are you going to do?

We walked slowly down the deserted avenue, I, meanwhile, talking of my plans.

'You love. Hope,' he said presently. 'You will marry her?

'If she will have me,' said I.

'You must wait,' he said, 'time enough!

He quickened his pace again as we came in sight of the scattering shops and houses of the upper city and no other word was spoken. On the corners we saw men looking into the sky and talking of the fallen moon. It was late bedtime when we turned into Gramercy Park.

'Come in,' said he as he opened an iron gate.

I followed him up a marble stairway and a doddering old English butler opened the door for us. We entered a fine hall, its floor of beautiful parquetry muffled with silken rugs. High and spacious rooms were all aglow with light.

He conducted me to a large smoking-room, its floor and walls covered with trophies of the hunt—antlers and the skins of carnivora. Here he threw off his coat and bade me be at home as he lay down upon a wicker divan covered with the tawny skin of some wild animal. He stroked the fur fondly with his hand.

'Hello Jock!' he said, a greeting that mystified me.

'Tried to eat me,' he added, turning to me.

Then he bared his great hairy arm and showed me a lot of ugly scars, I besought him to tell the story.

'Killed him,' he answered. 'With a gun?

'No—with my hands,' and that was all he would say of it.

He lay facing a black curtain that covered a corner. Now and then I heard a singular sound in the room—like some faint, far, night cry such as I have heard often in the deep woods. It was so weird I felt some wonder of it. Presently I could tell it came from behind the curtain where, also, I heard an odd rustle like that of wings.

I sat in a reverie, looking at the silent man before me, and in the midst of it he pulled a cord that hung near him and a bell rang.

'Luncheon!' he said to the old butler who entered immediately.

Then he rose and showed me odd things, carved out of wood, by his own hand as he told me, and with a delicate art. He looked at one tiny thing and laid it aside quickly.

'Can't bear to look at it now,' he said.

'Gibbet?' I enquired.

'Gibbet,' he answered.

It was a little figure bound hand and foot and hanging from the gallows tree.

'Burn it!' he said, turning to the old servant and putting it in his hands. Luncheon had been set between us, the while, and as we were eating it the butler opened a big couch and threw snowy sheets of linen over it and silken covers that rustled as they fell.

'You will sleep there,' said my host as his servant laid the pillows, 'and well I hope.

I thought I had better go to my own lodgings.

'Too late—too late,' said he, and I, leg-weary and half-asleep, accepted his proffer of hospitality. Then, having eaten, he left me and I got into bed after turning the lights out Something woke me in the dark of the night. There was a rustling sound in the room. I raised my head a bit and listened. It was the black curtain that hung in the corner. I imagined somebody striking it violently. I saw a white figure standing near me in the darkness. It moved away as I looked at it. A cold wind was blowing upon my face. I lay a long time listening and by and by I could hear the deep voice of Trumbull as if he were groaning and muttering in his sleep. When it began to come light I saw the breeze from an open window was stirring the curtain of silk in the corner. I got out of bed and, peering behind the curtain, saw only a great white owl, caged and staring out of wide eyes that gleamed fiery in the dim light. I went to bed again, sleeping until my host woke me in the late morning.

After breakfasting I went to the chalet. The postman had been there but he had brought no letter from Hope. I waited about home, expecting to hear from her, all that day, only to see it end in bitter disappointment.

Chapter 33

That very night, I looked in at the little shop beneath us and met Riggs. It was no small blessing, just as I was entering upon dark and unknown ways of life, to meet this hoary headed man with all his lanterns. He would sell you anchors and fathoms of chain and rope enough to hang you to the moon but his 'lights' were the great attraction of Riggs's. He had every kind of lantern that had ever swung on land or sea. After dark, when light was streaming out of its open door and broad window Riggs's looked like the side of an old lantern itself. It was a door, low and wide, for a time when men had big round bellies and nothing to do but fill them and heads not too far above their business. It was a window gone blind with dust and cobwebs so it resembled the dim eye of age. If the door were closed its big brass knocker and massive iron latch invited the passer. An old ship's anchor and a coil of chain lay beside it. Blocks and heavy bolts, steering wheels, old brass compasses, coils of rope and rusty chain lay on the floor and benches, inside the shop. There were rows of lanterns, hanging on the bare beams. And there was Riggs. He sat by a dusty desk and gave orders in a sleepy, drawling tone to the lad who served him. An old Dutch lantern, its light softened with green glass, sent a silver bean across the gloomy upper air of the shop that evening. Riggs held an old un lantern with little streams of light bursting through its perforated walls. He was blind. One would know it at a glance. Blindness is so easy to be seen. Riggs was showing it to a stranger.

'Turn down the lights,' he said and the boy got his step-ladder and obeyed him.

Then he held it aloft in the dusk and the little lantern was like a castle tower with many windows lighted, and, when he set it down, there was a golden sprinkle on the floor as if something had plashed into a magic pool of light there in the darkness.

Riggs lifted the lantern, presently, and stood swinging it in his hand. Then its rays were sown upon the darkness falling silently into every nook and corner of the gloomy shop and breaking into flowing dapples on the wall.

'See how quick it is!' said he as the rays flashed with the speed of lightning. 'That is the only traveller from Heaven that travels fast enough to ever get to earth.

Then came the words that had a mighty fitness for his tongue.

'Hail, holy light! Offspring of Heaven first born.

His voice rose and fell, riding the mighty rhythm of inspired song. As he stood swinging the lantern, then, he reminded me of a chanting priest behind the censer. In a moment he sat down, and, holding the lantern between his knees, opened its door and felt the candle. Then as the light streamed out upon his hands, he rubbed them a time, silently, as if washing them in the bright flood.

'One dollar for this little box of daylight,' he said.

'Blind?' said the stranger as he paid him the money.

'No,' said Riggs, 'only dreaming as you are.

I wondered what he meant by the words 'dreaming as you are.

'Went to bed on my way home to marry,' he continued, stroking his long white beard, 'and saw the lights go out an' went asleep and it hasn't come morning yet—that's what I believe. I went into a dream. Think I'm here in a shop talking but I'm really in my bunk on the good ship Arid coming home. Dreamed everything since then—everything a man could think of. Dreamed I came home and found Annie dead, dreamed of blindness, of old age, of poverty, of eating and drinking and sleeping and of many people who pass like dim shadows and speak to me—you are one of them. And sometimes I forget I am dreaming and am miserable, and then I remember and am happy. I know when the morning comes I shall wake and laugh at all these phantoms. And I shall pack my things and go up on deck, for we shall be in the harbour probably—ay! maybe Annie and mother will be waving their hands on the dock!

The old face had a merry smile as he spoke of the morning and all it had for him.

'Seems as if it had lasted a thousand years,' he continued, yawning and rubbing his eyes. 'But I've dreamed the like before, and, my God! how glad I felt when I woke in the morning.

It gave me an odd feeling—this remarkable theory of the old man. I thought then it would be better for most of us if we could think all our misery a dream and have his faith in the morning—that it would bring back the things we have lost. I had come to buy a lock for my door, but I forgot my errand and sat down by Riggs while the stranger went away with his lantern.

'You see no reality in anything but happiness,' I said.

'It's all a means to that end,' he answered. 'It is good for me, this dream. I shall be all the happier when I do wake, and I shall love Annie all the better, I suppose.

'I wish I could take my bad luck as a dream and have faith only in good things,' I said.

'All that is good shall abide,' said he, stroking his white beard, 'and all evil shall vanish as the substance of a dream. In the end the only realities are God and love and Heaven. To die is just like waking up in the morning.

'But I know I'm awake,' I said.

'You think you are—that's a part of your dream. Sometimes I think I'm awake—it all seems so real to me. But I have thought it out, and I am the only man I meet that knows he is dreaming. When you'do wake, in the morning, you may remember how you thought you came to a certain shop and made some words with a man as to whether you were both dreaming, and you will laugh and tell your friends about it. Hold on! I can feel the ship lurching. I believe I am going to wake.

He sat a moment leaning back in his chair with closed eyes, and a silence fell upon us in the which I could hear only the faint ticking of a tall clock that lifted its face out of the gloom beyond me.

'You there?' he whispered presently.

'I am here,' I said.

'Odd!' he muttered. 'I know how it will be—I know how it has been before. Generally come to some high place and a great fear seizes me. I slip, I fall—fall—fall, and then I wake.

After a little silence I heard him snoring heavily. He was still leaning back in his chair. I walked on tiptoe to the door where the boy stood looking out.

'Crazy?' I whispered.

'Dunno,' said he, smiling.

I went to my room above and wrote my first tale, which was nothing more or less than some brief account of what I had heard and seen down at the little shop that evening. I mailed it next day to the Knickerbocker, with stamps for return if unavailable.

Chapter 34

New York was a crowded city, even then, but I never felt so lonely anywhere outside a camp in the big woods, The last day of the first week came, but no letter from Hope. To make an end of suspense I went that Saturday morning to the home of the Fullers. The equation of my value had dwindled sadly that week. Now a small fraction would have stood for it—nay, even the square of it.

Hope and Mrs Fuller had gone to Saratoga, the butler told me. I came away with some sense of injury. I must try to be done with Hope. There was no help for it. I must go to work at something and cease to worry and lie awake of nights. But I had nothing to do but read and walk and wait. No word had come to me from the 'Tribune'—evidently it was not languishing for my aid. That day my tale was returned to me with thanks with nothing but thanks printed in black type on a slip of paper—cold, formal, prompt, ready-made thanks. And I, myself, was in about the same fix—rejected with thanks—politely, firmly, thankfully rejected. For a moment I felt like a man falling. I began to see there was no very clamourous demand for me in 'the great emporium', as Mr Greeley called it. I began to see, or thought I did, why Hope had shied at my offer and was now shunning me. I went to the Tribune office. Mr Greeley had gone to Washington; Mr Ottarson was too busy to see me. I concluded that I would be willing to take a place on one of the lesser journals. I spent the day going from one office to another, but was rejected everywhere with thanks. I came home and sat down to take account of stock. First, I counted my money, of which there were about fifty dollars left. As to my talents, there were none left. Like the pies at the Hillsborough tavern, if a man came late to dinner—they were all out. I had some fine clothes, but no more use for them than a goose for a peacock's feathers. I decided to take anything honourable as an occupation, even though it were not in one of the learned professions. I began to answer advertisements and apply at business offices for something to give me a living, but with no success. I began to feel the selfishness of men. God pity the warm and tender heart of youth when it begins to harden and grow chill, as mine did then; to put away its cheery confidence forever; to make a new estimate of itself and others. Look out for that time, O ye good people! that have sons and daughters.

I must say for myself that I had a mighty courage and no small capital of cheerfulness. I went to try my luck with the newspapers of Philadelphia, and there one of them kept me in suspense a week to no purpose. When I came back reduced in cash and courage Hope had sailed.

There was a letter from Uncle Eb telling me when and by what steamer they were to leave. 'She will reach there a Friday,' he wrote, 'and would like to see you that evening at Fuller's'.

I had waited in Philadelphia, hoping I might have some word, to give her a better thought of me, and, that night, after such a climax of ill luck, well—I had need of prayer for a wayward tongue. I sent home a good account of my prospects. I could not bring myself to report failure or send for more money. I would sooner have gone to work in a scullery.

Meanwhile my friends at the chalet were enough to keep me in good cheer. There were William McClingan, a Scotchman of a great gift of dignity and a nickname inseparably connected with his fame. He wrote leaders for a big weekly and was known as Waxy McClingan, to honour a pale ear of wax that took the place of a member lost nobody could tell how. He drank deeply at times, but never to the loss of his dignity or self possession. In his cups the natural dignity of the man grew and expanded. One could tell the extent of his indulgence by the degree of his dignity. Then his mood became at once didactic and devotional. Indeed, I learned in good time of the rumour that he had lost his ear in an argument about the Scriptures over at Edinburgh.

I remember he came an evening, soon after my arrival at the chalet, when dinner was late. His dignity was at the full. He sat awhile in grim silence, while a sense of injury grew in his bosom.

'Mrs Opper,' said he, in a grandiose manner and voice that nicely trilled the r's, 'in the fourth chapter and ninth verse of Lamentations you will find these words—here he raised his voice a bit and began to tap the palm of his left hand with the index finger of his right, continuing: "They that be slain with the sword are better than they that be slain with hunger. For these pine away stricken through want of the fruits of the field." Upon my honour as a gentleman, Mrs Opper, I was never so hungry in all my life.'

The other boarder was a rather frail man with an easy cough and a confidential manner, he wrote the 'Obituaries of Distinguished Persons' for one of the daily papers. Somebody had told him once, his head resembled that of Washington. He had never forgotten it, as I have reason to remember. His mind lived ever among the dead. His tongue was pickled in maxims; his heart sunk in the brine of recollection; his humour not less unconscious and familiar than that of an epitaph; his name was Lemuel Framdin Force. To the public of his native city he had introduced Webster one fourth of July—a perennial topic of his lighter moments.

I fell an easy victim to the obituary editor that first evening in the chalet. We had risen from the table and he came and held me a moment by the coat lapel. He released my collar, when he felt sure of me, and began tapping my chest with his forefinger to drive home his point. I stood for quite an hour out of sheer politeness. By that time he had me forced to the wall—a God's mercy, for there I got some sense of relief in the legs. His gestures, in imitation of the great Webster, put my head in some peril. Meanwhile he continued drumming upon my chest. I looked longingly at the empty chairs. I tried to cut him off with applause that should be condusive and satisfying, but with no success. It had only a stimulating effect. I felt somehow like a cheap hired man badly overworked. I had lost all connection. I looked, and smiled, and nodded, and exclaimed, and heard nothing. I began to plan a method of escape. McClingan—the great and good Waxy McClingan—came out of his room presently and saw my plight.

'What is this?' he asked, interrupting, 'a serial stawry?

Getting no answer he called my name, and when Force had paused he came near.

'In the sixth chapter and fifth verse of Proverbs,' said he, 'it is written:

"Deliver thyself as a roe from the hand of the hunter and as a bird from the hand of the fowler." Deliver thyself, Brower.

I did so, ducking under Force's arm and hastening to my chamber.

'Ye have a brawling, busy tongue, man,' I heard McClingan saying. 'By the Lord! ye should know a dull tongue is sharper than a serpent's tooth.

'You are a meddlesome fellow,' said Force.

'If I were you,' said McClingan, 'I would go and get for myself the long ear of an ass and empty my memory into it every day. Try it, man. Give it your confidence exclusively. Believe me, my dear Force, you would win golden opinions.

'It would be better than addressing an ear of wax,' said Force, hurriedly withdrawing to his own room.

This answer made McClingan angry.

'Better an ear of wax than a brain of putty,' he called after him. 'Blessed is he that hath no ears when a fool's tongue is busy,' and then strode up and down the floor, muttering ominously.

I came out of my room shortly, and then he motioned me aside.

'Pull your own trigger first, man,' he said to me in a low tone. 'When ye see he's going to shoot, pull your own trigger first. Go right up to him and tap him on the chest quiddy and say, "My dear Force, I have a glawrious stawry to tell you," and keep tapping him—his own trick, you know, and he can't complain. Now he has a weak chest, and when he begins to cough—man, you are saved.

Our host, Opper, entered presently, and in removing the tablecloth inadvertently came between us. McClingan resented it promptly.

'Mr Opper,' said he, leering at the poor German, 'as a matter of personal obligement, will you cease to interrupt us?

'All right! all right! gentlemens,' he replied, and then, fearing that he had not quite squared himself, turned back, at the kitchen door, and added, 'Oxcuse me.

McClingan looked at him with that leering superior smile of his, and gave him just the slightest possible nod of his head.

McClingan came into my room with me awhile then. He had been everywhere, it seemed to me, and knew everybody worth knowing. I was much interested in his anecdotes of the great men of the time. Unlike the obituary editor his ear was quite as ready as his tongue, though I said little save now and then to answer a question that showed a kindly interest in me.

I went with him to his room at last, where he besought me to join him in drinking 'confusion to the enemies of peace and order'. On my refusing, he drank the toast alone and shortly proposed 'death to slavery'. This was followed in quick succession by 'death to the arch traitor, Buchanan'; 'peace to the soul of John Brown'; 'success to Honest Abe' and then came a hearty 'here's to the protuberant abdomen of the Mayor'.

I left him at midnight standing in the middle of his room and singing 'The Land o' the Leal' in a low tone savoured with vast dignity.

Chapter 35

I was soon near out of money and at my wit's end, but my will was unconquered. In this plight I ran upon Fogarty, the policeman who had been the good angel of my one hopeful day in journalism. His manner invited my confidence.

'What luck?' said he.

'Bad luck' I answered. 'Only ten dollars in my pocket and nothing to do.'

He swung his stick thoughtfully.

'If I was you,' said he, 'I'd take anything honest. Upon me wurred, I'd ruther pound rocks than lay idle.'

'So would I.'

'Wud ye?' said he with animation, as he took my measure from head to foot.

'I'll do anything that's honest.'

'Ah ha!' said he, rubbing his sandy chin whiskers. 'Don't seem like ye'd been used to hard wurruk.'

'But I can do it,' I said.

He looked at me sternly and beckoned with his head.

'Come along,' said he.

He took me to a gang of Irishmen working in the street near by.

'Boss McCormick!' he shouted.

A hearty voice answered, 'Aye, aye, Counsellor,' and McCormick came out of the crowd, using his shovel for a staff.

'A happy day to ye!' said Fogarty.

'Same to youse an' manny o' thim,' said McCormick.

'Ye'll gi'me one if ye do me a favour,' said Fogarty.

'An' what?' said the other.

'A job for this lad. Wull ye do it?'

'I wall,' said McCormick, and he did.

I went to work early the next morning, with nothing on but my underclothing and trousers, save a pair of gloves, that excited the ridicule of my fellows. With this livery and the righteous determination of earning two dollars a day, I began the inelegant task of 'pounding rocks no merry occupation, I assure you, for a hot summer's day on Manhattan Island.

We were paving Park Place and we had to break stone and lay them and shovel dirt and dig with a pick and crowbar.

My face and neck were burned crimson when we quit work at five, and I went home with a feeling of having been run over by the cars. I had a strong sense of soul and body, the latter dominated by a mighty appetite. McClingan viewed me at first with suspicion in which there was a faint flavour of envy. He invited me at once to his room, and was amazed at seeing it was no lark. I told him frankly what I was doing and why and where.

'I would not mind the loaning of a few dollars,' he said, 'as a matter o' personal obligement I would be most happy to do it—most happy, Brower, indeed I would.'

I thanked him cordially, but declined the favour, for at home they had always taught me the danger of borrowing, and I was bound to have it out with ill luck on my own resources.

'Greeley is back,' said he, 'and I shall see him tomorrow. I will put him in mind o'you.'

I went away sore in the morning, but with no drooping spirit. In the middle of the afternoon I straightened up a moment to ease my back and look about me.

There at the edge of the gang stood the great Horace Greeley and Waxy McClingan. The latter beckoned me as he caught my eye. I went aside to greet them. Mr Greeley gave me his hand.

'Do you mean to tell me that you'd rather work than beg or borrow?' said he.

'That's about it,' I answered.

'And ain't ashamed of it?

'Ashamed! Why?' said I, not quite sure of his meaning. It had never occurred to me that one had any cause to be ashamed of working.

He turned to McClingan and laughed.

'I guess you'll do for the Tribune,' he said. 'Come and see me at twelve tomorrow.

And then they went away.

If I had been a knight of the garter I could not have been treated with more distinguished courtesy by those hard-handed men the rest of the day. I bade them goodbye at night and got my order for four dollars. One Pat Devlin, a great-hearted Irishman, who had shared my confidence and some of my doughnuts on the curb at luncheon time, I remember best of all.

'Ye'll niver fergit the toime we wurruked together under Boss McCormick,' said he.

And to this day, whenever I meet the good man, now bent and grey, he says always, 'Good-day to ye, Mr Brower. D'ye mind the toime we pounded the rock under Boss McCormick?

Mr Greeley gave me a place at once on the local staff and invited me to dine with him at his home that evening. Meanwhile he sent me to the headquarters of the Republican Central Campaign Committee, on Broadway, opposite the New York Hotel. Lincoln had been nominated in May, and the great political fight of 1860 was shaking the city with its thunders.

I turned in my copy at the city desk in good season, and, although the great editor had not yet left his room, I took a car at once to keep my appointment. A servant showed me to a seat in the big back parlour of Mr Greeley's home, where I spent a lonely hour before I heard his heavy footsteps in the hail. He immediately rushed upstairs, two steps at a time, and, in a moment, I heard his high voice greeting the babies. He came down shortly with one of them clinging to his hand.

'Thunder!' said he, 'I had forgotten all about you. Let's go right in to dinner.

He sat at the head of the table and I next to him. I remember how, wearied by the day's burden, he sat, lounging heavily, in careless attitudes. He stirred his dinner into a hash of eggs, potatoes, squash and parsnips, and ate it leisurely with a spoon, his head braced often with his left forearm, its elbow resting on the table. It was a sort of letting go, after the immense activity of the day, and a casual observer would have thought he affected the uncouth, which was not true of him.

He asked me to tell him all about my father and his farm. At length I saw an absent look in his eye, and stopped talking, because I thought he had ceased to listen.

'Very well! very well!' said he.

I looked up at him, not knowing what he meant.

'Go on! Tell me all about it,' he added.

'I like the country best,' said he, when I had finished, 'because there I see more truth in things. Here the lie has many forms—unique, varied, ingenious. The rouge and powder on the lady's cheek—they are lies, both of them; the baronial and ducal crests are lies and the fools who use them are liars; the people who soak themselves in rum have nothing but lies in their heads; the multitude who live by their wits and the lack of them in others—they are all liars; the many who imagine a vain thing and pretend to be what they are not liars everyone of them. It is bound to be so in the great cities, and it is a mark of decay. The skirts of Elegabalus, the wigs and rouge pots of Madame Pompadour, the crucifix of Machiavelli and the innocent smile of Fernando Wood stand for something horribly and vastly false in the people about them. For truth you ve got to get back into the woods. You can find men there a good deal as God made them, genuine, strong and simple. When those men cease to come here you'll see grass growing in Broadway.

I made no answer and the great commoner stirred his coffee a moment in silence.

'Vanity is the curse of cities,' he continued, 'and Flattery is its handmaiden. Vanity, flattery and Deceit are the three disgraces. I like a man to be what he is—out and out. If he's ashamed of himself it won't be long before his friends'll be ashamed of him. There's the trouble with this town. Many a fellow is pretending to be what he isn't. A man cannot be strong unless he is genuine.

One of his children—a little girl—came and stood close to him as he spoke. He put his big arm around her and that gentle, permanent smile of his broadened as he kissed her and patted her red cheek.

'Anything new in the South?' Mrs Greeley enquired.

'Worse and worse every day,' he said. 'Serious trouble coming! The Charleston dinner yesterday was a feast of treason and a flow of criminal rhetoric. The Union was the chief dish. Everybody slashed it with his knife and jabbed it with his fork. It was slaughtered, roasted, made into mincemeat and devoured. One orator spoke of "rolling back the tide of fanaticism that finds its root in the conscience of the people." Their metaphors are as bad as their morals.

He laughed heartily at this example of fervid eloquence, and then we rose from the table. He had to go to the office that evening, and I came away soon after dinner. I had nothing to do and went home reflecting upon all the great man had said.

I began shortly to see the truth of what he had told me—men licking the hand of riches with the tongue of flattery, men so stricken with the itch of vanity that they grovelled for the touch of praise; men even who would do perjury for applause. I do not say that most of the men I saw were of that ilk, but enough to show the tendency of life in a great town.

I was filled with wonder at first by meeting so many who had been everywhere and seen everything, who had mastered all sciences and all philosophies and endured many perils on land and sea. I had met liars before—it was no Eden there in the north country—and some of them had attained a good degree of efficiency, but they lacked the candour and finish of the metropolitan school. I confess they were all too much for me at first. They borrowed my cash, they shared my confidence, they taxed my credulity, and I saw the truth at last.

'Tom's breaking down,' said a co-labourer on the staff one day. 'How is that?' I enquired.

'Served me a mean trick.'

'Indeed!'

'Deceived me,' said he sorrowfully.

'Lied, I suppose?'

'No. He told the truth, as God's my witness.'

Tom had been absolutely reliable up to that time.

Chapter 36

Those were great days in mid autumn. The Republic was in grave peril of dissolution. Liberty that had hymned her birth in the last century now hymned her destiny in the voices of bard and orator. Crowds of men gathered in public squares, at bulletin boards, on street corners arguing, gesticulating, exclaiming and cursing. Cheering multitudes went up and down the city by night, with bands and torches, and there was such a howl of oratory and applause on the lower half of Manhattan Island that it gave the reporter no rest. William H. Seward, Charles Sumner, John A. Dix, Henry Ward Beecher and Charles O'Connor were the giants of the stump. There was more violence and religious fervour in the political feeling of that time than had been mingled since '76. A sense of outrage was in the hearts of men. 'Honest Abe' Lincoln stood, as they took it, for their homes and their country, for human liberty and even for their God.

I remember coming into the counting-room late one evening. Loud voices had halted me as I passed the door. Mr Greeley stood back of the counter; a rather tall, wiry grey-headed man before it. Each was shaking a right fist under the other's nose. They were shouting loudly as they argued. The stranger was for war; Mr Greeley for waiting. The publisher of the Tribune stood beside the latter, smoking a pipe; a small man leaned over the counter at the stranger's elbow, putting in a word here and there; half a dozen people stood by, listening. Mr Greeley turned to his publisher in a moment.

'Rhoades,' said he, 'I wish ye'd put these men out. They holler 'n yell, so I can't hear myself think.

Then there was a general laugh.

I learned to my surprise, when they had gone, that the tall man was William H. Seward, the other John A. Dix.

Then one of those fevered days came the Prince of Wales—a Godsend, to allay passion with curiosity.

It was my duty to handle some of 'the latest news by magnetic telegraph', and help to get the plans and progress of the campaign at headquarters. The Printer, as they called Mr Greeley, was at his desk when I came in at noon, never leaving the office but for dinner, until past midnight, those days. And he made the Tribune a mighty power in the state. His faith in its efficacy was sublime, and every line went under his eye before it went to his readers. I remember a night when he called me to his office about twelve o clock. He was up to his knees in the rubbish of the day-newspapers that he had read and thrown upon the floor; his desk was littered with proofs.

'Go an' see the Prince o' Wales,' he said. (That interesting young man had arrived on the Harriet Lane that morning and ridden up Broadway between cheering hosts.) 'I've got a sketch of him here an' it's all twaddle. Tell us something new about him. If he's got a hole in his sock we ought to know it.'

Mr Dana came in to see him while I was there.

'Look here, Dana,' said the Printer, in a rasping humour. 'By the gods of war! here's two columns about that performance at the Academy and only two sticks of the speech of Seward at St Paul. I'll have to get someone to go an' burn that theatre an' send the bill to me.

In the morning Mayor Wood introduced me to the Duke of Newcastle, who in turn presented me to the Prince of Wales—then a slim, blue-eyed youngster of nineteen, as gentle mannered as any I have ever met. It was my unpleasant duty to keep as near as possible to the royal party in all the festivities of that week.

The ball, in the Prince's honour, at the Academy of Music, was one of the great social events of the century. No fair of vanity in the western hemisphere ever quite equalled it. The fashions of the French Court had taken the city, as had the Prince, by unconditional surrender. Not in the palace of Versailles could one have seen a more generous exposure of the charms of fair women. None were admitted without a low-cut bodice, and many came that had not the proper accessories. But it was the most brilliant company New York had ever seen.

Too many tickets had been distributed and soon 'there was an elbow on every rib and a heel on every toe', as Mr Greeley put it. Every miss and her mamma tiptoed for a view of the Prince and his party, who came in at ten, taking their seats on a dais at one side of the crowded floor. The Prince sat with his hands folded before him, like one in a reverie. Beside him were the Duke of Newcastle, a big, stern man, with an aggressive red beard; the blithe and sparkling Earl of St Germans, then Steward of the Royal Household; the curly Major Teasdale; the gay Bruce, a major-general, who behaved himself always like a lady. Suddenly the floor sank beneath the crowd of people, who retired in some disorder. Such a compression of crinoline was never seen as at that moment, when periphery pressed upon periphery, and held many a man captive in the cold embrace of steel and whalebone. The royal party retired to its rooms again and carpenters came in with saws and hammers. The floor repaired, an area was roped off for dancing—as much as could be spared. The Prince opened the dance with Mrs Governor Morgan, after which other ladies were honoured with his gallantry.

I saw Mrs Fuller in one of the boxes and made haste to speak with her. She had just landed, having left Hope to study a time in the Conservatory of Leipzig.

'Mrs Livingstone is with her,' said she, 'and they will return together in April.

'Mrs Fuller, did she send any word to me?' I enquired anxiously. 'Did she give you no message?

'None,' she said coldly, 'except one to her mother and father, which I have sent in a letter to them.

I left her heavy hearted, went to the reporter's table and wrote my story, very badly I must admit, for I was cut deep with sadness. Then I came away and walked for hours, not caring whither. A great homesickness had come over me. I felt as if a talk with Uncle Eb or Elizabeth Brower would have given me the comfort I needed. I walked rapidly through dark, deserted streets. A steeple clock was striking two, when I heard someone coming hurriedly on the walk behind me. I looked over my shoulder, but could not make him out in the darkness, and yet there was something familiar in the step. As he came near I felt his hand upon my shoulder.

'Better go home, Brower,' he said, as I recognised the voice of Trumbull. 'You've been out a long time. Passed you before tonight.'

'Why didn't you speak?'

'You were preoccupied.'

'Not keeping good hours yourself,' I said.

'Rather late,' he answered, 'but I am a walker, and I love the night. It is so still in this part of the town.'

We were passing the Five Points.

'When do you sleep,' I enquired.

'Never sleep at night,' he said, 'unless uncommonly tired. Out every night more or less. Sleep two hours in the morning and two in the afternoon—that's all I require. Seen the hands o' that clock yonder on every hour of the night.'

He pointed to a lighted dial in a near tower.

Stopping presently he looked down at a little waif asleep in a doorway, a bundle of evening papers under his arm. He lifted him tenderly.

'Here, boy,' he said, dropping corns in the pocket of the ragged little coat, 'I'll take those papers—you go home now.

We walked to the river, passing few save members of 'the force, who always gave Trumbull a cheery 'hello, Cap!' We passed wharves where the great sea horses lay stalled, with harnesses hung high above them, their noses nodding over our heads; we stood awhile looking up at the looming masts, the lights of the river craft.

'Guess I've done some good,' said he turning into Peck Slip. 'Saved two young women. Took 'em off the streets. Fine women now both of them—respectable, prosperous, and one is beautiful. Man who's got a mother, or a sister, can't help feeling sorry for such people.

We came up Frankfort to William Street where we shook hands and parted and I turned up Monkey Hill. I had made unexpected progress with Trumbull that night. He had never talked to me so freely before and somehow he had let me come nearer to him than I had ever hoped to be. His company had lifted me out of the slough a little and my mind was on a better footing as I neared the chalet.

Riggs's shop was lighted—an unusual thing at so late an hour. Peering through the window I saw Riggs sleeping at his desk An old tin lantern sat near, its candle burning low, with a flaring flame, that threw a spray of light upon him as it rose and fell. Far back in the shop another light was burning dimly. I lifted the big iron latch and pushed the door open. Riggs did not move. I closed the door softly and went back into the gloom. The boy was also sound asleep in his chair. The lantern light flared and fell again as water leaps in a stopping fountain. As it dashed upon the face of Riggs

I saw his eyes half-open. I went close to his chair. As I did so the light went out and smoke rose above the lantern with a rank odour.

'Riggs!' I called but he sat motionless and made no answer.

The moonlight came through the dusty window lighting his face and beard. I put my hand upon his brow and withdrew it quickly. I was in the presence of death. I opened the door and called the sleeping boy. He rose out of his chair and came toward me rubbing his eyes.

'Your master is dead,' I whispered, 'go and call an officer.

Riggs's dream was over—he had waked at last. He was in port and I doubt not Annie and his mother were hailing him on the shore, for I knew now they had both died far back in that long dream of the old sailor.

My story of Riggs was now complete. It soon found a publisher because it was true.

'All good things are true in literature,' said the editor after he had read it. 'Be a servant of Truth always and you will be successful.'

Chapter 37

As soon as Lincoln was elected the attitude of the South showed clearly that 'the irrepressible conflict', of Mr Seward's naming, had only just begun. The Herald gave columns every day to the news of 'the coming Revolution', as it was pleased to call it. There was loud talk of war at and after the great Pine Street meeting of December 15. South Carolina seceded, five days later, and then we knew what was coming, albeit, we saw only the dim shadow of that mighty struggle that was to shake the earth for nearly five years. The Printer grew highly irritable those days and spoke of Buchanan and Davis and Toombs in language so violent it could never have been confined in type. But while a bitter foe none was more generous than he and, when the war was over, his money went to bail the very man he had most roundly damned.

I remember that one day, when he was sunk deep in composition, a negro came and began with grand airs to make a request as delegate from his campaign club. The Printer sat still, his eyes close to the paper, his pen flying at high speed. The coloured orator went on lifting his voice in a set petition. Mr Greeley bent to his work as the man waxed eloquent. A nervous movement now and then betrayed the Printer's irritation. He looked up, shortly, his face kindling with anger.

'Help! For God's sake!' he shrilled impatiently, his hands flying in the air. The Printer seemed to be gasping for breath.

'Go and stick your head out of the window and get through,' he shouted hotly to the man.

He turned to his writing—a thing dearer to him than a new bone to a hungry dog.

'Then you may come and tell me what you want,' he added in a milder tone.

Those were days when men said what they meant and their meaning had more fight in it than was really polite or necessary. Fight was in the air and before I knew it there was a wild, devastating spirit in my own bosom, insomuch that I made haste to join a local regiment. It grew apace but not until I saw the first troops on their way to the war was I fully determined to go and give battle with my regiment.

The town was afire with patriotism. Sumter had fallen; Lincoln had issued his first call. The sound of the fife and drum rang in the streets. Men gave up work to talk and listen or go into the sterner business of war. Then one night in April, a regiment came out of New England, on its way to the front. It lodged at the Astor House to leave at nine in the morning. Long before that hour the building was flanked and fronted with tens of thousands, crowding Broadway for three blocks, stuffing the wide mouth of Park Row and braced into Vesey and Barday Streets. My editor assigned me to this interesting event. I stood in the crowd, that morning, and saw what was really the beginning of the war in New York. There was no babble of voices, no impatient call, no sound of idle jeering such as one is apt to hear in a waiting crowd. It stood silent, each man busy with the rising current of his own emotions, solemnified by the faces all around him. The soldiers filed out upon the pavement, the police having kept a way clear for them, Still there was silence in the crowd save that near me I could hear a man sobbing. A trumpeter lifted his bugle and sounded a bar of the reveille. The clear notes clove the silent air, flooding every street about us with their silver sound. Suddenly the band began playing. The tune was Yankee Doodle. A wild, dismal, tremulous cry came out of a throat near me. It grew and spread to a mighty roar and then such a shout went up to Heaven, as I had never heard, and as I know full well I shall never hear again. It was like the riving of thunderbolts above the roar of floods—elemental, prophetic, threatening, ungovernable. It did seem to me that the holy wrath of God Almighty was in that cry of the people. It was a signal. It declared that they were ready to give all that a man may give for that he loves—his life and things far dearer to him than his life. After that, they and their sons begged for a chance to throw themselves into the hideous ruin of war.

I walked slowly back to the office and wrote my article. When the Printer came in at twelve I went to his room before he had had time to begin work.

'Mr Greeley,' I said, 'here is my resignation. I am going to the war.'

His habitual smile gave way to a sober look as he turned to me, his big white coat on his arm. He pursed his lips and blew thoughtfully. Then he threw his coat in a chair and wiped his eyes with his handkerchief.

'Well! God bless you, my boy,' he said. 'I wish I could go, too.'

Chapter 38

I worked some weeks before my regiment was sent forward. I planned to be at home for a day, but they needed me on the staff, and I dreaded the pain of a parting, the gravity of which my return would serve only to accentuate. So I wrote them a cheerful letter, and kept at work. It was my duty to interview some of the great men of that day as to the course of the government. I remember Commodore Vanderbilt came down to see me in shirt-sleeves and slippers that afternoon, with a handkerchief tied about his neck in place of a collar—a blunt man, of simple manners and a big heart, one who spoke his mind in good, plain talk, and, I suppose, he got along with as little profanity as possible, considering his many cares. He called me 'boy' and spoke of a certain public man as a 'big sucker'. I soon learned that to him a 'sucker' was the lowest and meanest thing in the world. He sent me away with nothing but a great admiration of him. As a rule, the giants of that day were plain men of the people, with no frills upon them, and with a way of hitting from the shoulder. They said what they meant and meant it hard. I have heard Lincoln talk when his words had the whiz of a bullet and his arm the jerk of a piston.

John Trumbull invited McClingan, of whom I had told him much, and myself to dine with him an evening that week. I went in my new dress suit—that mark of sinful extravagance for which Fate had brought me down to the pounding of rocks under Boss McCormick. Trumbull's rooms were a feast for the eye—aglow with red roses. He introduced me to Margaret Hull and her mother, who were there to dine with us. She was a slight woman of thirty then, with a face of no striking beauty, but of singular sweetness. Her dark eyes had a mild and tender light in them; her voice a plaintive, gentle tone, the like of which one may hear rarely if ever. For years she had been a night worker in the missions of the lower city, and many an unfortunate had been turned from the way of evil by her good offices. I sat beside her at the table, and she told me of her work and how often she had met Trumbull in his night walks.

'Found me a hopeless heathen,' he remarked.

'To save him I had to consent to marry him,' she said, laughing.

'"Who hath found love is already in Heaven,"'said McClingan. 'I have not found it and I am in" he hesitated, as if searching for a synonym.

'A boarding house on William Street,' he added.

The remarkable thing about Margaret Hull was her simple faith. It looked to no glittering generality for its reward, such as the soul's highest good, much talked of in the philosophy of that time. She believed that, for every soul she saved, one jewel would be added to her crown in Heaven. And yet she wore no jewel upon her person. Her black costume was beautifully fitted to her fine form, but was almost severely plain. It occurred to me that she did not quite understand her own heart, and, for that matter, who does? But she had somewhat in her soul that passeth all understanding—I shall not try to say what, with so little knowledge of those high things, save that I know it was of God. To what patience and unwearying effort she had schooled herself I was soon to know.

'Can you not find anyone to love you?' she said, turning to McClingan. 'You know the Bible says it is not good for man to live alone.

'It does, Madame,' said he, 'but I have a mighty fear in me, remembering the twenty-fourth verse of the twenty-fifth chapter of Proverbs: "It is better to dwell in the corner of the housetops than with a brawling woman in a wide house." We cannot all be so fortunate as our friend Trumbull. But I have felt the great passion.

He smiled at her faintly as he spoke in a quiet manner, his r s coming off his tongue with a stately roll. His environment and the company had given him a fair degree of stimulation. There was a fine dignity in his deep voice, and his body bristled with it, from his stiff and heavy shock of blonde hair parted carefully on the left side, to his high-heeled boots. The few light hairs that stood in lonely abandonment on his upper lip, the rest of his lean visage always well shorn, had no small part in the grand effect of McClingan.

'A love story!' said Miss Hull. 'I do wish I had your confidence. I like a real, true love story.

'A simple stawry it is,' said McClingan, 'and Jam proud of my part in it. I shall be glad to tell the stawry if you are to hear it.'

We assured him of our interest.

'Well,' said he, 'there was one Tom Douglass at Edinburgh who was my friend and classmate. We were together a good bit of the time, and when we had come to the end of our course we both went to engage in journalism at Glasgow. We had a mighty conceit of ourselves—you know how it is, Brower, with a green lad—but we were a mind to be modest, with all our learning, so we made an agreement: I would blaw his horn and he would blaw mine. We were not to lack appreciation. He was on one paper and I on another, and every time he wrote an article I went up and down the office praising him for a man o' mighty skill, and he did the same for me. If anyone spoke of him in my hearing I said every word of flattery at my command. "What Tom Douglass?" I would say, "the man o' the Herald that's written those wonderful articles from the law court? A genius, sir! an absolute genius!" Well, we were rapidly gaining reputation. One of those days I found myself in love with as comely a lass as ever a man courted. Her mother had a proper curiosity as to my character. I referred them to Tom Douglass of the Herald—he was the only man there who had known me well. The girl and her mother both went to him.

"Your friend was just here," said the young lady, when I called again. "He is a very handsome man."

'"And a noble man!" I said.

'"And didn't I hear you say that he was a very skilful man, too?"

'"A genius!" I answered, "an absolute genius!"

McClingan stopped and laughed heartily as he took a sip of water.

'What happened then?' said Miss I-lull.

'She took him on my recommendation,' he answered. 'She said that, while he had the handsomer face, I had the more eloquent tongue. And they both won for him. And, upon me honour as a gentleman, it was the luckiest thing that ever happened to me, for she became a brawler and a scold. My mother says there is "no the like o' her in Scotland".

I shall never forget how fondly Margaret Hull patted the brown cheek of Trumbull with her delicate white band, as we rose.

'We all have our love stawries,' said McClingan.

'Mine is better than yours,' she answered, 'but it shall never be told.'

'Except one little part if it,' said Trumbull, as he put his hands upon her shoulders, and looked down into her face. 'It is the only thing that has made my life worth living.'

Then she made us to know many odd things about her work for the children of misfortune—inviting us to come and see it for ourselves. We were to go the next evening.

I finished my work at nine that night and then we walked through noisome streets and alleys—New York was then far from being so clean a city as now—to the big mission house. As we came in at the door we saw a group of women kneeling before the altar at the far end of the room, and heard the voice of Margaret Hull praying, a voice so sweet and tender that we bowed our heads at once, and listened while it quickened the life in us. She plead for the poor creatures about her, to whom Christ gave always the most abundant pity, seeing they were more sinned against than sinning. There was not a word of cant in her petition. It was full of a simple, unconscious eloquence, a higher feeling than I dare try to define. And when it was over she had won their love and confidence so that they clung to her hands and kissed them and wet them with their tears. She came and spoke to us presently, in the same sweet manner that had charmed us the night before, there was no change in it. We offered to walk home with her, but she said Trumbull was coming at twelve.

'So that is "The Little Mother" of whom I have heard so often,' said McClingan, as we came away.

'What do you think of her?' I enquired.

'Wonderful woman!' he said. 'I never heard such a voice. It gives me visions. Every other is as the crackling of thorns under a pot.'

I came back to the office and went into Mr Greeley's room to bid him goodbye. He stood by the gas jet, in a fine new suit of clothes, reading a paper, while a boy was blacking one of his boots. I sat down, awaiting a more favourable moment. A very young man had come into the room and stood timidly holding his hat.

'I wish to see Mr Greeley,' he said.

'There he is,' I answered, 'go and speak to him.'

'Mr Greeley,' said he, 'I have called to see if you can take me on the Tribune.'

The Printer continued reading as if he were the only man in the room.

The young man looked at him and then at me—with an expression that moved me to a fellow feeling. He was a country boy, more green and timid even than I had been.

'He did not hear you—try again,' I said.

'Mr Greeley,' said he, louder than before, 'I have called to see if you can take me on the Tribune.'

The editor's eyes glanced off at the boy and returned to their reading.

'No, boy, I can't,' he drawled, shifting his eyes to another article. And the boy, who was called to the service of the paper in time, but not until after his pen had made him famous, went away with a look of bitter disappointment.

In his attire Mr Greeley wore always the best material, that soon took on a friendless and dejected look. The famous white overcoat had been bought for five dollars of a man who had come by chance to the office of the New Yorker, years before, and who considered its purchase a great favour. That was a time when the price of a coat was a thing of no little importance to the Printer. Tonight there was about him a great glow, such as comes of fine tailoring and new linen.

He was so preoccupied with his paper that I went out into the big room and sat down, awaiting a better time.

'The Printer's going to Washington to talk with the president,' said an editor.

Just then Mr Greeley went running hurriedly up the spiral stair on his way to the typeroom. Three or four compositors had gone up ahead of him. He had risen out of sight when we heard a tremendous uproar above stairs. I ran up, two steps at a time, while the high voice of Mr Greeley came pouring down upon me like a flood. It had a wild, fleeting tone. He stood near the landing, swinging his arms and swearing like a boy just learning how. In the middle of the once immaculate shirt bosom was a big, yellow splash. Something had fallen on him and spattered as it struck. We stood well out of range, looking at it, undeniably the stain of nicotine. In a voice that was no encouragement to confession he dared 'the drooling idiot' to declare himself. In a moment he opened his waistcoat and surveyed the damage.

'Look at that!' he went on, complainingly. 'Ugh! The reeking, filthy, slobbering idiot! I'd rather be slain with the jaw bone of an ass.'

'You'll have to get another shirt,' said the pressman, who stood near. 'You can't go to Washington with such a breast pin.'

'I'd breast pin him if I knew who he was,' said the editor.

A number of us followed him downstairs and a young man went up the Bowery for a new shirt. When it came the Printer took off the soiled garment, flinging it into a corner, and I helped him to put himself in proper fettle again. This finished, he ran away, hurriedly, with his carpet-bag, and I missed the opportunity I wanted for a brief talk with him.

Chapter 39

My regiment left New York by night in a flare of torch and rocket. The streets were lined with crowds now hardened to the sound of fife and drum and the pomp of military preparation. I had a very high and mighty feeling in me that wore away in the discomfort of travel. For hours after the train started we sang and told stories, and ate peanuts and pulled and hauled at each other in a cloud of tobacco smoke. The train was sidetracked here and there, and dragged along at a slow pace.

Young men with no appreciation, as it seemed to me, of the sad business we were off upon, went roistering up and down the aisles, drinking out of bottles and chasing around the train as it halted. These revellers grew quiet as the night wore on. The boys began to close their eyes and lie back for rest. Some lay in the aisle, their heads upon their knapsacks. The air grew chilly and soon I could hear them snoring all about me and the chatter of frogs in the near marshes. I closed my eyes and vainly courted sleep. A great sadness had lain hold of me. I had already given up my life for my country—I was only going away now to get as dear a price for it as possible in the hood of its enemies. When and where would it be taken? I wondered. The fear had mostly gone out of me in days and nights of solemn thinking. The feeling I had, with its flavour of religion, is what has made the volunteer the mighty soldier he has ever been, I take it, since Naseby and Marston Moor. The soul is the great Captain, and with a just quarrel it will warm its sword in the enemy, however he may be trained to thrust and parry. In my sacrifice there was but one reservation—I hoped I should not be horribly cut with a sword or a bayonet. I had written a long letter to Hope, who was yet at Leipzig. I wondered if she would care what became of me. I got a sense of comfort thinking I would show her that I was no coward, with all my littleness. I had not been able to write to Uncle Eb or to my father or mother in any serious tone of my feeling in this enterprise. I had treated it as a kind of holiday from which I should return shortly to visit them.

All about me seemed to be sleeping—some of them were talking in their dreams. As it grew light, one after another rose and stretched himself, rousing his seat companion. The train halted, a man shot a musket voice in at the car door. It was loaded with the many syllables of 'Annapolis Junction'. We were pouring out of the train shortly, to bivouac for breakfast in the depot yard. So I began the life of a soldier, and how it ended with me many have read in better books than this, but my story of it is here and only here.

We went into camp there on the lonely flats of east Maryland for a day or two, as we supposed, but really for quite two weeks. In the long delay that followed, my way traversed the dead levels of routine. When Southern sympathy had ceased to wreak its wrath upon the railroads about Baltimore we pushed on to Washington. There I got letters from Uncle Eb and Elizabeth Brower. The former I have now in my box of treasures—a torn and faded remnant of that dark period.

DEAR SIR 'pen in hand to hat you know that we are all wel. also that we was sorry you could not come horn. They took on terribul. Hope she wrote a letter. Said she had not herd from you. also that somebody wrote to her you was goin to be married. You had oughter write her a letter, Bill. Looks to me so you hain't used her right. Shes a comm horn in July. Sowed corn to day in the gardin. David is off byin catul. I hope God will take care uv you, boy, so goodbye from yours truly

EBEN HOLDEN

I wrote immediately to Uncle Eb and told him of the letters I had sent to Hope, and of my effort to see her.

Late in May, after Virginia had seceded, some thirty thousand of us were sent over to the south side of the Potomac, where for weeks we tore the flowery fields, lining the shore with long entrenchments.

Meantime I wrote three letters to Mr Greeley, and had the satisfaction of seeing them in the Tribune. I took much interest in the camp drill, and before we crossed the river I had been raised to the rank of first lieutenant. Every day we were looking for the big army of Beauregard, camping below Centreville, some thirty miles south.

Almost every night a nervous picket set the camp in uproar by challenging a phantom of his imagination. We were all impatient as hounds in leash. Since they would not come up and give us battle we wanted to be off and have it out with them. And the people were tired of delay. The cry of 'ste'boy!' was ringing all over the north. They wanted to cut us loose and be through with dallying.

Well, one night the order came; we were to go south in the morning—thirty thousand of us, and put an end to the war. We did not get away until afternoon—it was the 6th of July. When we were off, horse and foot, so that I could see miles of the blue column before and behind me, I felt sorry for the mistaken South. On the evening of the 18th our camp-fires on either side of the pike at Centreville glowed like the lights of a city. We knew the enemy was near, and began to feel a tightening of the nerves. I wrote a letter to the folks at home for post mortem delivery, and put it into my trousers pocket. A friend in my company called me aside after mess.

'Feel of that,' he said, laying his hand on a full breast.

'Feathers!' he whispered significantly. 'Balls can't go through 'em, ye know. Better n a steel breastplate! Want some?

'Don't know but I do,' said I.

We went into his tent, where he had a little sack full, and put a good wad of them between my two shirts.

'I hate the idee o'bein'hit 'n the heart,' he said. 'That's too awful.

I nodded my assent.

'Shouldn't like t'have a ball in my lungs, either,' he added. "Tain't necessary fer a man t'die if he can only breathe. If a man gits his leg shot off an' don't lose his head an' keeps drawin' his breath right along smooth an even, I don't see why he can't live.

Taps sounded. We went asleep with our boots on, but nothing happened.

Three days and nights we waited. Some called it a farce, some swore, some talked of going home. I went about quietly, my bosom under its pad of feathers. The third day an order came from headquarters. We were to break camp at one-thirty in the morning and go down the pike after

Beauregard. In the dead of the night the drums sounded. I rose, half-asleep, and heard the long roll far and near. I shivered in the cold night air as I made ready, the boys about me buckled on knapsacks, shouldered their rifles, and fell into line. Muffled in darkness there was an odd silence in the great caravan forming rapidly and waiting for the word to move. At each command to move forward I could hear only the rub of leather, the click, click of rifle rings, the stir of the stubble, the snorting of horses. When we had marched an hour or so I could hear the faint rumble of wagons far in the rear. As I came high on a hill top, in the bending column, the moonlight fell upon a league of bayonets shining above a cloud of dust in the valley—a splendid picture, fading into darkness and mystery. At dawn we passed a bridge and halted some three minutes for a bite. After a little march we left the turnpike, with Hunter's column bearing westward on a crossroad that led us into thick woods. As the sunlight sank in the high tree-tops the first great battle of the war began. Away to the left of us a cannon shook the earth, hurling its boom into the still air. The sound rushed over us, rattling in the timber like a fall of rocks. Something went quivering in me. It seemed as if my vitals had gone into a big lump of jelly that trembled every step I took. We quickened our pace; we fretted, we complained. The weariness went out of our legs; some wanted to run. Before and behind us men were shouting hotly, 'Run, boys! run!' The cannon roar was now continuous. We could feel the quake of it. When we came over a low ridge, in the open, we could see the smoke of battle in the valley. Flashes of fire and hoods of smoke leaped out of the far thickets, left of us, as cannon roared. Going at double quick we began loosening blankets and haversacks, tossing them into heaps along the line of march, without halting. In half an hour we stood waiting in battalions, the left flank of the enemy in front. We were to charge at a run. Half-way across the valley we were to break into companies and, advancing, spread into platoons and squads, and at last into line of skirmishers, lying down for cover between rushes.

'Forward!' was the order, and we were off, cheering as we ran. O, it was a grand sight! our colours flying, our whole front moving, like a blue wave on a green, immeasurable sea. And it had a voice like that of many waters. Out of the woods ahead of us came a lightning flash. A ring of smoke reeled upward. Then came a deafening crash of thunders—one upon another, and the scream of shells overhead. Something stabbed into our column right beside me. Many went headlong, crying out as they fell. Suddenly the colours seemed to halt and sway like a tree-top in the wind. Then down they went!—squad and colours—and we spread to pass them. At the order we halted and laid down and fired volley after volley at the grey coats in the edge of the thicket A bullet struck in the grass ahead of me, throwing a bit of dirt into my eyes. Another brushed my hat off and I heard a wailing death yell behind me. The colonel rode up waving a sword.

'Get up an' charge!' he shouted.

On we went, cheering loudly, firing as we ran, Bullets went by me hissing in my ears, and I kept trying to dodge them. We dropped again flat on our faces.

A squadron of black-horse cavalry came rushing out of the woods at us, the riders yelling as they waved their swords. Fortunately we had not time to rise. A man near me tried to get up.

'Stay down!' I shouted.

In a moment I learned something new about horses. They went over us like a flash. I do not think a man was trampled. Our own cavalry kept them busy as soon as they had passed.

Of the many who had started there was only a ragged remnant near me. We fired a dozen volleys lying there. The man at my elbow rolled upon me, writhing like a worm in the fire.

'We shall all be killed!' a man shouted. 'Where is the colonel?'

'Dead,' said another.

'Better retreat,' said a third.

'Charge!' I shouted as loudly as ever I could, jumping to my feet and waving my sabre as I rushed forward. 'Charge!'

It was the one thing needed—they followed me. In a moment we had hurled ourselves upon the grey line thrusting with sword and bayonet.

They broke before us—some running, some fighting desperately.

A man threw a long knife at me out of a sling. Instinctively I caught the weapon as if it had been a ball hot off the bat. In doing so I dropped my sabre and was cut across the fingers. He came at me fiercely, clubbing his gun—a raw-boned, swarthy giant, broad as a barn door. I caught the barrel as it came down. He tried to wrench it away, but I held firmly. Then he began to push up to me. I let him come, and in a moment we were grappling hip and thigh. He was a powerful man, but that was my kind of warfare. It gave me comfort when I felt the grip of his hands. I let him tug a jiffy, and then caught him with the old hiplock, and he went under me so hard I could hear the crack of his bones. Our support came then. We made him prisoner, with some two hundred other men. Reserves came also and took away the captured guns. My comrades gathered about me, cheering, but I had no suspicion of what they meant. I thought it a tribute to my wrestling. Men lay thick there back of the guns—some dead, some calling faintly for help. The red puddles about them were covered with flies; ants were crawling over their faces. I felt a kind of sickness and turned away.

What was left of my regiment formed in fours to join the advancing column. Horses were galloping riderless, rein and stirrup flying, some horribly wounded. One hobbled near me, a front leg gone at the knee.

Shells were flying overhead; cannonballs were ricocheting over the level valley, throwing turf in the air, tossing the dead and wounded that lay thick and helpless.

Some were crumpled like a rag, as if the pain of death had withered them in their clothes; some swollen to the girth of horses; some bent backward, with arms outreaching like one trying an odd trick, some lay as if listening eagerly, an ear close to the ground; some like a sleeper, their heads upon their arms; one shrieked loudly, gesturing with bloody hands, 'Lord God Almighty, have mercy on me!

I had come suddenly to a new world, where the lives of men were cheaper than blind puppies. I was a new sort of creature, and reckless of what came, careless of all I saw and heard.

A staff officer stepped up to me as we joined the main body.

'You ve been shot, young man,' he said, pointing to my left hand.

Before he could turn I felt a rush of air and saw him fly into pieces, some of which hit me as I fell backward. I did not know what had happened; I know not now more than that I have written. I remember feeling something under me, like a stick of wood, bearing hard upon my ribs. I tried to roll off it, but somehow, it was tied to me and kept hurting. I put my hand over my hip and felt it there behind me—my own arm! The hand was like that of a dead man—cold and senseless. I pulled it from under me and it lay helpless; it could not lift itself. I knew now that I, too, had become one of the bloody horrors of the battle.

I struggled to my feet, weak and trembling, and sick with nausea. I must have been lying there a long time. The firing was now at a distance: the sun had gone half down the sky. They were picking up the wounded in the near field. A man stood looking at me. 'Good God!' he shouted, and then ran away like one afraid. There was a great mass of our men back of me some twenty rods. I staggered toward them, my knees quivering.

'I can never get there,' I heard myself whisper.

I thought of my little flask of whiskey, and, pulling the cork with my teeth, drank the half of it. That steadied me and I made better headway. I could hear the soldiers talking as I neared them.

'Look a there!' I heard many saying. 'See 'em come! My God! Look at 'em on the hill there!

The words went quickly from mouth to mouth. In a moment I could hear the murmur of thousands. I turned to see what they were looking at. Across the valley there was a long ridge, and back of it the main position of the Southern army. A grey host was pouring over it—thousand upon thousand—in close order, debouching into the valley.

A big force of our men lay between us and them. As I looked I could see a mighty stir in it. Every man of them seemed to be jumping up in the air. From afar came the sound of bugles calling 'retreat, the shouting of men, the rumbling of wagons. It grew louder. An officer rode by me hatless, and halted, shading his eyes. Then he rode back hurriedly.

'Hell has broke loose!' he shouted, as he passed me.

The blue-coated host was rushing towards us like a flood: artillery, cavalry, infantry, wagon train. There was a mighty uproar in the men behind me—a quick stir of feet. Terror spread over them like the travelling of fire. It shook their tongues. The crowd began caving at the edge and jamming at the centre. Then it spread like a swarm of bees shaken off a bush.

'Run! Run for your lives!' was a cry that rose to heaven.

'Halt, you cowards!' an officer shouted.

It was now past three o clock.

The raw army had been on its feet since midnight. For hours it had been fighting hunger, a pain in the legs, a quivering sickness at the stomach, a stubborn foe. It had turned the flank of Beauregard; victory was in sight. But lo! a new enemy was coming to the fray, innumerable, unwearied, eager for battle. The long slope bristled with his bayonets. Our army looked and cursed and began letting go. The men near me were pausing on the brink of awful rout. In a moment they were off, pell-mell, like a flock of sheep. The earth shook under them. Officers rode around them, cursing, gesticulating, threatening, but nothing could stop them. Half a dozen trees had stood in the centre of the roaring mass. Now a few men clung to them—a remnant of the monster that had torn away. But the greater host was now coming. The thunder of its many feet was near me; a cloud of dust hung over it. A squadron of cavalry came rushing by and broke into the fleeing mass. Heavy horses, cut free from artillery, came galloping after them, straps flying over foamy flanks. Two riders clung to the back of each, lashing with whip and rein. The nick of wagons came after them, wheels rattling, horses running, voices shrilling in a wild hoot of terror. It makes me tremble even now, as I think of it, though it is muffled under the cover of nearly forty years! I saw they would go over me. Reeling as if drunk, I ran to save myself. Zigzagging over the field I came upon a grey-bearded soldier lying in the grass and fell headlong. I struggled madly, but could not rise to my feet. I lay, my face upon the ground, weeping like a woman. Save I be lost in hell, I shall never know again the bitter pang of that moment. I thought of my country. I saw its splendid capital in ruins; its people surrendered to God's enemies.

The rout of wagons had gone by I could now hear the heavy tramp of thousands passing me, the shrill voices of terror. I worked to a sitting posture somehow—the effort nearly smothered me. A mass of cavalry was bearing down upon me. They were coming so thick I saw they would trample me into jelly. In a flash I thought of what Uncle Eb had told me once. I took my hat and covered my face quickly, and then uncovered it as they came near. They sheared away as I felt the foam of their nostrils. I had split them as a rock may split the torrent. The last of them went over me—their tails whipping my face. I shall not soon forget the look of their bellies or the smell of their wet flanks. They had no sooner passed than I fell back and rolled half over like a log. I could feel a warm flow of blood trickling down my left arm. A shell, shot at the retreating army, passed high above me, whining as it flew. Then my mind went free of its trouble. The rain brought me to as it came pelting down upon the side of my face. I wondered what it might be, for I knew not where I had come. I lifted my head and looked to see a new dawn—possibly the city of God itself. It was dark—so dark I felt as if I had no eyes. Away in the distance I could hear the beating of a drum. It rang in a great silence—I have never known the like of it. I could hear the fall and trickle of the rain, but it seemed only to deepen the silence. I felt the wet grass under my face and hands. Then I knew it was night and the battlefield where I had fallen. I was alive and might see another day—thank God! I felt something move under my feet I heard a whisper at my shoulder.

'Thought you were dead long ago,' it said.

'No, no,' I answered, 'I'm alive—I know I'm alive—this is the battlefield.

''Fraid I ain't goin' t' live,' he said. 'Got a terrible wound. Wish it was morning.'

'Dark long?' I asked.

'For hours,' he answered. 'Dunno how many.'

He began to groan and utter short prayers.

'O, my soul waiteth for the Lord more than they that watch for the morning,' I heard him cry in a loud, despairing voice.

Then there was a bit of silence, in which I could hear him whispering of his home and people.

Presently he began to sing:

'Guide me, O thou great Jehovah!

Pilgrim through this barren land

I am weak but thou art mighty'

His voice broke and trembled and sank into silence.

I had business of my own to look after—perhaps I had no time to lose—and I went about it calmly. I had no strength to move and began to feel the nearing of my time. The rain was falling faster. It chilled me to the marrow as I felt it trickling over my back. I called to the man who lay beside me—again and again I called to him—but got no answer. Then I knew that he was dead and I alone. Long after that in the far distance I heard a voice calling. It rang like a trumpet in the still air. It grew plainer as I listened. My own name! William Brower? It was certainly calling to me, and I answered with a feeble cry. In a moment I could hear the tramp of someone coming. He was sitting beside me presently, whoever it might be. I could not see him for the dark. His tongue went clucking as if he pitied me.

'Who are you?' I remember asking, but got no answer.

At first I was glad, then I began to feel a mighty horror of him.

In a moment he had picked me up and was making off. The jolt of his step seemed to be breaking my arms at the shoulder. As I groaned he ran. I could see nothing in the darkness, but he went ahead, never stopping, save for a moment, now and then, to rest I wondered where he was taking me and what it all meant. I called again, 'Who are you?' but he seemed not to hear me. 'My God!' I whispered to myself, 'this is no man—this is Death severing the soul from the body. The voice was that of the good God.' Then I heard a man hailing near by.

'Help, Help!' I shouted faintly.

'Where are you?' came the answer, now further away. 'Can't see you.' My mysterious bearer was now running. My heels were dragging upon the ground; my hands were brushing the grass tops. I groaned with pain.

'Halt! Who comes there?' a picket called. Then I could hear voices.

'Did you hear that noise?' said one. 'Somebody passed me. So dark can't see my hand before me.

'Darker than hell!' said another voice.

It must be a giant, I thought, who can pick me up and carry me as if I were no bigger than a house cat. That was what I was thinking when I swooned.

From then till I came to myself in the little church at Centreville I remember nothing. Groaning men lay all about me; others stood between them with lanterns. A woman was bending over me. I felt the gentle touch of her hand upon my face and heard her speak to me so tenderly I cannot think of it, even now, without thanking God for good women. I clung to her hand, clung with the energy of one drowning, while I suffered the merciful torture of the probe, the knife and the needle. And when it was all over and the lantern lights grew pale in the dawn I fell asleep.

But enough of blood and horror. War is no holiday, my merry people, who know not the mighty blessing of peace. Counting the cost, let us have war, if necessary, but peace, peace if possible.

Chapter 40

But now I have better things to write of, things that have some relish of good in them. I was very weak and low from loss of blood for days, and, suddenly, the tide turned. I had won recognition for distinguished gallantry they told me—that day they took me to Washington. I lay three weeks there in the hospital. As soon as they heard of my misfortune at home Uncle Eb wrote he was coming to see me. I stopped him by a telegram, assuring him that I was nearly well and would be home shortly.

My term of enlistment had expired when they let me out a fine day in mid August. I was going home for a visit as sound as any man but, in the horse talk of Faraway, I had a little 'blemish'on the left shoulder. Uncle Eb was to meet me at the jersey City depot. Before going I, with others who had been complimented for bravery, went to see the president. There were some twenty of us summoned to meet him that day. It was warm and the great Lincoln sat in his shirt-sleeves at a desk in the middle of his big office. He wore a pair of brown carpet slippers, the rolling collar and black stock now made so familiar in print. His hair was tumbled. He was writing hurriedly when we came in. He laid his pen away and turned to us without speaking. There was a careworn look upon his solemn face.

'Mr President,' said the general, who had come with us, 'here are some of the brave men of our army, whom you wished to see.

He came and shook hands with each and thanked us in the name of the republic, for the example of courage and patriotism we and many others had given to the army. He had a lean, tall, ungraceful figure and he spoke his mind without any frill or flourish. He said only a few words of good plain talk and was done with us.

'Which is Brower?' he enquired presently.

I came forward more scared than ever I had been before.

'My son,' he said, taking my hand in his, 'why didn't you run?'

'Didn't dare,' I answered. 'I knew it was more dangerous to run away than to go forward.'

'Reminds me of a story,' said he smiling. 'Years ago there was a bully in Sangamon County, Illinois, that had the reputation of running faster and fighting harder than any man there. Everybody thought he was a terrible fighter. He'd always get a man on the run; then he'd ketch up and give him a licking. One day he tadded a lame man. The lame man licked him in a minute.

'"Why didn't ye run?" somebody asked the victor.

'"Didn't dast," said he. "Run once when he tackled me an I've been lame ever since."

"How did ye manage to lick him?" said the other.

'"Wall," said he, "I hed to, an' I done it easy."

'That's the way it goes,' said the immortal president, 'ye do it easy if ye have to.

He reminded me in and out of Horace Greeley, although they looked no more alike than a hawk and a handsaw. But they had a like habit of forgetting themselves and of saying neither more nor less than they meant. They both had the strength of an ox and as little vanity. Mr Greeley used to say that no man could amount to anything who worried much about the fit of his trousers; neither of them ever encountered that obstacle.

Early next morning I took a train for home. I was in soldier clothes I had with me, no others—and all in my car came to talk with me about the now famous battle of Bull Run.

The big platform at Jersey City was crowded with many people as we got off the train. There were other returning soldiers—some with crutches, some with empty sleeves.

A band at the further end of the platform was playing and those near me were singing the familiar music,

'John Brown's body lies a mouldering in the grave.

Somebody shouted my name. Then there rose a cry of three cheers for Brower. It's some of the boys of the Tribune, I thought—I could see a number of them in the crowd. One brought me a basket of flowers. I thought they were trying to have fun with me.

'Thank you!' said I, 'but what is the joke?'

'No joke,' he said. 'It's to honour a hero.'

'Oh, you wish me to give it to somebody.'

I was warming with embarrassment

'We wish you to keep it,' he answered.

In accounts of the battle I had seen some notice of my leading a charge but my fame had gone farther—much farther indeed—than I knew. I stood a moment laughing—an odd sort of laugh it was that had in it the salt of tears—and waving my hand to the many who were now calling my name.

In the uproar of cheers and waving of handkerchiefs I could not find Uncle Eb for a moment. When I saw him in the breaking crowd he was cheering lustily and waving his hat above his head. His enthusiasm increased when I stood before him. As I was greeting him I heard a lively rustle of skirts. Two dainty, gloved hands laid hold of mine; a sweet voice spoke my name. There, beside me, stood the tall, erect figure of Hope. Our eyes met and, before there was any thinking of propriety, I had her in my arms and was kissing her and she was kissing me.

It thrilled me to see the splendour of her beauty that day; her eyes wet with feeling as they looked up at me; to feel again the trembling touch of her lips. In a moment I turned to Uncle Eb.

'Boy,' he said, 'I thought you...' and then he stopped and began brushing his coat sleeve.

'Come on now,' he added as he took my grip away from me. 'We're goin' t' hev a gran' good time. I'll take ye all to a splendid tavern somewheres. An' I ain't goin' to count the cost nuther.

He was determined to carry my grip for me. Hope had a friend with her who was going north in the morning on our boat. We crossed the ferry and took a Broadway omnibus, while query followed query.

'Makes me feel like a flapjack t'ride 'n them things,' said Uncle Eb as we got out.

He hired a parlour and two bedrooms for us all at the St Nicholas.

'Purty middlin' steep!' he said to me as we left the office. 'It is, sartin! but I don't care—not a bit. When folks has to hev a good time they've got t' hev it.

We were soon seated in our little parlour. There was a great glow of health and beauty in Hope's face. It was a bit fuller but had nobler outlines and a colouring as delicate as ever. She wore a plain grey gown admirably fitted to her plump figure. There was a new and splendid 'dignity in her carriage, her big blue eyes, her nose with its little upward slant. She was now the well groomed young woman of society in the full glory of her youth.

Uncle Eb who sat between us pinched her cheek playfully. A little spot of white showed a moment where his fingers had been. Then the pink flooded over it.

'Never see a girl git such a smack as you did,' he said laughing.

'Well,' said she, smiling, 'I guess I gave as good as I got.'

'Served him right,' he said. 'You kissed back good 'n hard. Gran sport!' he added turning to me.

'Best I ever had,' was my humble acknowledgement.

'Seldom ever see a girl kissed so powerful,' he said as he took Hope's hand in his. 'Now if the Bible said when a body kissed ye on one cheek ye mus' turn if other I wouldn't find no fault. But ther's a heap o differ'nce 'tween a whack an' a smack.

When we had come back from dinner Uncle Eb drew off his boots and sat comfortably in his stocking feet while Hope told of her travels and I of my soldiering. She had been at the Conservatory, nearly the whole period of her absence, and hastened home when she learned of the battle and of my wound. She had landed two days before.

Hope's friend and Uncle Eb went away to their rooms in good season. Then I came and sat beside Hope on the sofa.

'Let's have a good talk,' I said.

There was an awkward bit of silence.

'Well,' said she, her fan upon her lips, 'tell me more about the war.

'Tired of war,' I answered; 'love is a better subject.

She rose and walked up and down the room, a troubled look in her face. I thought I had never seen a woman who could carry her head so proudly.

'I don't think you are very familiar with it,' said she presently.

'I ought to be,' I answered, 'having loved you all these years.

'But you told me that—that you loved another girl,' she said, her elbow leaning on the mantel, her eyes looking down soberly.

'When? Where?' I asked.

'In Mrs Fuller's parlour.'

'Hope,' I said, 'you misunderstood me; I meant you.

She came toward me, then, looking up into my eyes. I started to embrace her but she caught my hands and held them apart and came close to me.

'Did you say that you meant me?' she asked in a whisper.

'I did.'

'Why did you not tell me that night?

'Because you would not listen to me and we were interrupted.

'Well if I loved a girl,' she said, 'I'd make her listen.'

'I would have done that but Mrs Fuller saved you.'

'You might have written,' she suggested in a tone of injury.

'I did.'

'And the letter never came—just as I feared.'

She looked very sober and thoughtful then.

'You know our understanding that day in the garden,' she added. 'If you did not ask me again I was to know you—you did not love me any longer. That was long, long ago.

'I never loved any girl but you,' I said. 'I love you now, Hope, and that is enough—I love you so there is nothing else for me. You are dearer than my life. It was the thought of you that made me brave in battle. I wish I could be as brave here. But I demand your surrender—I shall give you no quarter now.

'I wish I knew,' she said, 'whether—whether you really love me or not?

'Don't you believe me, Hope?

'Yes, I believe you,' she said, 'but—but you might not know your own heart.

'It longs for you,' I said, 'it keeps me thinking of you always. Once it was so easy to be happy; since you have been away it has seemed as if there were no longer any light in the world or any pleasure. It has made me a slave. I did not know that love was such a mighty thing.

'Love is no Cupid—he is a giant,' she said, her voice trembling with emotion as mine had trembled. 'I tried to forget and he crushed me under his feet as if to punish me.

She was near to crying now, but she shut her lips firmly and kept back the tears. God grant me I may never forget the look in her eyes that moment. She came closer to me. Our lips touched; my arms held her tightly.

'I have waited long for this,' I said—'the happiest moment of my life! I thought I had lost you.

'What a foolish man,' she whispered. 'I have loved you for years and years and you—you could not see it, I believe now.'

She hesitated a moment, her eyes so close to my cheek I could feel the beat of their long lashes.

'That God made you for me,' she added.

'Love is God's helper,' I said. 'He made us for each other.

'I thank Him for it—I do love you so,' she whispered.

The rest is the old, old story. They that have not lived it are to be pitied.

When we sat down at length she told me what I had long suspected, that Mrs Fuller wished her to marry young Livingstone.

'But for Uncle Eb,' she added, 'I think I should have done so—for I had given up all hope of you.'

'Good old Uncle Eb!' I said. 'Let's go and tell him.

He was sound asleep when we entered his room but woke as I lit the gas.

'What's the matter?' he whispered, lifting his head.

'Congratulate us,' I said. 'We're engaged.

'Hey ye conquered her?' he enquired smiling.

'Love has conquered us both,' I said.

'Wall, I swan! is thet so?' he answered. 'Guess I won't fool away any more time here in bed. If you childen'll go in t'other room I'll slip into my trousers an' then ye'll hear me talk some conversation.

'Beats the world!' he continued, coming in presently, buttoning his suspenders. 'I thought mos' likely ye'd hitch up t'gether sometime. 'Tain't often ye can find a pair s'well matched. The same style an gaited jest about alike. When ye goin' t' git married?

'She hasn't named the day,' I said.

'Sooner the better,' said Uncle Eb as he drew on his coat and sat down. 'Used to be so t'when a young couple hed set up 'n held each other's han's a few nights they was ready fer the minister. Wish't ye could fix it fer 'bout Crissmus time, by jingo! They's other things goin' to happen then. S'pose yer s'happy now ye can stan' a little bad news. I've got to tell ye—David's been losin' money. Hain't never wrote ye 'bout it—not a word—'cause I didn't know how 'twas comin' out.

'How did he lose it?' I enquired.

'Wall ye know that Ow Barker—runs a hardware store in Migleyville—he sold him a patent right. Figgered an' argued night an' day fer more 'n three weeks. It was a new fangled wash biler. David he thought he see a chance if put out agents an' make a great deal o'money. It did look jest as easy as slidin' downhill but when we come slide—wall, we found out we was at the bottom o the hill 'stid o' the top an' it wan't reel good slidin. He paid five thousan' dollars fer the right o'ten counties. Then bym bye Barker he wanted him t'go security fer fifteen hunderd bilers thet he was hevin' made. I to!' David he hedn't better go in no deeper but Barker, he promised big things an' seemed to be sech a nice man 'at fin'ly David he up 'n done it. Wall he's hed 'em t' pay fer an' the fact is it costs s'much if sell 'em it eats up all the profits.

'Looks like a swindle,' I said indignantly.

'No,' said Uncle Eb, "tain't no swindle. Barker thought he hed a gran' good thing. He got fooled an' the fool complaint is very ketchin'. Got it myself years ago an' I've been doctorin' fer it ever sence.

The story of David's undoing hurt us sorely. He had gone the way of most men who left the farm late in life with unsatisfied ambition.

'They shall never want for anything, so long as I have my health,' I said.

'I have four hundred dollars in the bank,' said Hope, 'and shall give them every cent of it.

'Tain' nuthin'if worry over,' said Uncle Eb. 'If I don' never lose more'n a little money I shan't feel terrible bad. We're all young yit. Got more'n a million dollars wuth o' good health right here 'n this room. So well, I'm 'shamed uv it! Man's more decent if he's a leetle bit sickly. An' thet there girl Bill's agreed t'marry ye! Why! 'Druther hev her 'n this hull city o' New York.

'So had I,' was my answer.

'Wall, you am'no luckier 'n she is—not a bit,' he added. 'A good man's better 'n a gol'mine ev'ry time.

'Who knows,' said Hope. 'He may be president someday.

'Ther's one thing I hate,' Uncle El continued. 'That's the idee o hevin' the woodshed an' barn an' garret full o' them infernal wash bilers. Ye can't take no decent care uv a hoss there 'n the stable' they're so piled up. One uv 'em tumbled down top o' me t'other day. 'Druther 'twould a been a panther. Made me s'mad I took a club an' knocked that biler into a cocked hat. 'Tain't right! I'm sick o' the sight uv 'em.

'They'll make a good bonfire someday,' said Hope.

'Don't believe they'd burn,' he answered sorrowfully, 'they're tin.

'Couldn't we bury 'em?' I suggested.

'Be a purty costly funeral,' he answered thoughtfully. 'Ye'd hev to dig a hole deeper n Tupper's dingle.

'Couldn't you give them away?' I enquired.

'Wall,' said he, helping himself to a chew of tobacco, 'we ve tried thet. Gin 'em t'everybody we know but there ain't folks enough' there's such a slew o'them bilers. We could give one to ev'ry man, woman an' child in Faraway an' hex enough left t'fill an acre lot. Dan Perry druv in t'other day with a double buggy. We gin him one fer his own fam'ly. It was heavy t'carry an' he didn't seem t' like the looks uv it someway. Then I asked him if he wouldn't like one fer his girl. "She ain't married," says he. "She will be some time," says I, "take it along," so he put in another. "You've got a sister over on the turnpike hain't ye?" says I. "Yes," says he. "Wall," I says, "don' want a hex her feel slighted." "She won't know 'bout my hevin' 'em," says he, lookin' 's if he'd hed enough. "Yis she will," I says, "she'll hear uv it an' mebbe make a fuss." Then we piled in another. "Look here," I says after that, "there s yer brother Bill up there 'bove you. Take one along fer him." "No," says he, "I don' tell ev'ry body, but Bill an' I ain't on good terms. We ain't spoke fer more'n a year."

'Knew he was lyin',' Uncle Eb added with a laugh, 'I'd seen him talkin' with Bill a day er two before.

'Whew!' he whistled as he looked at his big silver watch. 'I declare it's mos' one o'clock They's jes' one other piece o' business to come before this meetin'. Double or single, want ye to both promise me t'be hum Crissmus.

We promised.

'Now childern,' said he. "S time to go to bed. B'lieve ye'd stan' there swappin' kisses 'till ye was kner sprung if I didn't tell ye t' quit.

Hope came and put her arms about his neck, fondly, and kissed him good-night.

'Did Bill prance right up like a man?' he asked, his hand upon her shoulder.

'Did very well,' said she, smiling, 'for a man with a wooden leg.

Uncle Eb sank into a chair, laughing heartily, and pounding his knee. It seemed he had told her that I was coming home with a wooden leg! 'That is the reason I held your arm,' she said. 'I was expecting to hear it squeak every moment as we left the depot. But when I saw that you walked so naturally I knew Uncle Eb had been trying to fool me.

'Purty good sort uv a lover, ain't he?' said he after we were done laughing.

'He wouldn't take no for an answer,' she answered.

'He was alwuss a gritty cuss,' said Uncle Eb, wiping his eyes with a big red handkerchief as he rose to go. 'Ye'd oughter be mighty happy an' ye will, too—their am'no doubt uv it—not a bit. Trouble with most young folks is they wan' to fly tew high, these days. If they'd only fly clus enough t'the ground so the could alwuss touch one foot, they'd be all right. Glad ye ain't thet kind.

We were off early on the boat—as fine a summer morning as ever dawned. What with the grandeur of the scenery and the sublimity of our happiness it was a delightful journey we had that day. I felt the peace and beauty of the fields, the majesty of the mirrored cliffs and mountains, but the fair face of her I loved was enough for me. Most of the day Uncle Eb sat near us and I remember a woman evangelist came and took a seat beside him, awhile, talking volubly of the scene.

'My friend,' said she presently, 'are you a Christian?

'Fore I answer I'll hev to tell ye a story,' said Uncle Eb. 'I recollec' a man by the name o' Ranney over 'n Vermont—he was a pious man. Got into an argyment an' a feller slapped him in the face. Ranney turned t'other side an' then t'other an' the feller kep' a slappin' hot 'n heavy. It was jes' like strappin' a razor fer half a minnit. Then Ranney sailed in—gin him the wust lickin' he ever hed.

'"I declare," says another man, after 'twas all over, "I thought you was a Christian."

"Am up to a cert in p'int," says he. "Can't go tew fur not 'n these parts—men are tew powerful. 'Twon't do 'less ye wan' to die sudden. When he begun poundin' uv me I see I wan't eggzac'ly prepared."

"Fraid 's a good deal thet way with most uv us. We're Christians up to a cert'in p'int. Fer one thing, I think if a man'll stan' still an' see himself knocked into the nex' world he's a leetle tew good fer this.'

The good lady began to preach and argue. For an hour Uncle Eb sat listening unable to get in a word. When, at last, she left him he came to us a look of relief in his face.

'I b'lieve,' said he, 'if Balaam's ass hed been rode by a woman he never 'd hev spoke.'

'Why not?' I enquired.

'Never'd hev hed a chance,' Uncle Eb added.

We were two weeks at home with mother and father and Uncle Eb. It was a delightful season of rest in which Hope and I went over the sloping roads of Faraway and walked in the fields and saw the harvesting. She had appointed Christmas Day for our wedding and I was not to go again to the war, for now my first duty was to my own people. If God prospered me they were all to come to live with us in town and, though slow to promise, I could see it gave them comfort to know we were to be for them ever a staff and refuge.

And the evening before we came back to town Jed Feary was with us and Uncle Eb played his flute and sang the songs that had been the delight of our childhood.

The old poet read these lines written in memory of old times in Faraway and of Hope's girlhood.

'The red was in the clover an' the blue was in the sky:

There was music in the meadow, there was dancing in the rye;

An' I heard a voice a calling to the flocks o' Faraway

An' its echo in the wooded hills—Go'day! Go'day! Go'day!

O fair was she—my lady love—an' lithe as the willow tree,

An' aye my heart remembers well her parting words t' me.

An' I was sad as a beggar-man but she was blithe an' gay

An' I think o' her as I call the flocks Go'day! Go'day! Go'day!

Her cheeks they stole the dover's red, her lips the odoured air,

An' the glow o' the morning sunlight she took away in her hair;

Her voice had the meadow music, her form an' her laughing eye

Have taken the blue o' the heavens an' the grace o' the bending rye.

My love has robbed the summer day—the field, the sky, the dell,

She has taken their treasures with her, she has taken my heart as well;

An' if ever, in the further fields, her feet should go astray

May she hear the good God calling her Go'day! Go'day! Go'day!

Chapter 41

I got a warm welcome on Monkey Hill. John Trumbull came to dine with us at the chalet the evening of my arrival. McGlingan had become editor-in-chief of a new daily newspaper. Since the war began Mr Force had found ample and remunerative occupation writing the 'Obituaries of Distinguished Persons. He sat between Trumbull and McGlingan at table and told again of the time he had introduced the late Daniel Webster to the people of his native town.

Reciting a passage of the immortal Senator he tipped his beer into the lap of McClingan. He ceased talking and sought pardon.

'It is nothing, Force—nothing,' said the Scotchman, with great dignity, as he wiped his coat and trousers. 'You will pardon me if I say that I had rather be drenched in beer than soaked in recollections.

'That's all right,' said Mr Opper, handing him a new napkin. 'Yes, in the midst of such affliction I should call it excellent fun, McClingan added. 'If you ever die, Force, I will preach the sermon without charge.

'On what text?' the obituary editor enquired.

'"There remaineth therefore, a rest for the people of God,"'quoth McClingan solemnly. 'Hebrews, fourth chapter and ninth verse.

'If I continue to live with you I shall need it,' said Force.

'And if I endure to the end,' said McClingan, 'I shall have excellent Christian discipline; I shall feel like opening my mouth and making a loud noise.

McGlingan changed his garments and then came into my room and sat with us awhile after dinner.

'One needs ear lappers and a rubber coat at that table,' said he.

'And a chest protector,' I suggested, remembering the finger of Force.

'I shall be leaving here soon, Brower,' said McGlingan as he lit a cigar.

'Where shall you go?' I asked.

'To my own house.

'Going to hire a housekeeper?

'Going to marry one,' said he.

'That's funny,' I said. We're all to be married—every man of us.

'By Jove!' said McClingan, 'this is a time for congratulation. God save us and grant for us all the best woman in the world.

Chapter 42

For every man he knew and loved Mr Greeley had a kindness that filled him to the fingertips. When I returned he smote me on the breast—an unfailing mark of his favour—and doubled my salary.

'If he ever smites you on the breast,' McClingan had once said to me, 'turn the other side, for, man, your fortune is made.'

And there was some truth in the warning.

He was writing when I came in. A woman sat beside him talking. An immense ham lay on the marble top of the steam radiator; a basket of eggs sat on the floor near Mr Greeley's desk All sorts of merchandise were sent to the Tribune those days, for notice, and sold at auction, to members of the staff, by Mr Dana.

'Yes, yes, Madame, go on, I hear you,' said the great editor, as his pen flew across the white page.

She asked him then for a loan of money. He continued writing but, presently, his left hand dove into his trousers pocket coming up full of bills.

'Take what you want,' said he, holding it toward her, 'and please go for I am very busy.' Whereupon she helped herself liberally and went away.

Seeing me, Mr Greeley came and shook my hand warmly and praised me fer a good soldier.

'Going down town,' he said in a moment, drawing on his big white overcoat, 'walk along with me—won't you?

We crossed the park, he leading me with long strides. As we walked he told how he had been suffering from brain fever. Passing St Paul's churchyard he brushed the iron pickets with his hand as if to try the feel of them. Many turned to stare at him curiously. He asked me, soon, if I would care to do a certain thing for the Tribune, stopping, to look in at a shop window, as I answered him. I waited while he did his errand at a Broadway shop; then we came back to the office. The publisher was in Mr Greeley's room.

'Where's my ham, Dave?' said the editor as he looked at the slab of marble where the ham had lain.

'Don't know for sure,' said the publisher, 'it's probably up at the house of the—editor by this time.

'What did you go 'n give it to him for?' drawled Mr Greeley in a tone of irreparable injury. 'I wanted that ham for myself.

'I didn't give it to him,' said the publisher. 'He came and helped himself. Said he supposed it was sent in for notice.

'The infernal thief!' Mr Greeley piped with a violent gesture. 'I'll swear! if I didn't keep my shirt buttoned tight they'd have that, too.

The ham was a serious obstacle in the way of my business and it went over until evening. But that and like incidents made me to know the man as I have never seen him pictured—a boy grown old and grey, pushing the power of manhood with the ardours of youth.

I resumed work on the Tribune that week. My first assignment was a mass meeting in a big temporary structure—then called a wigwam—over in Brooklyn. My political life began that day and all by an odd chance. The wigwam was crowded to the doors. The audience bad been waiting half an hour for the speaker. The chairman had been doing his best to kill time but had run out of ammunition. He had sat down to wait, an awkward silence had begun. The crowd was stamping and whistling and clapping with impatience. As I walked down the centre aisle, to the reporter's table, they seemed to mistake me for the speaker. Instantly a great uproar began. It grew louder every step I took. I began to wonder and then to fear the truth. As I neared the stage the chairman came forward beckoning to me. I went to the flight of steps leading up to that higher level of distinguished citizens and halted, not knowing just what to do. He came and leaned over and whispered down at me. I remember he was red in the face and damp with perspiration.

'What is your name?' he enquired.

'Brower,' said I in a whisper.

A look of relief came into his face and I am sure a look of anxiety came into mine. He had taken the centre of the stage before I could stop him.

'Lathes and gentlemen,' said he, 'I am glad to inform you that General Brower has at last arrived.

I remembered then there was a General Brower in the army who was also a power in politics.

In the storm of applause that followed this announcement, I beckoned him to the edge of the platform again. I was nearer a condition of mental panic than I have ever known since that day.

'I am not General Brower,' I whispered.

'What!' said he in amazement.

'I am not General Brower,' I said.

'Great heavens!' he whispered, covering his mouth with his band and looking very thoughtful. 'You'll have to make a speech, anyway—there's no escape.

I could see no way out of it and, after a moment's hesitation, ascended the platform took off my overcoat and made a speech.

Fortunately the issue was one with which I had been long familiar. I told them how I had been trapped. The story put the audience in good humour and they helped me along with very generous applause. And so began my career in politics which has brought me more honour than I deserved although I know it has not been wholly without value to my country. It enabled me to repay in part the kindness of my former chief at a time when he was sadly in need of friends. I remember meeting him in Washington a day of that exciting campaign of '72. I was then in Congress.

'I thank you for what you have done, Brower,' said he, 'but I tell you I am licked. I shall not carry a single state. I am going to be slaughtered.

He had read his fate and better than he knew. In politics he was a great prophet.

Chapter 43

The north country lay buried in the snow that Christmastime. Here and there the steam plough had thrown its furrows, on either side of the railroad, high above the window line. The fences were muffled in long ridges of snow, their stakes showing like pins in a cushion of white velvet. Some of the small trees on the edge of the big timber stood overdrifted to their boughs. I have never seen such a glory of the morning as when the sun came up, that day we were nearing home, and lit the splendour of the hills, there in the land I love. The frosty nap of the snow glowed far and near with pulsing glints of pale sapphire.

We came into Hillsborough at noon the day before Christmas. Father and Uncle Eb met us at the depot and mother stood waving her handkerchief at the door as we drove up. And when we were done with our greetings and were standing, damp eyed, to warm ourselves at the fire, Uncle Eb brought his palms together with a loud whack and said:

'Look here, Lizbeth Brower! I want to hev ye tell me if ye ever see a likelier pair o' colts.

She laughed as she looked at us. In a moment she ran her hand down the side of Hope's gown. Then she lifted a fold of the cloth and felt of it thoughtfully.

'How much was that a yard?' she asked a dreamy look in her eyes. 'Wy! w'y!' she continued as Hope told her the sum. 'Terrible steep! but it does fit splendid! Oughter wear well too! Wish ye'd put that on if ye go t' church nex' Sunday.

'O mother!' said Hope, laughing, 'I'll wear my blue silk.

'Come boys 'n girls,' said Elizabeth suddenly, 'dinner's all ready in the other room.

'Beats the world!' said Uncle Eb, as we sat down at the table. 'Ye do look gran' to me—ree-markable gran', both uv ye. Tek a premium at any fair—ye would sartin.'

'Has he won yer affections?' said David laughing as he looked over at Hope.

'He has,' said she solemnly.

'Affections are a sing'lar kind o' prop'ty,' said Uncle Eb. 'Hain't good fer nuthin till ye've gin em away. Then, like as not, they git very valyble.

'Good deal that way with money too,' said Elizabeth Brower.

'I recollec' when Hope was a leetle bit uv a girl' said Uncle Eb, 'she used to say 'et when she got married she was goin' to hev her husban' rub my back fer me when it was lame.

'I haven't forgotten it,' said Hope, 'and if you will all come you will make us happier.

'Good many mouths if feed!' Uncle Ebb remarked.

'I could take in sewing and help some,' said Elizabeth Brower, as she sipped her tea.

There was a little quiver in David's under lip as he looked over at her. 'You ain't able t' do hard work any more, mother,' said he. 'She won't never hev to nuther,' said Uncle Eb. 'Don't never pay if go bookin' fer trouble—it stew easy if find. There ain' no sech thing 's trouble 'n this world 'less ye look for it. Happiness won't hey nuthin if dew with a man thet likes trouble. Minnit a man stops lookin' fer trouble happiness 'II look fer him. Things came puny nigh's ye like 'em here 'n this world—hot er cold er only middlin'. Ye can either laugh er cry er fight er fish er go if meetin'. If ye don't like erry one you can fin fault. I'm on the lookout fer happiness—suits me best, someway, an don't hurt my feelin's a bit.

'Ev'ry day's a kind uv a circus day with you, Holden,' said David Brower. 'Alwuss hevin' a good time. Ye can hev more fun with yerseif 'n any man I ever see.'

'If I hev as much hereafter es I've hed here, I ain't a goin'if fin' no fault,' said Uncle Eb. "S a reel, splendid world. God's fixed it up so ev'ry body can hev a good time if they'll only hev it. Once I heard uv a poor man 'at hed a bushel o' corn give tew him. He looked up kind o' sad an' ast if they wouldn't please shell it. Then they tuk it away. God's gin us happiness in the ear, but He ain't a goin' t' shell it fer us. You n 'Lizabeth oughter be very happy. Look a' them tew childern!

There came a rap at the door then. David put on his cap and went out with Uncle Eb.

'It's somebody for more money,' Elizabeth whispered, her eyes filling. 'I know 'tis, or he would have asked him in. We're goin't lose our home.

Her lips quivered; she covered her eyes a moment.

'David ain't well,' she continued. 'Worries night 'n day over money matters. Don't say much, but I can see it's alwuss on his mind. Woke up in the middle o' the night awhile ago. Found him sittin' by the stove. "Mother," he said, "we can't never go back to farmin'. I've ploughed furrows enough if go 'round the world. Couldn't never go through it ag'in." "Well," said I, "if you think best we could start over see how we git along. I'm willin' if try it." "No, we re too old," he says. "Thet's out o' the question. I've been thinkin' what'll we do there with Bill 'n Hope if we go t'live with 'em? Don't suppose they'll hev any hosses if take care uv er any wood if chop. What we'll hev if do is more'n I can make out. We can't do nuthin; we've never learnt how."

'We've thought that all over,' I said. 'We may have a place in the country with a big garden.

'Well,' said she, 'I'm very well if I am over sixty. I can cook an wash an' mend an' iron just as well as I ever could.'

Uncle Eb came to the door then.

'Bill,' he said, 'I want you 'n Hope if come out here 'n look at this young colt o' mine. He's playful 's a kitten.

We put on our wraps and went to the stable. Uncle Eb was there alone.

'If ye brought any Cnssmus presents,' he whispered, 'slip 'em into my hands. I'm goin' if run the cirkis t'morrow an' if we don't hev fun a plenty I'll miss my guess.

'I'll lay them out in my room,' said Hope.

'Be sure 'n put the names on 'em,' Uncle Eb whispered, as Hope went away.

'What have ye done with the "bilers"?' I enquired.

'Sold 'em,' said he, laughing. 'Barker never kep' his promise. Heard they'd gone over t' the 'Burg an' was tryin' t' sell more territory. I says if Dave, "You let me manage 'em an' I'll put 'em out o business here 'n this part o' the country." So I writ out an advertisement fer the paper. Read about this way: "Fer sale. Twelve hunderd patented suction Wash Bilers. Anyone at can't stan' prosperity an' is learnin' if swear 'll find 'em a great help. If he don't he's a bigger fool 'n I am. Nuthin' in 'em but tin—that's wuth somethin'. Warranted t' hold water."

'Wall ye know how that editor talks? 'Twant a day 'fore the head man o' the biler business come 'n bought 'em. An' the advertisement was never put in. Guess he wan't hankerin' to hev his business spilt.

Uncle Eb was not at the supper table that evening.

'Where's Holden?' said Elizabeth Brower.

'Dunno,' said David. 'Goin' after Santa Claus he tol' me.

'Never see the beat o' that man!' was the remark of Elizabeth, as she poured the tea. 'Jes' like a boy ev'ry Crissmus time. Been so excited fer a week couldn't hardly contain himself.'

'Ketched him out 'n the barn t'other day laffin' like a fool,' said David. 'Thought he was crazy.'

We sat by the fire after the supper dishes were put away, talking of all the Christmas Days we could remember. Hope and I thought our last in Faraway best of all and no wonder, for we had got then the first promise of the great gift that now made us happy. Elizabeth, sitting in her easy-chair, told of Christmas in the olden time when her father had gone to the war with the British.

David sat near me, his face in the firelight—the broad brow wrinkled into furrows and framed in locks of iron-grey. He was looking thoughtfully at the fire. Uncle Eb came soon, stamping and shaking the snow out of his great fur coat.

'Col'night,' he said, warming his hands.

Then he carried his coat and cap away, returning shortly, with a little box in his hand.

'Jes' thought I'd buy this fer fun,' said he, holding it down to the firelight. 'Dummed if I ever see the like uv it. Whoa!' he shouted, as the cover flew open, releasing a jumping-jack. 'Quicker n a grasshopper! D'ye ever see sech a sassy little critter?

Then he handed it to Elizabeth.

'Wish ye Merry Christmas, Dave Brower!' said he.

'Ain't as merry as I might be,' said David.

'Know what's the matter with ye,' said Uncle Eb. 'Searchin' after trouble—thet's what ye're doin'. Findin' lots uv it right there 'n the fire. Trouble 's goiti' t' git mighty scurce 'round here this very selfsame night. Ain't goin' t' be nobody lookin' fer it—thet's why. Fer years ye've been takin' care o' somebody et I'll take care 'o you, long's ye live—sartin sure. Folks they said ye was fools when ye took 'em in. Man said I was a fool once. Alwuss hed a purty fair idee o'myself sence then. When some folks call ye a fool 's a ruther good sign ye ain't. Ye've waited a long time fer yer pay—ain't much longer to wait now.'

There was a little quaver in his voice, We all looked at him in silence. Uncle Eb drew out his wallet with trembling hands, his fine old face lit with a deep emotion. David looked up at him as he wondered what joke was coming, until he saw his excitement.

'Here's twenty thousan' dollars,' said Uncle Eb, 'a reel, genuwine bank check! Jist as good as gold. Here 'tis! A Crissmus present fer you 'n Elizabeth. An' may God bless ye both!'

David looked up incredulously. Then he took the bit of paper. A big tear rolled down his cheek.

'Why, Holden! What does this mean?' he asked.

''At the Lord pays His debts,' said Uncle Eb. 'Read it.'

Hope had lighted the lamp.

David rose and put on his spectacles. One eyebrow had lifted above the level of the other. He held the check to the lamplight. Elizabeth stood at his elbow.

'Why, mother!' said he. 'Is this from our boy? From Nehemiah? Why, Nehemiah is dead!' he added, looking over his spectacles at Uncle Eb.

'Nehemiah is not dead,' said the latter.

'Nehemiah not dead!' he repeated, looking down at the draft. They turned it in the light, reading over and over again the happy tidings pinned to one corner of it. Then they looked into each other's eyes.

Elizabeth put her arms about David's neck and laid her head upon his shoulder and not one of us dare trust himself to speak for a little. Uncle Eb broke the silence.

'Got another present,' he said. 'S a good deal better 'n gold er silver.' A tall, bearded man came in.

'Mr Trumbull!' Hope exclaimed, rising.

'David an' Elizabeth Brower,' said Uncle Eb, 'the dead hes come to life. I give ye back yer son—Nehemiah.'

Then he swung his cap high above his head, shouting in a loud voice:

'Merry Crissmus! Merry Crissmus!'

The scene that followed I shall not try to picture. It was so full of happiness that every day of our lives since then has been blessed with it and with a peace that has lightened every sorrow; of it, I can truly say that it passeth all understanding.

'Look here, folks!' said Uncle Eb, after awhile, as he got his flute, 'my feelin's hev been teched hard. If I don't hev some jollification I'll bust. Bill Brower, limber up yer leather a leetle bit.'

Chapter 44

Nehemiah, whom I had known as John Trumbull, sat a long time between his father and mother, holding a hand of each, and talking in a low tone, while Hope and I were in the kitchen with Uncle Eb. Now that father and son were side by side we saw how like they were and wondered we had never guessed the truth.

'Do you remember?' said Nehemiah, when we returned. 'Do you remember when you were a little boy, coming one night to the old log house on Bowman's Hill with Uncle Eb?

'I remember it very well,' I answered.

'That was the first time I ever saw you,' he said.

'Why, you are not the night man?'

'I was the night man,' he answered.

I stared at him with something of the old, familiar thrill that had always come at the mention of him years agone.

'He's grown a leetle since then,' said Uncle Eb.

'I thought so the night I carried him off the field at Bull Run,' said Nehemiah.

'Was that you?' I asked eagerly.

'It was,' he answered. 'I came over from Washington that afternoon. Your colonel told me you had been wounded.

'Wondered who you were, but I could not get you to answer. I have to thank you for my life.

Hope put her arms about his neck and kissed him.

'Tell us,' said she, 'how you came to be the night man.'

He folded his arms and looked down and began his story.

'Years ago I had a great misfortune. I was a mere boy at the time. By accident I killed another boy in play. It was an old gun we were playing with and nobody knew it was loaded. I had often quarrelled with the other boy—that is why they thought I had done it on purpose. There was a dance that night. I had got up in the evening, crawled out of the window and stolen away. We were in Rickard's stable. I remember how the people ran out with lanterns. They would have hung me—some of them—or given me the blue beech, if a boy friend had not hurried me away. It was a terrible hour. I was stunned; I could say nothing. They drove me to the 'Burg, the boy's father chasing us. I got over into Canada, walked to Montreal and there went to sea. It was foolish, I know, but I was only a boy of fifteen. I took another name; I began a new life. Nehemiah Brower was like one dead. In 'Frisco I saw Ben Gilman. He had been a school mate in Faraway. He put his hand on my shoulder and called me the old name. It was hard to deny it—the hardest thing I ever did. I was homesick; I wanted to ask him about my mother and father and my sister, who was a baby when I left. I would have given my life to talk with him. But I shook my head.

'"No," I said, "my name is not Brower. You are mistaken."

'Then I walked away and Nemy Brower stayed in his grave.

'Well, two years later we were cruising from Sidney to Van Dieman's Land. One night there came a big storm. A shipmate was washed away in the dark. We never saw him again. They found a letter in his box that said his real name was Nehemiah Brower, son of David Brower, of Faraway, NY, USA. I put it there, of course, and the captain wrote a letter to my father about the death of his son. My old self was near done for and the man Trumbull had a new lease of life. You see in my madness I had convicted and executed myself.

He paused a moment. His mother put her hand upon his shoulder with a word of gentle sympathy. Then he went on.

'Well, six years after I had gone away, one evening in midsummer, we came into the harbour of Quebec. I had been long in the southern seas. When I went ashore, on a day's leave, and wandered off in the fields and got the smell of the north, I went out of my head—went crazy for a look at the hills o' Faraway and my own people. Nothing could stop me then. I drew my pay, packed my things in a bag and off I went. Left the 'Burg afoot the day after; got to Faraway in the evening. It was beautiful—the scent o' the new hay that stood in cocks and rows on the hill—the noise o' the crickets—the smell o' the grain—the old house, just as I remembered them; just as I had dreamed of them a thousand times. And—when I went by the gate Bony—my old dog—came out and barked at—me and I spoke to him and he knew me and came and licked my hands, rubbing upon my leg. I sat down with him there by the stone wall and—the kiss of that old dog—the first token of love I had known for years' called back the dead and all that had been his. I put my arms about his—neck and was near crying out with joy.

'Then I stole up to the house and looked in at a window. There sat father, at a table, reading his paper; and a little girl was on her knees by mother saying her prayers. He stopped a moment, covering his eyes with his handkerchief.

'That was Hope,' I whispered.

'That was Hope,' he went on. 'All the king's oxen could not have dragged me out of Faraway then. Late at night I went off into the woods. The old dog followed to stay with me until he died. If it had not been for him I should have been hopeless. I had with me enough to eat for a time. We found a cave in a big ledge over back of Bull Pond. Its mouth was covered with briars. It had a big room and a stream of cold water trickling through a crevice. I made it my home and a fine place it was—cool in summer and warm in winter. I caught a cub panther that fall and a baby coon. They grew up with me there and were the only friends I had after Bony, except Uncle Eb.

'Uncle Eb!' I exclaimed.

'You know how I met him,' he continued. 'Well, he won my confidence. I told him my history. I came into the clearing almost every night. Met him often. He tried to persuade me to come back to my people, but I could not do it. I was insane; I feared something—I did not know what. Sometimes I doubted even my own identity. Many a summer night I sat talking for hours, with Uncle Eb, at the foot of Lone Pine. O, he was like a father to me! God knows what I should have done without him. Well, I stuck to my life, or rather to my death, O—there in the woods—getting fish out of the brooks and game out of the forest, and milk out of the cows in the pasture. Sometimes I went through the woods to the store at Tifton for flour and pork. One night Uncle Eb told me if I would go out among men to try my hand at some sort of business he would start me with a thousand dollars. Well, I did—it. I had also a hundred dollars of my own. I came through the woods afoot. Bought fashionable clothing at Utica, and came to the big city—you know the rest. Among men my fear has left me, so I wonder at it. I am a debtor to love—the love of Uncle Eb and that of a noble woman I shall soon marry. It has made me whole and brought me back to my own people.

'And everybody knew he was innocent the day after he left,' said David.

'Three cheers for Uncle Eb!' I demanded.

And we gave them.

'I declare!' said he. 'In all my born days never see sech fun. It's tree-menjious! I tell ye. Them 'et takes care uv others'll be took care uv—'less they do it o'purpose.'

And when the rest of us had gone to bed Uncle Eb sat awhile by the fire with David. Late at night he came upstairs with his candle. He came over to my bed on tiptoe to see if I were awake, holding the candle above my head. I was worn out and did not open my eyes. He sat down snickering.

'Tell ye one thing, Dave Brower,' he whispered to himself as he drew off his boots, 'when some folks calls ye a fool 's a purty good sign ye ain't.'

Chapter 45

Since that day I have seen much coming and going.

We are now the old folks—Margaret and Nehemiah and Hope and I. Those others, with their rugged strength, their simple ways, their undying youth, are of the past. The young folks—they are a new kind of people. It gives us comfort to think they will never have to sing in choirs or 'pound the rock' for board money; but I know it is the worse luck for them. They are a fine lot of young men and women—comely and well-mannered—but they will not be the pathfinders of the future. What with balls and dinners and clubs and theatres, they find too great a solace in the rear rank.

Nearly twenty years after that memorable Christmas, coming from Buffalo to New York one summer morning, my thoughts went astray in the north country. The familiar faces, the old scenes came trooping by and that very day I saw the sun set in Hillsborough as I had often those late years.

Mother was living in the old home, alone, with a daughter of Grandma Bisnette. It was her wish to live and die under that roof. She cooked me a fine supper, with her own hands, and a great anxiety to please me.

'Come Willie!' said she, as if I were a small boy again, 'you fill the woodbox an' I'll git supper ready. Lucindy, you clear out,' she said to the hired girl, good-naturedly. 'You dunno how t'cook for him.'

I filled the woodbox and brought a pail of water and while she was frying the ham and eggs read to her part of a speech I had made in Congress. Before thousands I had never felt more elation. At last I was sure of winning her applause. The little bent figure stood, thoughtfully, turning the ham and eggs. She put the spider aside, to stand near me, her hands upon her hips. There was a mighty pride in her face when I had finished.

I rose and she went and looked out of the window.

'Grand!' she murmured, wiping her eyes with the corner of her handkerchief.

'Glad you like it,' I said, with great satisfaction.

'O, the speech!' she answered, her elbow resting on the window sash, her hand supporting her head. 'I liked it very well—but—but I was thinking of the sunset. How beautiful it is.

I was weary after my day of travel and went early to bed there in my old room. I left her finishing a pair of socks she had been knitting for me. Lying in bed, I could hear the creak of her chair and the low sung, familiar words:

'On the other side of Jordan, In the sweet fields of Eden, Where the tree of life is blooming, There is rest for you.

Late at night she came into my room with a candle. I heard her come softly to the bed where she stood a moment leaning over me. Then she drew the quilt about my shoulder with a gentle hand.

'Poor little orphan!' said she, in a whisper that trembled. She was thinking of my childhood—of her own happier days.

Then she went away and I heard, in the silence, a ripple of measureless waters.

Next morning I took flowers and strewed them on the graves of David and Uncle Eb; there, Hope and I go often to sit for half a summer day above those perished forms, and think of the old time and of those last words of my venerable friend now graven on his tombstone:

I AIN'T AFRAID.

'SHAMED O'NUTHIN' I EVER DONE.

ALWUSS KEP'MY TUGS TIGHT,

NEVER SWORE 'LESS 'TWAS NECESSARY,

NEVER KETCHED A FISH BIGGER 'N 'TWAS

ER LIED 'N A HOSS TRADE

ER SHED A TEAR I DIDN'T HEV TO.

NEVER CHEATED ANYBODY BUT EBEN HOLDEN.

GOIN' OFF SOMEWHERES, BILL

DUNNO THE WAY NUTHER

DUNNO 'F IT'S EAST ER WEST ER NORTH ER SOUTH,

ER ROAD ER TRAIL;

BUT I AIN'T AFRAID.

68962037R00105

Made in the USA
Lexington, KY
23 October 2017